CHRIST AND COMMUNITY

CHRIST AND COMMUNITY

By GILBERT A. BEAVER

*an exploration of
co-operative fellowship*

(KOINONIA)

ASSOCIATION PRESS : 1950

Printed in the United States of America

To
JEAN KEIR BEAVER
whose insight and genius
for evoking fellowship
shine through this
book

PREFACE

THE WRITING of this book has placed me under a debt of gratitude to more people than I can possibly name. It is especially gratifying that a book about the sharing of life should have brought forth such a demonstration of its theme.

There are, of course, the scores of writers and publishers whose permissions to use their materials have been cheerfully given. In the back of the book these sources are listed, and we hope that in many cases the citations will lead to further reading.

Dr. John Oliver Nelson, of the Yale Divinity School, prepared the questions which, at the ends of the chapters, will encourage thought, discussion, and application. His skill and enthusiasm illustrate what scores of others have done in criticism, questioning, and suggestion. Some of them brought specialized knowledge and wide experience; some adopted what was for them a new working hypothesis in order to take part in our inquiry. Their varied points of view add significance to the fact that all who continued in the inquiry came to share increasingly the conclusion of Eugene Lyman that "the fullest experience of the God whose nature is Creative Reason and Creative Love will be entered into by those who take as their supreme end the building of a world-wide community in which reason and love prevail—what Professor Royce called the Beloved Community."

It has been gratifying, too, to find in a busy publishing office an illustration of the application of the principles of this book to the business of getting the day's work done. I must express my gratitude to the staff of Association Press for the way in which they have made *koinonia* a reality for me in the whole process of getting the book edited and manufactured.

I must add a word of special gratitude to Jean Keir Beaver, my wife, who has reviewed and criticized every part of this manuscript, and who makes our home a place where increasing numbers of neighbors and friends and strangers of various nations and beliefs share in a fellowship of thought and prayer and action—a good place for thinking and writing in fellowship.

GILBERT A. BEAVER

Yorktown Heights
September, 1950

CONTENTS

9

Part I

THE APPROACH THROUGH RE-CREATIVE FELLOWSHIP

I

LEARNING HARMONY THROUGH
FELLOWSHIP

The Range and Method of Our Inquiry

IN THIS BOOK we explore the possibilities, hindrances, and
tested ways of living in creative communities. We do not
assume that Jesus proposed any exact form of political or
economic organization. Rather we invite readers to unite in
testing the attitudes, principles, and way of living in the
world-uniting communion and community through which
he sought abundant life for all. This way of living, covering
all aspects of life and furthered in part by leaders of different races, came to most potent influence through Jesus, yet
still waits to be tried by others on a scale commensurate with
its importance. The present inquiry is a co-operative gathering and testing of some of the best thought and experience
available in this neglected art of living.

As we examine such experience in various fields, we shall
try to see clearly how a scientific and public-spirited use of
the resources now available may improve the interactions of
men and nature for general well-being, and why science
alone is inadequate. We see science reaching out in many
directions, placing new knowledge at our disposal and offering boundless possibilities of good or evil. Therefore we
must examine the limitations as well as the possibilities of
science. For we need to see more clearly, as we shall find

15

leading scientists explaining, why an impersonal science, strictly speaking, is confined to the physical world and necessarily lacks personal and spiritual values and moral directiveness—why science, therefore, though needed to help solve man's personal and social problems, is by itself powerless to solve them and, in fact, often complicates them.

Accordingly we shall here seek such advances as may now be possible if the interactions of men and nature are energized and directed by a Creative Spirit that works toward world-uniting communities of good will. For such communities, large and small, give us opportunity to understand and love one another in the various relationships of life. They are training grounds where everyone may practice the attitudes and methods that make world-wide fellowship possible. In sufficient numbers, therefore, they may become a decisive factor in the immediate future of this atomic age, an essential condition of peace and security.

Thus we may find with Arthur Morgan that "the preservation and perfecting of the small community is one of the greatest issues facing our time. . . . Yet of all major factors which enter into the determination of our national life, few if any are receiving so inadequate attention as is the welfare of the community or primary group."[1]

Our inquiry, however, takes a wider range. It has to deal with conditions, both perilous and promising, in which everyone is involved more deeply than he knows. For instance, when widespread unemployment and physical or mental disorders augment fears, when underhand methods destroy confidence, when self-seeking and racial or class prejudice hinder neighborliness, whole populations are so affected that no one escapes. Everyone is cramped by the results, whether in himself or in his neighbors. Therefore everyone needs a society in which such dehumanizing conditions can be forestalled and all may enjoy manifold opportunities both to serve the commonweal and to find scope for their own best powers. Without this kind of society, neither individuals nor communities come to their best estate.

Moreover, in testing and improving the conditions for such a society, every possible participant is needed to help forestall the encroachments of an aggressive communism, for this wily aggressor abets the failures of an incomplete democracy and a partly Christian society and tries to take advantage of them. Therefore all who desire true freedom and democracy should take part in continuing inquiries, more or less like ours, because the extension of communism can be prevented only by those who have a sounder faith and a better program to meet human needs and unsolved problems.

Whoever explores the possibilities of this sounder faith and better program needs evidence not only of encouraging achievements but also of conditions that will foster a better state of mind and of affairs. To enlarge the range of evidence, quotations from experts are woven into our discussion, like apt remarks at a round-table conference. The remarks, though brief, are so pertinent that it is hoped they will stimulate further reading.* Moreover, what is cited is no mere theory. It embodies tested experience. The pooling of this experience yields common ground and workable suggestions for those who differ on many matters, yet desire such solutions of personal and social problems as will avert world chaos.

Readers who approach this book without convictions such as Jesus held about the meaning of life may be encouraged to know that certain participants in our inquiry began without such convictions. Though they could not feel sure, as Jesus did, of a fatherlike God or of any intimately co-operating reality at the heart of the universe, they saw the necessity of beginning such an inquiry by taking attitudes and aims like his as a working hypothesis. Thus we have found that the very diversity of thinking and working in this way for kindred aims cultivates the most fruitful attitudes in an ever-expanding community of interests. For only in so far

---

* See explanation of references, placed before the notes at the end of the book.

as persons transcend self-interest in wholehearted devotion
to a "beloved community" that exercises all their faculties,
do they find better ways to make the resources of the universe
widely available and to further a corresponding growth of
their own powers.

Fellowship in the Author's Experience

To show the background of our inquiry, friends urged the
writer to tell certain of his own experiences that led to discoveries of how community of interests can grow in daily life.
Some of these experiences came to him through parents and
teachers who were themselves bright exemplars of the spirit
of community. They encouraged him to apply his studies to
the life about him, to learn carpentry, gardening, and farming in comradeship with good workmen, and to cultivate a
growing awareness of his partnership with nature through
these pursuits. Making friends of spirited horses and dogs,
or helping to meet the needs of growing chicks and tender
plants, deepened this sense of partnership. Doubtless his
father's friendly way with animals helped to shut out fear
of them from the growing boy and increased his confidence
and adaptability in dealing with them. Moreover, the fellowship of family prayer, often with guests participating, was a
daily reminder of the source of his father's power to evoke
fellowship in the private and public relations of a many-
sided life. For instance, his father, James Addams Beaver,
when Chairman of the Board of Trustees of the Pennsylvania
State College, was elected an honorary member of a succession of college classes and was invited to attend class meetings. Students came to him freely with their problems.
Through comradeship with such a father, richer experience
than the boy could then appreciate was brought into his
other relationships, including growing up with younger
brothers and later with his own daughter. The co-operative
fellowship of the family in prayer and action gave invaluable preparation for solving later problems.

Other experiences came through family obligations for

fair practices in industry and agriculture, through service in state and local government, and through life in a city neighborhood house. Still others came through years of intimate work with students when they were making life decisions, and through later years of dealing with manifold human relations as a Justice of the Peace, keeping in view the safety and maturing of both the persons concerned and the community. All this became clearer because of our expanding fellowship. Serving later as executive secretary of The Committee on Friendly Relations among Foreign Students in many lands, and helping to federate national groups of Christian Associations in South America brought direct evidence of the need and possibility of better international relations.

All of these ventures in fellowship have continued to gain significance through participation in movements dealing with the causes, aftermath, and cure of war. Thus questions have been raised about a state of things long taken for granted. And these questions have induced rethinking of the meaning and methods of life. Such thinking has been helped also by close touch with the realities of life on a farm.

During forty years this farm near New York, where suburbs and open country meet, has given many opportunities for testing the kind of life we are examining. Our life on the farm went deeper and involved far more than we had expected. Yet many a seeming failure has been more educative than was an apparent success. For often, when rightly considered, a lack of response from plants, animals, or men led to discovery of the cause and to readjustment of conditions. For instance, a man who was often irritable and troublesome when working with others, because his nerves had been unstrung by periodic drinking, was found to be a kind and devoted worker with horses. When he was assigned to work with a team, given the care of all the horses, and encouraged in other ways to overcome his craving for alcohol, he became a most thoughtful member of the farm family.[2] The chance to learn through fellowship in solving practical problems brought good workers to the farm and helped those who suffered from limitations. Thanks to the education, skill, and disposition of Halsey Palmer, partner and alert manager of our farming, dairy, and cattle raising enterprise, willing workers were often on a waiting list, eager to learn by working with him. Such thinking and working together by members of different races, all seeking community development, confirm the validity of the experience.

And the rambling old farmhouse, whose spacious, book-lined rooms invite a sharing of the best thought of past and present, has become a congenial center for conference. Here groups representing many interests have gathered from far and near to think together about particular problems. Here many young people, seeking a way through the perplexities of social, scientific, and religious questions, have helped to give variety and point to our inquiry. They have seen to it that the contributions used from science, economics, psychology, and philosophy are expressed in nontechnical words, and have helped thereby to clear common ground for both lay and professional workers in many fields. On this point, the eagerness of our many helpers to share and to work out ideas, regardless of public recognition, suggests that countless more would surmount their differences and live effectively if they were given a better chance to think and to act in the kind of fellowship that we are seeking.

Others, with wide knowledge of men and affairs, some of them specialists within the range of our inquiry, have contributed generously to the making of this book. We shared throughout, whether in city or in country, an attitude well expressed by Zona Gale: "I am determined to increase the area of my awareness."

As a result of all this we found with Richard Roberts that "there seems to be no reason why men could not become possessed by the passion for fellowship, as in times past they have been possessed by the passion for freedom. And this is the moral impulse which will make in the coming days the difference between a social revolution which is a dance of death and one that shall be a pageant of life. For the old single slogan of Freedom we must adopt the double slogan of Freedom and Fellowship. We have before us larger tasks than the redemption of a class. Our business is with God's help to create a living society."[3]

Fellowship at the Source of Civilization

Those who would experience the saving influence of freedom and fellowship in a distraught world need more than co-operative thinking. They need the clarifying effect of co-operative action for brotherly communities, including the deepest source of brotherhood they can find. This means, in terms which any one may take as a starting point, that the whole man, intellect, affections, imagination, conscience, and will must seek the whole truth and work with the most enlightening and co-ordinating influence to be found through fellowship.

The need for such an integrating influence becomes more evident in view of the increased specialization of our time. Often, by the departmentalizing of life, our awareness of our environment is limited, our purpose is distorted, and our energies are curtailed. Absorbed in details of divergent affairs, we see life in fragments and miss its unifying power.

Yet unity and power have come again and again to divergent people through such inclusive fellowship as the early Christians enjoyed. The word for their fellowship (*koinonia* in Greek, variously translated in the English New Testament as communion, fellowship, participation, and partnership) originally meant partnership in business or in some common treasure. This was the word chosen by them to express the import of their relationship with one another and with the Spirit of truth and love, that Jesus promised would be their "Helper" in a world-uniting community of service.[a] Through such participation in the Spirit they and their spiritual successors found ever wider ways to share with various races and conditions of people an influence that could energize, unify, and enlighten them in the development of this expanding community.[b] Now, more than ever, as people are enlightened and quickened through similar fellowship in their relations with nature, their fellow men, and "the Spirit of life," they discover in natural resources, and in productive power, enlarging possibilities of abundant life.[c] They learn that the root of their trouble is neither in nature nor in God. They find that the real trouble is in man and his works, in those attitudes, customs, and institutions which hinder comprehensive spiritual fellowship as a transforming influence in society.

We shall sift the evidence for tested ways of overcoming these man-made hindrances when attitudes and institutions are made tributary to the general well-being. This evidence is found, for instance, when scientists, other workers, and corporations collaborate for adequate housing, nutrition, medicine, agriculture, and other factors in an economy of potential plenty. The evidence multiplies also when we study what Lecomte du Noüy, in his scientific study of human destiny, calls "the dawn of a new phase of evolution, no longer on the physiological and anatomical plane but on the spiritual and moral plane." Here we enter an area of expanding possibilities where sensitiveness, adaptability, and mutual aid develop in the higher forms of life, and where self-giving love emerges in man as the power in fellowship that can hold the world together.[4] We shall study such developments, and the influence of suffering upon them, in order to see how far these qualities, which make for inventive and co-operant ways of living, receive the powers of survival and growth, and whether they are essential for the most creative living.

Following such clues, many have found that the growth of these creative qualities depends not only upon man's awareness of his environment, physical, mental and spiritual, but also upon the adequacy of his adjustment to it, including his adjustment to the deepest Reality of the universe. Anything short of this, such as giving way to the craze for self-expression, has often led into one of the many bypaths that deflect the ascent of man.

We shall seek, therefore, a more thoroughgoing and continuous adjustment, "which is not simply a yearning for a better world through some new manifestation of religion coming to us from afar; but which is a finding of divine reality in the actual process of discovering and fulfilling the conditions through which the better world may begin to come."[5] Thus any one may test in practice a central idea of the life and teaching of Jesus, that a God who is love is the father of men, and that men are at least potential members, even when prodigal sons, of the family of God. This means seeking always, as sons and brothers, such communion and community as will foster the fullest possible development of individual personality in the widest and deepest possible fellowship.

Questions for Further Thought and Discussion*

Are there ways other than "co-operative community" to find inner integration today?

What groups can we name which might be described in the quoted phrase, "possessed by the passion for fellowship"?

Is the author's own experience so distinctive that no one can get the same results in conviction without sharing such a varied and full life as he has had?

Are the disintegrative effects of modern life likely to be arrested or neutralized by the integrative ones of Christianity, in this generation?

* The questions at the ends of chapters were prepared by Dr. John O. Nelson of the Yale University Divinity School.

2

THE RELEVANCE OF JESUS FOR ENDURING COMMUNITIES

He Uses Situations to Teach Community Principles

WHY, it is asked, do you turn to an impractical idealist like Jesus, Do you expect him to answer the complicated questions of modern life?

This much is clear at the outset: No one should expect, and Jesus did not suppose, that any set of ready-made answers could meet all the questions that arise. He never tried to answer in this way the questions even of his own time. He sought to develop, not to supplant, every one's capacity for unfettered thinking and voluntary, co-operating action. So he taught, not by rigid rules or abstractions but by parables, by the application of principles to concrete situations, by the light of a universal purpose, by the spirit and method of his own life. He dealt with those creative attitudes which transcend mere rules, survive the changes of time, and underlie all the relations of a co-operating world. Through fellowship with others in seeking this new order of life, which he conceived as a real community of God and men, Jesus nurtured in his disciples the attitudes and principles that foster a corresponding way of living.

Facing each actual situation as it arose, Jesus dealt with it in a way that would further a neighborly society. He did not hesitate, for instance, to heal men on the Sabbath, despite all the prohibitions of those in authority, for he had found a surer clue to the conduct of life in the facts of human need than in the hair-splitting regulations of a legalized religion. When a man with a withered hand stood before him and his critics watched whether he would heal on the Sabbath, he said to them, "I ask you, is it lawful on the Sabbath to do good or to do harm, to save life or to destroy it?"[a]

So the spontaneous talk and acts of Jesus, springing from some immediate need or question, illustrate far better than could any formal treatise the spirit and the principles that are creative of the commonwealth to come. His talk was full of vivid sayings in the oriental manner, and to our more matter-of-fact western minds these sayings have often seemed like rules. But the whole tenor of his life shows that he meant them to be concrete, unforgettable illustrations of the principles and characteristics of the neighborly life. He was asked, for instance, "How often am I to forgive my brother when he wrongs me? As many as seven times?" Jesus answered: "Not seven times, but seventy times seven."[b] Here is no mathematical formula. Jesus was not imposing a mechanical rule of conduct: such rules he held to be deadening. He was making vivid the necessity for a forgiving spirit to heal a breach between brothers. He meant that his disciples should persevere in this spirit rather than give way to resentment or revenge. These embittering attitudes and acts, he knew, would keep brothers at variance, and to that extent would preclude a better state of mind and heart, a better mode of living. Thus the sayings and acts of Jesus, which grew out of and aptly fitted each occasion, far surpassed abstract moralizing in meeting the needs of daily living. For this reason they are still most helpful in times of need to all sorts of men and women.

Those who followed faithfully the way of Jesus in the early stage of its trial, despite persecution and the rule of dictators, found much to confirm the wisdom of all that he had said about it. In the new freedom and fellowship of their voluntary, co-operant life, they found release from depressing fears, deliverance from inner conflicts, and harmonious use for all their powers. Some were deflected by the selfish pursuit of lesser things and lost thereby, as Jesus said they would lose, the divine energy, wisdom, and love. But so far as his disciples sought communion and community for all, they lost pettiness and provincialism, they found enlargement of heart and mind in thoroughgoing devotion to his purpose.

William Lecky, though not always a lenient critic of much that was later called Christian, said in his *History of European Morals*: "There can indeed be little doubt that, for nearly two hundred years after its establishment in Europe, the Christian community exhibited a moral purity which, if it has been equalled, has never for any long period been surpassed." In comparing the wide influence of Jesus and his early disciples upon all sorts of men and women throughout the Empire with the limited influence of moralists like Marcus Aurelius and Seneca, Lecky said: "The ethics of Paganism were part of a philosophy. The ethics of Christianity were part of a religion. The first were the speculations of a few highly cultivated individuals, and neither had nor could have any direct influence upon the masses of mankind. The second were indissolubly connected with the worship, hopes and fears of a vast religious system, that act at least as powerfully on the most ignorant as on the most educated."[1] This transforming influence of Jesus and his followers in the first two centuries, confirmed by similar experience to this day, shows how sufficiently he can meet the needs of men and women in the actual conduct of life.

He Shows Purpose, Attitudes, Methods of Community

Yet some say this early experience with Jesus seems too remote and too uncertain to be significant today. We shall inquire later whether this experience is uncertain or whether, on the contrary, it is confirmed by historical evidence and progressive experience in ways that give it unusual value for us. Leaving these queries for the moment, let us examine the purpose, the attitudes, the spirit and methods of Jesus when put to the test of daily living. By thus "exploring and enjoying him," as many penetrating studies of his influence show, men have found more and more in him, have had clearer glimpses into the depths of their own natures, and have seen greater things possible in the life of the world. Whether they consider Jesus as disclosing the nature and initiative of God, or the possibilities of man, he gives them a higher conception of what men may become, and he helps them to realize it.

This creative influence of Jesus is confirmed by physicians and psychiatrists of wide experience, who recognize more than ever the necessity for such attitudes and objectives as he exemplified. A leading practitioner of applied psychology, having examined and advised some four thousand patients, wrote about his return to religion and the Church: "A great variety of incidents gradually forced me to realize that the findings of psychology in respect to personality and happiness were largely a rediscovery of old religious truths. . . . I found myself explaining the psychological significance of the Christian religion as exemplified by the social aggressiveness of its Founder and its emphasis on forgetting oneself in the service of others. . . . No discovery of modern psychology is, in my opinion, so important as its scientific proof of the necessity of self-sacrifice to self-realization. It requires religion, something higher than the individual, to overcome the selfish impulses of the natural man and to lead him to a more successful and a fuller life."[2]

Dr. A. J. Hadfield, in his experience at the Oxford Neurological War Hospital and in his general practice of psychotherapy, found further evidence of unrealized possibilities in the religion of the New Testment: "In its fundamental doctrine of love to God and man, it harmonizes the emotions of the soul into one inspiring purpose, thereby abolishing all conflicts, and liberating instead of suppressing the free energies of men." Dr. Hadfield calls attention to the great increase of power among the earlier Christians, which they attributed to a divine energy within them called "the Spirit."

Such release of energy he found corroborated by "the experience of applied psychology, and especially of psychotherapy. . . . It points toward the conclusion that we are living far below the limits of our possible selves; and that there are open to us resources of power which, if directed to noble purposes, will free our minds from the worries, anxieties, and morbid fatigues which spoil our lives, and will free us for a life of energy and strength."[3] The conditions under which such energy can be more generally released will be considered later. We shall see then how people, meeting these conditions, have experienced the abundant life that an early disciple found to be the intention of Jesus: "I have come that they may have life and have it to the full."[c]

Jesus gave men assurance of this abundant life only in so far as they were willing to share the spirit and way of life that they found in him. No greater requirement than this was made by Jesus of his disciples. He did not try to commit them in advance to any particular explanation of himself. Such questions, we shall see, he was willing to leave to their unhurried answer in the light of their intimate acquaintance with him and of their continuous endeavor to live with others and with God as they saw him living. He had found a way to meet the temptations and to resolve the conflicts that defeat men and wreck society. And he desired that everyone should profit by his experience. He saw too clearly to be blinded by the popularity or power that has beguiled many an otherwise able man. He deplored the hatreds and ambitions of his own countrymen, obsessed by ideas of racial superiority. He faced acute problems at a time of national crisis and withstood the lure of expediency. "It was because he faced problems hard to solve, and with immense possibilities of good and evil hanging upon his decisions, that Christian experience, though not always Christian theology, has recognized in him 'one who has been in all points tempted as we are,' " who "learned obedience through what he suffered," and "because he himself has suffered and been tempted, is able to help those who are tempted."[4]

As a modern critic and poet saw from the depths of his own self-inflicted misery, "Jesus realized in the entire sphere of human relations that imaginative sympathy which in the sphere of Art is the sole secret of creation. He understood the darkness of the blind, the fierce misery of those who live for pleasure, the strange poverty of the rich."[5] "There was in him a psychological and spiritual realism such as some of our greatest artists have shared. Dante knew the torments of those who refuse to choose, or choose their own hell and will not walk out the open door. Human sin swiftly hardens into psychic fetters, crippling all free movement."[6] Therefore Jesus, who had compassion for the sinner, warned against the estranging, antisocial consequences of sins that, unless repented of in deed, inevitably shut men out from true community. So fully did he comprehend the suffering, the temptation, the sin and need of others, that in a real sense he has borne the griefs and carried the sorrows of the world. Yet his presence has never been depressing. Not only is he "tinged with no ascetic gloom," but he has a rejuvenating way of imparting his deeper enjoyment of nature, his heartier appreciation of men, and his keener delight in God. In proportion as men have shared this experience of Jesus, he has made good the assurance, "Learn from me, and you will find your souls refreshed."[d]

Many, encouraged by his experience with nature, men, and God, have made daring experiments on the hypothesis of a cosmic trend toward harmony, fellowship, and mutual aid. Following such a clue, they have become convinced of what a modern interpreter calls the gist of the Christianity of Jesus: "At the centre of the Universe there is That which is more like a father's loving heart than like anything else we know."[7] Inadequate as is the analogy of fatherhood, or any symbol, to express this experience of Jesus, it is still to vast numbers of people the best analogy available. And this conviction that fatherlike love is the source and principle of life has come to men in largest measure (so leading students of comparative religion tell us) through the influence of

Jesus—not only his teaching but also his life and what he imparts of his experience to those who put it to the test. A testing of the possibility that there is in the universe an influence or power like that which came to men through Jesus has often saved the day in man's extremity. By giving this influence free course in his own life, many a discouraged soul has found new beauty in the world, greater possibilities in men, and a "new creature" in himself.

He Makes World Community a Test of Customs and Institutions

Life of the quality that Jesus showed to be possible for individuals is an essential part of his intention for society. His attitude toward the lawgivers and socially minded prophets of the Hebrews is typical: he came "not to destroy but to fulfill" the highest aspirations of every people for their collective life. Under his influence, far more than under any other, men of conflicting interests and hostile races have learned to live together in the enlightenment of brotherly co-operation. Such ventures have been far too limited in scope, yet they are more significant than is usually supposed. For example, there is the record of seventy-two unbroken years of harmonious relations between the friendly colonists and the Indians in Pennsylvania. Not until the Quakers were outvoted in the legislature did the vicious circle of suspicion, armaments, and atrocities begin. This "holy experiment," as the Friends called it, gives the weight of long experience to a conclusion of George Bernard Shaw: "I am ready to admit that after contemplating the world and human nature for nearly sixty years, I see no way out of the world's misery but the way which would have been found by Christ's will if he had undertaken the work of a modern practical statesman."[8]

Far more than we usually recognize, Jesus had a statesmanlike grasp of political and social conditions. Because he could read the signs of the times, he saw how little the rulers of his nation understood them. "They are blind guides," he said, "and if a blind man leads a blind man, both will fall into a pit."⁶ The catastrophe, which he saw as inevitable if existing conditions continued, came with the destruction of Jerusalem while some who remembered his warning were still living. Historical research into the political, economic, and religious conditions of the period in their relation to the life of Jesus shows his deep understanding of the situation.⁹

Issues complicated by racial and religious prejudice and by exaggerated nationalism, Jesus clarified in a way that is always relevant. "He made his ultimate appeal to the very nature of things. . . . His standard of judgment," as Ernest Burton shows, "was not some other literature or philosophy, but things as they are—the world as the revelation of divine thought."¹⁰ He penetrated the maze of tradition and prejudice that blinded his contemporaries, and disclosed illuminating facts. In this way, for example, he dealt with an intricate system of regulations about eating and about avoiding supposed contamination from various sources, especially from contact with other races. However well conceived was the beginning of these regulations, they had been amplified in ways that fostered a feeling of racial superiority and hindered the best relations with other peoples. They had become an oppressive part of the traditions by which a devout Jew was compelled to order his life. Jesus approached these regulations from a different point of view. "Do you not see," he said to his disciples, "that whatever goes into the mouth passes into the stomach and is afterward expelled? But the things that come out from the mouth proceed from the heart, and it is these that defile a man. For out of the heart proceed evil thoughts—murder, adultery, unchastity, theft, perjury, slander. These are the things that defile a man; but eating with unwashed hands does not defile a man."ᶠ How Jesus clarified other issues by appealing to fundamental needs and realities is seen in his treatment of fasting and the Sabbath.

Moreover, when Jesus said, "by their fruits ye shall know them," and "seek first the Kingdom of God,"[g] he gave his disciples, in the light of his own life and teaching, a timeless way for testing customs and institutions as well as personal conduct; and this way corresponds to that which leaders in different schools of thought now apply to our social institutions. As John Dewey says: "Democracy has many meanings, but if it has a moral meaning, it is found in resolving that the supreme test of all political institutions and industrial arrangements shall be the contributions they make to the all-round growth of every member of society."[11] Or, as another modern philosopher puts it, in full accord with the aims and principles of Jesus: "The intrinsic worth of persons, of their creative capacities, and of a world-wide community of creative personalities forms an objective principle of good by which ultimately all our interests and desires must be tested."[12]

He Gives True Community a Universal Appeal

Jesus' way of testing the conduct and customs of men by an ever expanding commonwealth of values discouraged all arbitrary and rigid institutionalism, and it helps to explain the universality of his influence. It illustrates how he kept his teaching free from the limitations of any particular time and place, even while he was dealing with concrete situations. It shows also how he tried to keep his disciples free from a too literal or legalistic observance of his teaching, and from the bondage of minute rules that might later fetter the influence of the same Spirit that inspired him.

Another way by which Jesus made his teaching universal is pointed out by a modern scientist: "The amazing insight of Jesus is revealed in his having kept himself free from creedal statements, particularly statements that reflect the state of man's knowledge or ignorance of the universe that was characteristic of his times. . . . The things that a man does not say often reveal the understanding and penetration of his mind even more than the things he says. The fact that

Jesus confined himself so largely to the statement of truths that still seem to us to have eternal value is what has made him a leader and teacher of such supreme influence throughout the centuries."[13]

This universality of Jesus is seen also in the response of people who have been educated in the philosophies of other great teachers. An elderly Chinese official, for instance, talking about the difference between Jesus and other foremost spiritual teachers—Laotse, Buddha, and Confucius—put his conclusion in these words: "He seems to me to have the power to create a more delicate conscience."[14] So also William Lecky, after comparing the influence of Jesus with that of earlier philosophers, concluded: "It was reserved for Christianity to present to the world an ideal character, which through all the changes of eighteen centuries has inspired the hearts of men with an impassioned love, has shown itself capable of acting on all ages, nations, temperaments, and conditions, has been not only the highest pattern of virtue but the strongest incentive to its practice, and has exercised so deep an influence that it may be truly said that the simple record of three short years of active life has done more to regenerate and to soften mankind than have all the disquisitions of philosophers and all the exhortations of moralists. This has indeed been the wellspring of whatever is best and purest in the Christian life."[15]

This universal appeal of Jesus and his expanding influence in all human relationships was made possible also by his unprecedented attitude toward women, and by his new departure in the treatment of children. He is, in fact, the first teacher on record to give the child a fair chance to contribute to its own education and to the moral and spiritual growth of its elders. According to Jesus, the child has at least as much to teach the man as the man the child, and there is a fellowship of the child with the man yet to be realized. The practice of such fellowship by Jesus may help to explain the quick response of children to him, and the eagerness of mothers to bring their children under his influ-

ence. Women trusted him spontaneously. In view of the
limitations they suffered at the time, it is the more significant
that Jesus welcomed their public co-operation, and was accompanied on at least one of his tours and on his last journey
to Jerusalem by women like "Joanna, the wife of Chuzza,
the chancellor of Herod, who ministered to him out of their
means."[h] Similarly, the relation between Jesus and the two
sisters, Martha and Mary, is prophetic of the unselfish friendships between men and women that have been realized so
much more completely since he led the way. His attitude,
though often disregarded in such relationships, now more
than ever encourages the freer co-operation of women with
men in the achievement of a contributive society.[16]

Thus differences, not only of age and sex but also of tem-
perament, occupational interests, and racial cultures, are
harmonized in so far as the influence of Jesus prevails. The
wider appreciations he inspires surmount age-old barriers and
reveal ever greater possibilities of intimacy and co-operation
to many whose differences once estranged them.

He Is "the Pioneer of Life" for Building Community

If we are to make the most of this universality of Jesus,
our inadequate opinions about him must be supplemented
by fellowship in the spirit that he communicates. Thus the
indifference and antipathy of some or the passing enthusiasm
of others, which often accompanies insufficient acquaintance
with a great man, will be transcended in the search for truth
which Jesus inspires. When an intimate disciple discouraged
a man who was doing good work because "he does not follow
us," Jesus said, "Do not stop him. He who is not against us
is for us."[i] His constant encouragement of the search for truth
from any quarter is reflected in the Fourth Gospel. The
words are typical of his attitude. They encourage the scientific spirit at its best. "No one who comes to me will I ever
turn away." "If you live in accordance with what I teach, . . .
you will know the truth and the truth will set you free."[j]

To those who put Jesus most completely to the test, he

was "the pioneer of life."[k] He sounded its depths and disclosed its resources as has no other master of the art of living. Who, then, can set limits to what might follow if the Spirit of love and truth living in him should unite and guide his disciples?

Questions for Further Thought and Discussion

What are the outcomes, in community and personality, of codifying Jesus' declared principles into set rules and dogmas? What are the outcomes, on the other hand, of considering them "mere ideals," by which we can never aspire actually to live?

Is it a new experience that in our generation psychological studies and neurotic needs point people to Christianity?

If first-century pagan ethics were "part of a philosophy," and those of Christians "part of a religion," what are the parallel systems and groups in today's world?

Is the Christian attitude to women and children unique among world faiths?

3

THE SCOPE OF COMMUNITY INSPIRED
BY JESUS

He Fulfills Ethics, Science, and Religion

THERE IS an alternative to exploitation, violence, and war, supported by good precedents, though it still waits to be tried on a scale commensurate with its importance. This alternative, whatever you call it, corresponds to the steadfast pursuit in all relationships of that new order of life which Jesus set forth as the controlling aim for mankind in this world: "Do not be troubled, then," he said, "and cry, 'What are we to eat?' or 'What are we to drink?' or 'How are we to be clothed?' The Gentiles seek all these things; and your heavenly Father knows that you need them all. But seek first his kingdom and his righteousness, and all these things shall be yours as well."ᵃ Jesus was not promising the necessities of life on a basis of individualistic attainment. On the contrary, his assurance of enough to make the good life possible for everyone was based on sound principles of co-operation. Had these principles been consistently applied, they would have done away with slavery, forestalled feudalism, and turned the inventive energies of men, which these institutions almost paralyzed, into constructive means for the common welfare. But, having discarded the co-operating way of Jesus, western civilization has maintained exploitations like those of slavery and feudalism throughout the industrial revolution to the present time. The economy of potential plenty that Jesus long ago envisaged is only now beginning to be appreciated by scientists, economists, and men of affairs. Those who do foresee this possibility, whatever their point of view, recognize that it cannot be realized by the present struggle of conflicting interests; and many are coming to see that a good life for everyone depends upon principles of control and motivation that correspond in general to the principals of Jesus. History and recent advance in the physical and social sciences help us to see more clearly than was possible in earlier generations that Jesus forecast no impossible Utopia, that, on the contrary, he set as a goal for humanity the most practical and comprehensive intention that has ever fired the imaginations of men.

The scope of this intention may be seen from different angles. It corresponds with what Eugene Lyman found to be the supreme principle of ethics: "the fullest development of every human personality through the co-operative creation of a world-wide community of persons." It corresponds also with what he found to be the supreme principle of religion: "the maximum of harmonious interaction between the personalities of men and the Deepest Reality of the universe."[1] Or, as Henry Wieman put it, "the Kingdom was Jesus' word for the total maximum of possibility for good which can be accomplished in us and through us and round about us in so far as we make right adaptation to God."[2] In its human relations Jesus portrayed it as nothing less than a world of brothers, living for the best welfare of the entire family.

This wide scope of his intention and influence is seen also in its encouragement of the scientific spirit, even in dark and reactionary times. Arthur Compton shows how Jesus gave this encouragement in the message that the future has in store for the race something better than anything it has known in the past. Neither India nor China ever offered this hope because they were always looking back on the Golden Age. Arthur Compton found the scientific spirit born before in Arabia and Greece, but without the spiritual content to keep it alive. The religious background, so essential for the continued development of science, he found given to Christendom as Jesus inspired His followers to know, to be, and to do the best. "He promised freedom of thought, liberty of action, democracy of spirit, the only setting in which science can thrive without fetters of fear. He gave to men the resistless urge to go forward, teaching them that faith begets courage and courage begets action."[3]

He Brings the Past to Fruition

The intention of Jesus that men should be concerned for the temporal life of their fellows becomes clearer to us the better we understand the foremost statesmen and social thinkers of Old Testament times, whose purposes Jesus said he had come to fulfill. On this point a statement by the Convocation of Canterbury goes so far as to say that we cannot discover what Jesus meant by the Kingdom of God without first considering the social and economic teachings of the Law and the prophets to which Jesus himself was continually referring his hearers.[4] The statement shows how the prophets dared to indict the religious and political leaders of their time for antisocial practices, quoting specific charges of Isaiah: "The Lord will enter into judgment with the elders of his people, and the princes thereof: for it is ye that have eaten up the vineyards; and the spoil of the poor is in your houses. What mean ye that ye crush my people, and grind the faces of the poor?"[b] In explaining legislation that was intended to forestall or to correct such abuses, the statement continues: "The tendency of the legislation was to raise the status of the Israelite slave to that of the hired workman who was to be treated as a brother. We find a prohibition of usury between Israelite and Israelite, and provision is taken against the permanent alienation of the land; various enactments protect labor. . . . The general well-being is a supreme consideration restricting the selfish acquisition of wealth. Manual labor is held in honor, it is the necessary basis of all society. . . . Christianity did not take over the formal legislation of the Old Testament, but it did inherit its moral principles which Jesus Christ deepened and universalized."[4]

Jesus, rather than the reputed leaders of his time, is in the true succession of these pioneers of the past. He charged the scribes and pharisees, the pretenders to leadership in his day, that they were "blind guides" who insisted upon legal technicalities or ritualistic minutiae, and "neglected the weightier requirements of the law—just judgment, mercy, and faithful dealing."[c] Jesus could see from Old Testament history that this neglect was in no way exceptional. Again and again the ruling classes in church and state had disregarded the economic provisions of the law and the warnings of the prophets, which were intended to further fair opportunity for everyone and helpful co-operation from everyone for the common welfare. Sharing this intention, Jesus "believes that his Father has sent him to found a new spiritual society, a new Order of Humanity. In spite of all the dangers involved in the use of the term, he links this new society to the ideal of Hebrew prophecy by describing it as 'the Kingdom of God.' "[5] By thus linking it with the most progressive ideal that men had espoused, Jesus strengthens its appeal for his disciples; he presents it as a continuous concern of God in history, and as a fulfillment of the persistent aspirations of men. He treats this new spiritual society both as a present possibility "within you" and as a future consummation in collective life, as dependent on God, yet not independent of men. He means that it is already germinally present among men; and that it grows on earth as they embody corresponding attitudes and conditions. Jesus, therefore, does not argue about this divine order of society as though it were merely a political or philosophical theory. He sees it as a potential fact. He lives on earth the life of this society, and dies rather than swerve from it.

He Shows Love at the Heart of the Universe

On what conviction about this new kind of society did Jesus stake his life? We need not try to define it precisely. There is general agreement that it was profoundly concerned with the possibilities of self-giving love. "Was there in the universe a behavior, however latent, which would respond to love? If men loved intelligently, honestly, without sentimentality, unreservedly, would the behavior of the world swing into line and support the venture? Was love truly more mighty than violence, more irresistible than logic or art or any social institution except as these embodied love? . . . Jesus made the experiment. The results are not yet all in: the experiment is not completed."[6] It has been interrupted, as we shall see, for centuries. But Jesus evidently intended his disciples to carry it forward in ways that would make more manifest and persuasive, throughout human living, such behavior of the universe as he believed to be in harmony with the nature of a God who is love.

In order to share this far-reaching confidence with his disciples, Jesus called them to continuous search and experiment with nature, men, and God: "Consider the lilies of the field, how they grow. . . . If God so clothes the grass of the field . . . will he not much more clothe you? O men, how little you trust him! Ask, . . . seek, . . . knock." By such persistent, experimental attempts to seek God's Realm and his goodness, and to do to others "whatever you would have men do to you,"[d] Jesus believed that his disciples would find more and more helpful response from within and beyond themselves. Yet how many of his disciples, even now, appreciate as Jesus did the intimate relations of men with one another and with nature, and the dependence of both upon "the Creator Spirit" for their proper functioning.

The responsibilities that flow from this intimate relation with nature are emphasized by William Temple: "Man is a part of the system of nature, whatever he may be beside. He must study the ways of nature and follow them, for he is utterly dependent on the natural world. Consequently, he must not think of natural resources as there for him to exploit to his own immediate advantage, but must rather co-operate with the natural process and so, in the long run, gain a far greater advantage. This is of primary importance in relation to man's treatment of the soil. The treatment of the earth by man the exploiter is not only imprudent but sacrilegious. We are not likely to correct our hideous mistakes in this realm unless we can recover the mystical sense of our oneness with nature. I labour this precisely because many people think it fantastic; I think it is fundamental to sanity."[7]

To practice such partnership with nature and to enjoy its varied ministry to men, as Jesus did, will surely help us to realize his convictions about an intimately co-operating God and a corresponding behavior of men and nature. Such convictions are of far greater reach and depth than an hypothesis. Yet if they do not come to us at first as convictions, we can at least take them as hypotheses to serve as a working basis for life. What we most need to know can be found out only by acting on the assumption that it may be so. This is true of the assumption that there is support in the universe for the moral aspirations of man, help for him in his ethical struggle. What if the universe is partly hostile or indifferent to man at certain points! "There is still room for the assumption that it is friendly to him at vital points. Not to make the effort to find out whether this assumption will hold is to miss the only chance to overcome the hostility and endure the indifference."[8]

It is just here that Jesus helps men to overcome the pessimism of the modern temper in dealing with the nature and possibilities of the universe. He carries this problem of the universe beyond the stage of abstract reasoning, and summons men to put it to the test of action in the co-operant use of all resources; for only as we experimentally develop such co-operation can we discover how far the universe supports it. We cannot solve this problem of the universe by the physical sciences alone. We must learn the nature and use of moral as well as physical energy. We know enough about the response of the universe to those who practice mutual aid to justify our advance in that direction. This is our only hope for truth and our only chance for life. "Those who are temperamentally unable to take the necessary attitude of trust in the universe and in their fellows at least owe this much to the scientific spirit they profess to serve, that they should encourage and not attack the explorers."[8]

Such a friendly attitude is further justified because this exploration, as proposed by Jesus, not only encourages the scientific spirit to the utmost but carries forward the only experience of the race that points toward its survival and growth. What he proposes is not a pattern that may be outgrown but a continuing process of life, deeply rooted in our racial inheritance. It develops the mutual aid and solidarity of tribal days which were gradually lost as city states and their class divisions supplanted village communities, only to be merged into great empires maintained by force. These empires succumbed to the same kind of force because, seeking power and glory, they forsook the life giving qualities of sharing and serving. "These values have been preserved in humble groups, many of whom have been wiped out in blood and most of them neglected by the historians who have told the might of the empires and the majesty of the churches that crushed them. Those who cannot find any continuity of ethical development, who think history must begin anew with us, and those who reject the ethic of Jesus because they hold the standards of simpler days to be unavailable for a complex society, might consider the process by which nervous organisms, species, and a social order came from simple cells. It now appears that mutual aid is not only the power of cohesion and continuance for human society, but is also, biologically speaking, the vital aspect of the race. It is the secret of man's emergence as a species and the hope for his continuance. It is thus the deathless part of man's racial inheritance which is embodied in Jesus, which he declares to be the life of God seeking to express itself in men."[9]

He Includes Nature, Men, and God in Community

When the life of God is given free course to express itself in a partnership of men and nature, those who take part in it can better detect the fallacies and avoid the pitfalls in the seductive craze for self-expression. The more fully they share in the purpose of God for the world, the more clearly they see how the craze for self-expression tends to make character egocentric and self-limited, how the putting foremost of one's own development, whether in art, science, business, or any other pursuit, interferes with the highest attainment in any sphere. What Ralph Sockman says about the distinguishing marks of the genuine artist is true of any really great soul: "He is trying to express something through himself rather than merely trying to express himself through something. . . . Michelangelo beholding unpainted beauty was yearning to express not himself but it. No great work of art, or of science, for that matter, has ever been inspired by the motive of self-expression. The doer has forgotten himself in his desire to give form or voice to something felt to be greater than himself. The old paradox holds true that he who would find himself must lose himself. It is in devotion to larger loyalties that man finds satisfying self-expression."[9]

When the disciple thus loses his self-centeredness by sharing in the partnership of men and nature with God, he finds the conditions that Jesus prescribed for man's fulfillment. He believed that when men seek the fulfillment of life for all possible partners in true fellowship with God and with nature, their own conflicting desires will be progressively transformed and unified by the Spirit of truth and love. Only in this way, as he showed, does one become in the full sense co-worker with a redeeming God who desires that all his children shall be as like himself as possible.[e] Jesus staked his own life on the conviction that when you thus devote yourself to the Kingdom of God on earth, and when you take the risks of making known in word and deed as much as you can apprehend of its aim and method, "it is the Spirit of your Father that will speak through you," and foster in you a disposition and conduct more and more like his own.[f]

All this suggests that Jesus intended his disciples to carry forward in their personal and corporate life the new beginning for mankind that came with the Incarnation of God, as seen in the life and conduct of Jesus himself, "stamped with God's own character."[g] In explaining this turning point in history, a book of apt experience for laymen says: "The good news of Christianity is that God has ennobled man through the Incarnation, showing that we can receive his very self, that he can be revealed in an ordinary life lived on earth. We are saved from our sinful selfhood because God was in Christ, reconciling the world unto himself.[h] But more: such a practical theology shows that this Incarnation was not something which became real just nineteen hundred years ago in Palestine. It is fact and experience in which we can live now. Just as Jesus was aware of being 'ordained to preach the gospel to the poor, to bind up the broken-hearted'—so we, as members of his continuing presence in today's world, are ordained to carry along such activity of God's spirit."[10]

This work of the Spirit manifest in Jesus comes to men not merely as individuals, but as members of the community inspired by him. "For God did not manifest himself in Jesus alone, but in the life of the group which was formed about him and in whose creation he was himself the decisive factor. It was in Jesus *as known in the Church* that the fresh activity of God among men, which we call the revelation in Christ, occurred. And that revelation is not merely remembered in the Church; it is constantly present wherever there is genuine Christian fellowship. . . . The sacrament of the Lord's Supper has its primary significance not as a mere memorial of something that happened centuries ago, but rather as an outward symbol of the fact that the God of truth and grace, of nature and history, who made himself known in the life of the group which Christ called into being, is constantly making himself known afresh in the life of the Christian community. . . . Needless to say, God's revelation of himself is not confined to the Church. . . . But it is safe to affirm as a common faith the conviction that as God revealed himself most effectively in the first century, so He does in the twentieth—in the fellowship of contrite hearts united in devotion to the God and Father of our Lord Jesus Christ. Into that fellowship all are invited to come—or to return. In that fellowship, transcending race, nation, culture—yea, time and death—are forgiveness, guidance, and strength for us and our children, the salvation which each one of us and our world so desperately need."[11]

Questions for Further Thought and Discussion

What are the closest parallels to the Christian community as a movement built about an actual historical person, and somehow living in that person?

What value do we find in the peculiarly modern idea (Wieman's) that Jesus was one who "made an experiment"?

Did our Lord's creating of community arise from the fact that his followers became like him in important respects? How far can we go in the "imitation of Christ" effort?

What do we mean today by "the Kingdom of God on earth"?

Considering the phrase, "the sustaining community": what sustains, and what is sustained in it?

4

VERIFICATION BY PAUL OF TARSUS

The Letters of a Contemporary Vouch for Jesus

SOME WELL ATTESTED LETTERS of a Roman citizen who was also a patriotic Jew, a contemporary of Jesus and at first his opponent, give important evidence at this stage of our inquiry. In the view of those well qualified to judge, these letters are a primary evidence today for the historicity of Jesus. They show how his influence brought a baffled but able young contemporary from inner conflict and nationalistic ambition to a world-uniting purpose of fellowship; and how this larger purpose works continuously, even through suffering, toward the development of more co-operant types of life.

These letters, particularly those which the most searching criticism still attributes to Paul of Tarsus, contain many of the earliest extant allusions to Jesus. They have led no less an authority than Gilbert Murray to characterize Paul as "certainly one of the great figures in Greek literature." This pre-eminence was due to the transforming influence in Paul of a life and character uniquely different from any ever before recorded. Paul's early purpose began to be changed within a few years after the crucifixion on Calvary. When he began to write of this change in himself, before the gospel narratives had been written, Paul attributed to Jesus, throughout his vivid correspondence, the same influence and characteristics that later appeared in the other writings of the New Testament.

It has been said that Paul's letters tell us little or nothing about the historical Jesus, and that Paul was not interested in the details of Jesus' life. "This is a superficial judgment. But details are not needed. What matters is that the Jesus Paul preached should not be different in character from the Jesus of gospel history. And he is not." Paul attributed to the influence of Jesus such fruits of the Spirit as love, joy, peace, good temper, kindliness, generosity, fidelity, gentleness, self-control.[a] These correspond exactly with the qualities evinced in life by the Jesus of Gospel history.[1] Moreover the changed purpose and attitude seen in Paul's own life and work, his affection for those he had won to the new way of living, his cheerful acceptance of suffering and possible death[b]—all reflect the same spirit that is seen in the Jesus of the gospels.

Paul was, above all, a representative of the Christlike temper of love which transcended as never before the barriers of class and race. "He wrote the greatest of all hymns to love.[c] There is not one line that does not fit the Christ of gospel story as it fits no one else. Why had no one described that quality before in all the glorious roll of the literature of Greece? Why did not Sophocles burst into such a song when he had before him the example of Antigone? Why did Euripides, the human, never compose such an ode though he pictured many a hero and heroine? The reason surely is that these princes of Greek literature had not met in life this phenomenon—love like that consistently manifested by Jesus. They knew the love of passion, of the home, of brother and sister, of friend and friend. But they had never seen that quality in its pre-eminence. Paul was not writing about a love he had dreamed of: he had experienced it and he had practiced it. He belonged to the most exclusive of peoples. . . . Never has there been a nation that has kept up the barriers against other nations so effectively throughout all ages. Yet members of that exclusive race had suddenly begun

to mix freely with men and women of other races. They did
not do it easily. They had qualms about eating with Gentiles.
But Paul had insisted they must and they did."[1,d] Thus began
a national, or rather an international revolution. And it began with the disciples of Jesus. He had taught them to love,
even enemies, despite differences of race or condition; and
apparently that amazing social conduct of his followers was a
proof of their historical faithfulness to his teaching.[1] To the
end of a life filled with unprecedented situations Paul taught
and practiced a new ethic, which he claimed to have derived
from Jesus and which corresponds with the ethical teaching
of Jesus as we find it in the synoptic gospels.

Thus the historicity and ethical temper of Jesus are
vouched for by a contemporary of penetrating mind who
had unusual access to first-hand evidence and every reason
for scrutinizing it closely. And of this contemporary there
can be no doubt. "Among all the great men of antiquity
there is none, with the exception of Cicero, whom we may
know so intimately as Saul of Tarsus. It is, however, only
in our own day that his personal characteristics have been
intelligently studied."[2] All the more impressive, therefore, is
a thorough study of Paul which concludes: "To know that
Paul was historical is to know the historicity of Jesus."[3]

This Nationalist Finds an International Purpose

This many-sided Paul, well called by Glover "a Garibaldi
for adventure and a Socrates for thought," is also one of the
best examples of how an adequate purpose helps a man to
grow toward the full use of his powers. Paul illustrates how
a traditional purpose, confined by race or nation, can blind
and frustrate a man; and how it can be transcended by a
purpose of universal scope, through which one's whole life
is enriched and a maximum of energy released. During this
process, as one writer puts it, "Paul became the pioneer for
European thought in the moral analysis of self"; and he
still helps many to find a solution for their inner conflicts.

Unfortunately, his letters, including passages that he wrote only for a passing emergency, have been used on both sides of later controversies in ways that do injustice to the man he came to be, and that prejudiced many against him. Yet this is no reason why we should hesitate to profit by his exhilarating experience for, in spite of all the misunderstanding, we can know the real Paul—his difficulties no less than the secret of his growth and influence—as we know no other person in Biblical history, scarcely any other person in antiquity. And the well-attested experience of this transformed Stoic-Pharisee is not invalidated by any of the conflicting theories that grew around it. On the contrary, the highest tides of creative life since Paul's day show that as long as men concentrate on a purpose akin to his, they accomplish more for a wholesome world-society and for their own fulfillment in it than do those who either lose themselves in irrelevant pursuits or seek first their own limited self-realization. Here is the authentic unfolding, still in process, of a more comprehensive purpose than has ever yet been given the place it deserves in education, religion, or current affairs.[4]

To understand Paul as personifying this purpose, we must read his letters in the light of the intense controversy occasioned by those who tried to compel the Gentile Christians to submit to circumcision and other Jewish ordinances. The false charges made by Paul's opponents and the gravity of the crisis account for much that otherwise might seem unduly personal or vehement in his letters. Some of his opponents had hounded Paul through the Greek and Roman world in order to destroy his influence by calumny, and to impose upon the churches he had founded an elaborate sectarian legalism. Well might the founder of these churches be aflame with indignation at the insidious attempt of these emissaries from Jerusalem to impose such practices upon Greek and Roman Christians. Had these emissaries succeeded, they would, as Peter admitted, "have put a yoke upon the neck of the disciples, which neither our fathers nor we have been able to bear."[e] What began as a religion of freedom and universal fellowship would have ended in the bondage of a divisive sect. It now appears that the whole future of civil and religious liberty, and of Christianity as a world-uniting religion, was at stake. Paul felt the issue acutely because he himself had been a sincere and baffled member of what he later characterized as "the strictest sect of our religion."[f] He believed however that no Jew should be compelled to give up rites which his conscience constrained him to observe. The issue arose over the attempt to compel Gentiles to be circumcised and to observe other Jewish rites as a condition of membership in the Christian Church; and here Paul believed that a principle of spiritual freedom was endangered.

It has been claimed that Paul's references to his earlier religion have not done justice to Judaism at its best. Doubtless Paul would have admitted that he was not dealing with Judaism at its best, "that at all times it was *possible,* even within Judaism, for men to transcend the purely legal attitude, and that as a matter of fact many saints of the old order had done so."[5] Even the letters occasioned by the great controversy show Paul's concern for the mission and fate of Israel, and his appreciation of the law as "a schoolmaster."[g]

He Finds Common Ground for Jews and Christians

It is high time for more Jews and Christians to seek a better understanding of the later Paul, and of the principles of religious and political development for which he stood. In so far as these principles are now applied in the light of a common Biblical background by those who worship the same God whom Paul and the great Hebrew prophets worshiped, we can co-operate as joint heirs of a common heritage. This heritage helped Paul to recognize in Jesus the hope of a universal fellowship. Better understood now, this common inheritance should help all of us to realize the significance of Jesus for our fateful time.

The significance of Jesus is illuminated by the impressive testimony of Sholem Asch. While still holding a Jewish point of view, he records this profound experience, culminating in

Jesus: "He, as no other, works in the human consciousness like a second, higher nature and leaves man no rest in his animal state, wakens him, raises him, and inspires him to the noblest deeds and sacrifices. . . . No one but he sheds about himself such an aura of moral power, which, with a divine touch, has moulded our world and our character, being the most potent influence in our everyday lives, the measure and scale for our deeds at every hour." Writing of what "God has given us through his chosen prophets, both of the Old and the New Testaments, and of the will of God, expressed through Christ and the Sermon on the Mount," Asch concludes: "These teachings created our civilization, which we call the civilization of the Jewish-Christian idea. I can see no hope of our unhappy world save that which lies in the renewal of the moral and spiritual estates which our common ideal of faith has created."[6]

Similarly, John Cournos, the Jewish novelist and critic, pleads for their closer co-operation, saying, "I have repeatedly stated that Jesus stands as the very apex of Jewish culture. . . . The Jews, in their later indifference to Jesus, were deflected from their own line of culture, of which Jesus was the highest representative. Notwithstanding this, the Jews' secret subconscious striving is toward Jesus, who stands for all those virtues for which the noblest Jews have been fighting through all the centuries of Christendom. Why, then, not acknowledge Jesus openly? The time is propitious. . . . The Christian and Jewish points of view have never before coincided as they do today. . . . Democracy stands or falls with them."[7]

Toward this better co-operation between Jews and Christians, Elton Trueblood has made an important contribution in a terse little book, *Foundations for Reconstruction*. He finds these foundations in the Ten Commandments, which he restates in universal terms, illustrated from contemporary life. He shows that they represent the cumulative insight of the greatest of the prophets, and "the moral principles which have provided, in large measure, the chief standard of conduct in the life of the West. . . . An important fact about these principles," he says, "is that they constitute a cementing element in our cultural life. All three chief groups in our spiritual federation, Jews, Roman Catholics, and Protestants, accept their validity. This, therefore, is ground upon which we as a people can meet and from which we can move forward. Incidentally, this body of teaching provides material which *can* be taught and *ought* to be taught in our public schools. This is not sectarian any more than the Twenty-third Psalm is sectarian. . . . Each of the commandments can be greatly expanded; each can be stated in positive rather than negative form and ought to be so stated. When this is done, we have positive principles of such a nature that a good society cannot be constructed or reconstructed without reference to them."[8]

Should not, then, the exigencies of our time lead both Jews and Christians to a better mutual understanding, not only of what once separated them but of what should now unite them in world-wide co-operation. Thus we might all profit by Paul's struggle to keep the future open for the very freedom and fellowship that is now endangered everywhere. We return, therefore, to the story of Paul's expanding purpose and world embracing hope, so relevant now to the present needs of mankind.

His New Purpose Clarifies the Purpose of Creation

As a young man, little dreaming that he was approaching a decisive moment in history, Paul was riding to Damascus with a group of attendants in behalf of what seemed to him the foremost cause of the world—the cause of his ancestral religion and of national unity. In his mind religion and nationalism were closely related because he thought of both as intended to promote the ascendency of his race. In repressing those who differed from him, he thought of himself as serving both God and his country.

As Paul rode forth on this "patriotic" errand, he showed no outward sign that before this decisive day was over he would be calling in question his whole conception of religion and government. He was apparently satisfied with his purpose and prospects in life. He was recognized as a man of learning and high ideals, of earnestness and courage. His determination to stamp out the dangerous sect associated with Jesus enhanced the esteem in which he was held by the ruling class of his nation, and gave him the leadership of this special mission.

Yet Paul was not really satisfied. He was hampered by his own inner conflict, which he later described with deep insight. He had yet to learn that his baffling struggle to attain a legalistic, self-confident righteousness arrested his development. He had to learn also the limitations imposed upon him by his pride of race and of personal achievement.[h]

As Paul drew near to Damascus, his difficulties began to clear in what later seemed to him a decisive spiritual experience, which gathered around Jesus. This experience made Paul doubt the wisdom of his own mission. It challenged his past ambitions by confronting him with a different purpose and type of life. Even before this experience, Paul had seen the influence of Jesus in the life and character of men like Stephen and others whom he had persecuted. Now, in his first intimate touch with Jesus himself, Paul found surprising meanings in the unusual life and death that had deeply influenced Stephen, and had now begun to influence him.[i]

The purpose and method of Jesus seemed so new and revolutionary to Paul that he had to gain time and detachment in order to fathom them. So, from the crumbling world of his past experience, he went away into Arabia. There he spent unhurried days, perhaps the best part of three years. He had to learn more about the nature and resources of his new mission in order to know what his own practice and preaching should be.[j]

As Paul saw the character and self-giving of Jesus in clearer light, he could no longer read the meaning of life in terms of self-centered righteousness and an exclusive class or nation. In the universal love revealed in Jesus, Paul saw the old

walls of racial and class intolerance broken down. He found
that any purpose worthy of a God whom Jesus called Father
involved the working of his Spirit in men on such a scale as
to develop a new type of character, a new race of human
beings, and consequently a new order of society. He came to
believe that the God and Father of Jesus desires all his children "to bear the likeness of his Son, that he might be the
Eldest in a vast family of brothers."[k]

In the attempt to realize this ideal, Paul became convinced that those who love God—those who are responsive
to his purpose for a new humanity, and eager to become like
him—may find that in everything God works for good toward the development in them of a new and Christlike character.[l] This conviction did not blind Paul to the evils that
hinder this purpose of life. On the contrary, it made him
more eager to overcome evil with good;[m] and it encouraged
him in the hope that this very work of overcoming evil might
help men and women to grow more like Jesus. So Paul
learned to make use of everything, privation and weakness,
persecution and sorrow, to enlarge his sympathies, and to
bring him into more effective accord with others through
whom the same Spirit works for the new manhood. He ex-
plored ways of turning whatever might befall him to good
account, not only for personal discipline but for social health.
He worked at tentmaking, for instance, not only to disarm
his critics who accused him of self-seeking but also to keep
himself from becoming a burden upon the churches he vis-
ited, and to further fellowship with them.

Personal and social aims, as Paul now saw them, were harmonized and fulfilled in the all-inclusive purpose that was
taking shape within him. He gave a glimpse of its vast outreach when he wrote to the Romans: "Even the creation
waits with eager longing for the sons of God to be revealed."
Paul had an inkling of what a good day it would be for
other living creatures also when the influence of men had
become like the influence of Jesus. He was encouraged by
the hope "that creation as well as men would one day be

freed from its bondage to decay, and gain the glorious freedom of the children of God."[n]

This expanding view of the goal of creation should help us to deal more wisely with nature and with common things in our daily living. "The goal tells us something important about the entire process. Ours is the kind of world which, from the beginning, was preparing for the emergence of creatures who, with all their sins, would be able to appreciate values and choose by reference to the good. *The fact that spirit is, at any point, part of the continuous cosmic process is the most important single fact we know about the process.* That the world should give rise to creatures sensitive to values and concerned with duty gives one clue to the secret of the nature of the world." Therefore, as Elton Trueblood shows in *The Common Ventures of Life,* "the more we identify our spirits with the rest of the natural order, and the more we see matter and spirit as a mutually beneficent combination, the more we are compelled, in reason, to posit the reality of a transcendent Creator of both. God is known best, not by separation from common things, but by such identification with them that we find the divine meaning latent in them."[9]

Questions for Further Thought and Discussion

In what ways did Paul add to the picture of Jesus he found that inspired the devotion of the community?

What evidence is there, in our general knowledge, that the early Christians may not have been "doing justice to Judaism at its best"?

To what extent are Christians and Jews today kept apart by mere proud group allegiance (on both sides), rather than by devotion to truth?

What are the pre-conditions for a "Damascus-road experience" in the life of a modern skeptical American?

5

CONTINUING VERIFICATION IN LIFE

The Universe a Field for Endless Growth

WHAT WE HAVE SEEN of Paul's hope for the development of more sensitive and co-operating types of human life seems even more significant in the brighter light now dawning on the evolutionary process. In a broad view of life, scientists now see that on the whole it has not paid to be cruel and self-seeking and unsociable and ugly. "It is, so we are now assured, the animals that have been helpful to one another and have cultivated kindly ways and have loved beautiful color and have elaborated and sharpened their minds that have tended, and are still tending, to survive. The dog is beating the lion in the race of life. Parasites who will not work, but cling on to some more vigorous life, and spend their lives in sucking, tend not only to be hideously ugly, but to degenerate. We find nature constantly experimenting in the direction of complexity of mind and elaboration of beauty."[1] In exploring the source of civilization, Gerald Heard found the essentials of progress in those forms of life which develop sensitiveness, adaptability, and concern for others, rather than in those which arrest their development through absorption in acquisitive or defensive measures or superficial aims. When such absorption prevails widely and long, it dooms both individuals and the species.[2] It is the morally alert and co-operating characters among mankind who find in the long run that the universe supports their efforts and survival.[3]

This degeneration of the cruel and self-seeking types of life, and the success in survival of the intelligent, sensitive, and co-operant types, points the direction in which man should now advance. It is not the direction taken by the great, heavily armored beasts of prehistoric times. "They piled up armaments to such an extent that at last they sank beneath their weight of armor and disappeared, to make room for more inventive and sociable forms of life." The human race need no longer imitate the extinct animals by trying all possible roads in the hope of finding the right one —the costly method of trial and error; for we have now come to a stage where we can see more or less clearly the direction in which we ought to move forward. We can avoid the unsuccessful experiments of the past. "We cannot create, apparently, what was not there originally, but of all the multitude of possibilities existent, and of all the new variations appearing, we can choose which shall be fostered, and which shall be checked and destroyed." Variations in a race appear without any reason that man has yet seen clearly; but, when once they appear, they remain unless they are forcibly checked.[1] By encouraging everything in ourselves and in our environment that increases our capacity to be other-regarding, we can foster the kind of changes that nature has already demonstrated as desirable.

As we survey the long process of nature, with its myriad delays and failures, its cruelties and bloodshed, we may be dismayed at what seems to be a ruthless severity of discipline, especially if we read back into the scene our own human sensitiveness. But if we would do justice to the process as a whole, we must be on guard against attributing our sensibilities to creatures differently organized. It may be doubted whether there is any real pain such as we know without "the highly sensitive nervous system which accompanies the development of the higher areas of the brain, the anticipation of hurt due to our fore-knowledge of what is

to come, and the sympathy which enables us to share the
suffering of our fellows. These are attributes of humanity.
The others suffer, each in the measure of its capacity; their
range is not ours nor anything at all closely resembling it.
And to assume it to be so is to set up the bogey of a night-
mare as truth."[4]

Neither should we see the earlier stages of life merely as
wastage, or as having only preparatory value for the evolution of man. At many stages below the human "the creature
is no mere puppet impelled solely from without, but itself
in some sort an entity capable alike of an ever more definite
individuality and of ever more complex interaction with its
surroundings and its fellows."[4]

Without some such freedom, some alternative possibilities
in this reaction to environment, carrying with them inevitable risks and difficult choices, the higher skills and co-
ordinating purposes never could have been developed. As
was pointed out long ago, if man had not been liable to die
of cold and hunger, he would never have developed his skill
as builder and weaver, gardener and farmer, his arts of
housewifery and social organization.[5] And without dangerous
hazards and decisions there would have been no opportunity
for "creating creators" who might work in partnership with
God.

This growing partnership, leading to ever closer intimacy
and likeness between *The Creator Spirit* and men, is well
explained by Charles E. Raven. As a geneticist, he once
thought of the universe as a mechanism, but now finds it
more significant as a school. "It has ordered conditions, a
rigid framework of law, without which, much as we rebel
against it, there could be no learning." Recognizing the
difficulties, and looking not only at the lowest grades of life
but also at the highest, Raven sees that in spite of apparent
ruthlessness the universe has been the training ground for
humanity, the medium for the production and perfection of
goodness in finite minds. In a survey of biology and psychology, he shows that new knowledge in these fields sup-

ports a view of the Creator Spirit as working not only for advance in nature but also for the development of Christlike character in men.[4]

Suffering and Evil Overcome for the Common Good

When we consider creation from this point of view, we gain better understanding of the sufferings and evils we meet and how to deal with them. Even though we recognize that no adequate explanation of evil has yet been formulated, we may share a view of the world as a place for the development of moral beings: "Its purpose cannot be to make the world a fit environment for perfect beings; it is not such, and there are no perfect beings on its surface. Nor can it be to return to each man the just rewards of his deeds, for it does not fulfill this purpose. . . . The struggle and pain of the world are the lot of the good as well as of the evil. But if they can be turned to the increase and refinement of goodness, to the lessening and conquest of evil, then their existence is not an insuperable obstacle to the ethical view of reality; it may even be regarded as an essential condition of such a view. Account for it how we may, the fact remains that the heroes and saints of history have passed through much tribulation, and that man is made perfect only through suffering. . . . A world of completely unerring finite beings, created and maintained so by the conditions of their life, would be a world of marionettes. Not such are the beings whom God is conceived as having created for communion with himself. They must fight their way upwards through the long stages of man's development. In this progress they have to attain reason and freedom, so that the good may be known and chosen, until, tried by every kind of circumstance, they find and assimilate the values which can transform the world and make themselves fit for the higher spiritual life."[6]

That these values, otherwise unattainable, may be won through the overcoming of evil is abundantly evident from our own experience and observation, and in the pages of biography. Jesus is the supreme illustration; and many an obscure soul has demonstrated the same truth by overcoming evil with good. Out of such experiences have come "insights which otherwise seem hidden, character which otherwise seems unattainable, and a transforming power for mankind's good which nothing else seems able to generate."[7]

To estimate the gains and the true inwardness of suffering "we must not go to the professional pessimist who counts up the grievances of humanity, as often as not from the vantage ground of a position of personal comfort. The sufferer himself has often a deeper sense of the significance of his experience. 'That which we suffer ourselves has no longer the same air of monstrous injustice and wanton cruelty that suffering wears when we see it in the case of others.'[8] This was the verdict of a man of letters whose whole life was a battle with disease and suffering, but who did his life's work with high courage and in serenity of soul. Such a judgment cannot be lightly set aside."[8]

This testimony of Robert Louis Stevenson may be supplemented by that of Katharine Mansfield, who died at the age of thirty-four with the promise of her best writing unfulfilled. Her latter years and her continuing influence show how physical and mental suffering wisely met may bring victory for one's self and the spirit of victory to others. After a long struggle with disease she wrote in her *Journal:* "I do not want to die without leaving a record of my belief that suffering can be overcome. For I do believe it. What must one do? . . . Accept it fully. Make it *part of life.* Everything in life that we really accept undergoes a change. So suffering must become love. This is the mystery. This is what I must do. I must pass from personal love to greater love." Thus pressing on through suffering to her appointed work, she wrote, a little later: "May I be found worthy to do it! Lord, make me crystal clear for thy light to shine through."[9]

That faith working through love is needed in dealing also with insidious social evils is seen in the life of the seventh Earl of Shaftesbury, England's greatest social reformer of the last century, whose faith was the mainspring of his work for reform. His faith was needed to meet the hazards and suffering which increased the more he sought the overthrow of evils deeply entrenched in the customs and institutions of his time. When the outlook for his factory legislation seemed dark, he wrote in his journal: "Twelve years of labor, anxiety, and responsibility! I have borrowed and spent in reference to my income enormous sums of money, and am shut out from every hope of emolument and path of honorable ambition. My own kinsfolk dislike my opinions and persecute me. I am excluded from my father's house because I have maintained the cause of the laborer. It has been toil by day and by night, fears and disappointments, prayers and tears, long journeys and unceasing letters."[10] Yet "Shaftesbury's pain and struggle bore their fruit, and at the time of his death it could be said that all the great social reforms of his generation were due more to his influence, character, and perseverance than to any other single cause. There could be no clearer demonstration that active faith is an indispensable part of the solution of the problem of evil."[11] This kind of faith does not accept the actual evils of the world as a necessary part of the good. Rather it seeks their defeat in the confidence that men are co-workers with God, consciously or unconsciously, wherever they are striving courageously and intelligently for the elimination of evils, and are changing the processes which produce evil into processes which produce good.[11]

In these changes, science is needed to take an important part through its effect upon physical and social conditions. But it appears that science, left to itself, will not always take this part. "Science may be used to entrench evils in society still more strongly, and to reinforce destructive agencies. Hence the conquest of evil is in the last analysis the responsibility of ethics and religion. The fight with evil becomes a matter of building a moral world and of evoking the fullest responsiveness to God in the depths of the human heart."[11]

This responsiveness to God grows into a better adjusted

world through men's Christlike self-giving. For such giving
evokes a kindred response from others. George Tyrrell tells
of his own response. Facing an agonizing obligation, he
wrote to a friend: "What a relief if one could conscien-
tiously wash one's hands of the whole concern! But then
there is that Strange Man upon his Cross who drives one
back again and again."[12] No one through the ages has so
moved men of every race and condition as has that Strange
Man, "lifted up" on his Cross, "bringing life and immortality to light," and drawing men to himself in deathless fellowship.[a] Thus through the years he has drawn men to his
Father also, leading them to pray and to work for a divine-
human Commonwealth that furthers the unity of his children in this world, and is, even now, "a colony of heaven,"
and a training school for citizenship there and here.[b] In
view of this destiny for men, the experience of co-operation
with God and nature has shown many disciples that the
suffering, self-giving love which they see in Jesus they may
discern also at the heart of the universe. And thus they have
begun to understand the universe as having a spiritual goal
toward which the Creator is still working through all who
seek to get the better of evil by doing good, in the spirit
of the divine self-sacrifice.[c]

Thus we can gain deeper insight and faith in divine Providence, which is so little understood. Without minimizing
what is wrong with the world and with ourselves, we can
see with Paul Tillich that "faith in divine Providence is the
faith that nothing can prevent us from fulfilling the ultimate meaning of our existence. Providence does not mean
a divine planning by which everything is predetermined,
as is an efficient machine. Rather, Providence means that
there is a creative and saving possibility implied in every
situation, which cannot be destroyed by any event. Providence means that the daemonic and destructive forces within
ourselves and our world can never have an unbreakable
grasp upon us, and that the bond which connects us with
the fulfilling love can never be disrupted. . . . It is not the

depth of our suffering, but the depth of our separation from God, which destroys our faith in Providence. Providence and the forgiveness of sins are not two separate aspects of the Christian faith; they are one and the same—the certainty that we can reach eternal life in spite of suffering and sin. Paul unites both words by saying, 'Who is he that condemneth? It is Christ Jesus . . . who maketh intercession for us,' and *therefore,* he continues, 'Who shall separate us from the love of Christ? Shall tribulation, or anguish, or persecution, or famine, or nakedness, or peril, or sword. . . ? In all these things we are more than conquerors through him who loved us. . . .' *This* is the faith in Providence, and this alone."[13]

"The Dawn of a New Phase of Evolution"

We may all help to verify this conception of life by cultivating the best religious, scientific, and artistic attitudes. "The artist uses the material world as means to the expression of that love of beauty which is one aspect of love of God, and thereby transfigures the material—delivers it, as Paul might say, from the bondage of decay into the liberty of glory. If we could all become artists over the whole of life, using our environment to express the highest spiritual relations within our reach, is it not possible that the influence of humanity upon the world might change its whole aspect? Paul at least thought that in some way the universe was waiting for men to attain right relations in the spiritual sphere—waiting for the revealing of the sons of God'! In attacking what was wrong with man he firmly believed that he was attacking the problem of the universe. Shall we put it this way, that the problem of reality is at bottom a problem of personal relations? No purely physical speculations will ever solve for us the problem of this tangled universe. Personality holds the cue; and the solution is personal and practical. The spiritual aspirations of men, faithfully followed, let us into the secret of evolution and give us the only [or the best] hint we can get of its purposes."[14]

This hint corresponds with what a leading biologist says about the present stage in the evolution of man: "As in former ages progress passed from individual cells to many-celled organisms, so now it is passing from individual organisms to society. . . . In man no less than in lower organisms the welfare and evolution of the species is of supreme concern. And the greatest and most practical work of religion is to further the evolution of a better race. A religion that looks merely to personal rewards or punishments in the present or future is not one of the highest type; on the other hand the religion of service and sacrifice for the good of others, the religion of which Christ was the great exemplar, must more and more become the religion of human society in future stages of evolution."[15]

Similarly, Lecomte du Noüy found in his searching study of *Human Destiny:* "Evolution continues in our time, *no longer on the physiological or anatomical plane but on the spiritual and moral plane.* We are at the dawn of a new phase of evolution. The evolved man has reached a state of development of his conscience which enables him to broaden his outlook, and to become fully aware of the magnificent role he can play as a responsible actor in Evolution. . . . Let him above all never forget that the divine spark is in him, in him alone, and that he is free to disregard it, to kill it, or to come closer to God by showing his eagerness to work with him, and for him."[16] With this conclusion of du Noüy, compare an early Christian experience: "We are God's children now; it does not yet appear what we shall be, but we know that when he appears we shall be like him, for we shall see him as he is. And every one who thus hopes in him purifies himself as he is pure."[d] Du Noüy found the experiences reflected in the New Testament to be typical of essential attitudes and purpose for the "new phase of evolution."

Questions for Further Thought and Discussion

*Typically, what does modern secularism set over against the sort of Christian
sense of destiny or philosophy of history outlined here: mechanism,
fatalism, chance progress or regression, emergent evolution, or other
claims?*

*In what specific areas of human experience does Christianity enable people
to "overcome evil with good"?*

*Has belief in evolution—in whatever form scientists have advanced it—fulfilled the dire predictions made some decades ago, as to its effect on
religion? Is this because the common man has never accepted it, or
because evolution has been assimilated by religion?*

*What do we mean by "Christian optimism" about the world, history, and
man, as opposed to secular optimism in these same fields?*

Part II

THE ROLE OF RELIGION AND SCIENCE IN COMMUNITY LIFE

6

RELIGION AND SCIENCE IN PARTNERSHIP

This Partnership Can Save the Future

CO-OPERATION between religion and science becomes more urgent as this generation decides whether atomic energy and biological science shall be used for wholesale destruction or for maximum increase of energy and health for all mankind. "When we consider what religion is for mankind, and what science is, it is no exaggeration to say that the future course of history depends upon the decision of this generation as to the relation between them. We have here the two strongest general forces (apart from the mere impulse of the various senses) which influence men."[1] This prophetic conclusion of a great mathematician and physicist, Alfred North Whitehead, who became a leading philosopher, is further confirmed by the second World War and its aftermath. A serious student of genetics, Charles E. Raven, who also became a foreward-looking philosopher, explains: "Both science and religion must take a share of blame for the appalling catastrophies which they ought to have been able to prevent. They represent the most important formative influences in the educational and indeed the intellectual life of the world. The complacency with which their leading representatives lay the blame [for the war] upon the social order, or Nazism, or the politicians, or the devil, makes it clear that they do not recognize their responsibility—or rather, since we are all involved, that we are all still impenitent and self-satisfied." Therefore, he shows the need to apply both science and religion in the development of ourselves and of society: "Knowledge divorced from life speedily becomes valueless and is always dangerous. For it is from experience as we live it out that the mind must constantly derive the provision of its raw material, the testing of its progress, the verification of its results. And here neither the senses nor the mind alone but the whole self is involved."[2] And here also not only whole selves but whole communities are involved. Under such conditions our problems become so many-sided and so interrelated that they require both science and religion applied harmoniously to the expanding tasks of community.

The necessity for such co-operation becomes clearer as foremost leaders of science explain its limitations and the catastrophe that will befall us unless we seek more help than science alone can give. For instance, Lecomte du Noüy concludes *The Road to Reason* by showing our present predicament: "We have forgotten that science limits itself to describing, interpreting, and predicting material phenomena, revealed by our senses. We have overlooked, behind the codified and conquered material forces, the directing forces that alone characterize man. We have looked solely for the things that connect him with brute matter and animals; we have lost interest in those that raise him above them. Yet this difference inspires the sentiment of that dignity which is inseparable from the unit we call Man. We had hoped that the transition between unorganized matter and thought was progressive. If this is so, we are still far from being able to prove it; if we wait to be sure of it before giving our attention to the moral factors of our evolution, we can be certain that it will be too late, and that this civilization of which we boast will have disappeared from the surface of the globe."[3]

With a similar warning, in his discussion of the role of

science in preserving democracy, Vannevar Bush, speaking from vast experience with atomic energy and other scientific problems, says: "Science has been misread. Science does not exclude faith. And faith alone can meet the threat that now hangs over us. . . . The course of history is determined by the faith that men are guided by. If they misread the lessons of expanding knowledge, and in their brazen egotism believe that all things are known or knowable, then they will see nothing but an endlessly repeating pattern of sordid strife. . . . If they see beyond this, they will see by faith, and not by reading instruments or combining numbers."[4]

Therefore, in order to discover what science and religion at their best may bring to our own lives and to a suffering world, we begin with them in a living partnership. For we find that they supplement and support rather than curtail or contradict each other when their followers "seek first" that universal community of good will and mutual aid which Jesus set before men as the unifying and also liberating aim of life in fellowship with God. This aim is kindred to the highest ideal of modern science. "What is distinctively modern in science," Sir Arthur Thomson declares, "is the ideal of bringing the light of science to bear on man's problems all along the line, on health of mind as well as of body, on education as well as on agriculture, on ethical development as well as on the more economical usage of natural resources, on eugenics as well as on utopias."[5] The nearer each scientist and citizen comes to this ideal in his own life and work, the more he will further and the less he will hinder the kind of society forecast by Jesus. For "the more we learn about the world we live in, the more we find it lends itself to our uses. The titanic forces that used to be our masters have become our servants. . . . With every passing year our power of control grows greater, and there seems no limit to what the future may make possible"—unless insuperable limitations are found to persist in human nature.[6]

Yet here also a conviction like that of Jesus about the possibilities of human beings is essential to the best adjustments

between men and nature; and it is essential to the most
effective application of the social sciences. In all these fields
the crucial question is how far men may rise to their new
opportunities. "The old dictum that human nature remains
always the same may be true," as William Adams Brown said,
"of the principles that govern it and the laws to which it is
subject, but not of the uses to be made of those principles or
the results that may follow from their application. All modern education is based upon the belief that human nature
can be improved. To the wise teacher, each new child is a
new opportunity." How great the opportunity is we seem
only beginning to learn in modern education and applied
psychology.[7]

Moreover, "what the psychologists propose for the life of
the individual, the sociologists would undertake for the life
of society. They, too, believe that by the study of process it
is possible to improve results." The wide response to James
Harvey Robinson's *The Mind in the Making* was due in
large measure to the conviction that by bringing scientific
methods to bear upon the study of social relations, conditions
can be improved for better political and economic life, as
they are being improved for better physical life. Yet the
whole process—educational, economic and political—requires habits of thought and life that we find at their best
in Jesus. For instance, such liberal and constructive interpretation as he gave to his nation's laws is essential if both
science and religion are to be set free for their utmost service
to men everywhere. Jesus came to fulfill, not the letter of
old laws, but their best spiritual and moral intention. Today
foremost judges take a similar aim. So able a jurist as the
late Justice Benjamin Cardozo "conceived it to be the function of the judge of the future not only to expound the law
as his predecessors have defined it, but to reinterpret it so
that it may more adequately conform to the social conscience
of his day."[7] And where no reinterpretation is adequate, the
test which Jesus would apply calls for a new law and a
greater purpose.

The more accurately we appraise the value of what the physical or social sciences or existing laws make possible, the more we find ourselves applying the test of Jesus. Though he differed in background from the modern scientist, he too had a way of judging by results. His test, "by their fruits ye shall know them,"[a] is applicable to modern processes and institutions no less than to the words and deeds of the individual man. The test by which Jesus judged the fruit was its effect on human lives. "He was the first to bring the value of every human soul to light, and what he did no man can any more undo."[8] It is now clearer than ever that if social experiments are to further the best growth of human souls and of society they must pass a test like that of Jesus. In agriculture and industry, for instance, final appraisals must be made "by the human balance sheet; not by the mountain of things produced, but by what happens to human agents in the process," and by the effect of the product upon human lives.[9]

It Fosters Experimental Living Grounded in Love

To apply this way of judging to ourselves, as we must if we are to be scientific and honest with ourselves, we must refuse, for instance, to harbor a fear of radical books, such as Gamaliel Bradford confessed in his Journal, lest they should lead him perforce to radical conclusions: "I do not dare to read the New Testament for fear of its awakening a storm of anxiety and self-reproach and doubt and dread of having taken the wrong path, of having been traitor to the plain and simple God."[10] Whatever our honest doubts and misgivings may be, we shall find encouragement in the attitude of Jesus towards fearless investigation. He called men to great adventures of living in good will. He expected them to learn in a fellowship of daring thought and deed. We can discover what such fellowship has meant in the experience of some who illustrate its less trammeled possibilities. We can examine this experience in the light of modern psychology and the scientific spirit. We can even go so far as to make honest experiments for ourselves. We can employ a truly scientific method in the art of living.

It was through experimental living, prompted by love, that Jesus expected higher possibilities of life to be realized. He was so sure of love at the heart of things, so sure of love as the very character of the creative energy in the universe, that he was willing to stake everything on a great experiment of love. He was convinced that this experiment would be justified eventually in a new way of living.

This confidence in the power of love to verify itself helps to explain why Jesus seemed to be so little concerned about the exact form in which his words should be recorded. More important apparently in his mind than a precise recording of his words or deeds (though the historical evidences for these have a cumulative value of their own), more important than any external evidence, is the self-evidencing power of love. For the evidence of its power should never be confined to the scholar's probing of the past; the evidence should come to every man at first hand through his own testing of love in the actual life of his day.

Such testing of love has been possible not only for the favored few but also for the unlettered many, for the rich but no less for the poor—for a gay youth like Francis of Assisi, finding, despite his pleasure-loving circle, the joy and power of simple living; for a favorite at court like William Penn, turning from bright prospects of preferment to make a colonial experiment in good will; for a man of business like John Woolman, applying truly Christian tests in an economic order that his contemporaries thought dangerous or unprofitable to change; for a poor lad like David Livingstone, learning the power of love, and later proving it in his epoch-making work for Africa; for illiterate natives like the attendants of Livingstone, hazarding their own lives in a last service of love on the strength of what his love had taught them; and for a leader in prison reform like Mrs. Maude Ballington Booth, reclaiming thousands of men and women from lives of crime and inspiring countless citizens to employ and to befriend them.

Despite all differences of antecedent and circumstance, the long succession of disciples of Jesus, so far as they have centered on love, corroborates this chief emphasis of his life and teaching. They show also that by kindred applications of love in daily living, rather than by mere discussion of his teaching, we too may come to a better understanding of him.

The assumption that we can understand Jesus and his influence only "by getting at his teachings in the form in which he actually expressed them would be true if he were only a moral lecturer, or if (whatever he was) he had come only to replace old creeds by a new creed, and old codes of law by a new code." But these suppositions fall far short of explaining him. An essential question for our understanding of him is this: "What is that moral impulse which is the starting point of the whole movement set forth in the New Testament? In every sphere of life we find that *a thing is what it does*. The meaning of the moral impulse given by Jesus is shown in its results."[11] The first results are found in the new type of character and community reflected in the New Testament. And, whenever the emphasis is placed where these records place it, we find a kindred type of character and society. We see love now as then passing from person to person as a living transforming influence. And the more this influence has become like that of Jesus, the more profound have been the changes in the individual and in society.

Suppose, then, that we should make this experience the basis of more thoroughgoing experiments, using freely the resources of both science and religion, without imposing any limitations born of our own inadequate past! Such experiments have led to illuminating co-operation between those of quite different points of view. They have brought together both those who find benefit in the sacraments, and others who have been repelled by organized religion as they have seen it, yet desire some effective unity to prevent the disintegration of the world. What if all these should co-operate under conditions where the spirit of truth and love prevails? Then they would be more alert to give and to receive in the pooling of varied experience. They would be more inventive in applying their discoveries. Such attempts, now in progress, are releasing unexpected energies. They are verifying the experience of that small but dynamic fellowship which first set out with Jesus for the renewal of life through love.

Its Local Practice Prepares for World Issues

The possibilities for fellowship of like quality in the present relations of science and religion throughout the world are illustrated in the lives of many who have served the common good through agriculture and related arts. The writer has had experience, in his own family and beyond, which illuminates this very point. He has lived under the abiding influence of a father and a grandfather, Hugh Nelson McAllister, who added to their active practice of law a voluntary and absorbing devotion to scientific agriculture, not merely on their own farm but especially in the founding and development of a State College and Experiment Station as part of a nation-wide movement.[12] He bears witness to how patiently in the early stages of this movement they overcame indifference and continued opposition (often from leaders of so-called Christian colleges). Through his relations to these pioneers and in his own work he has come to know many others who gave themselves with a religious sense of vocation to various applications of science to the general welfare. They work in many lands and under many auspices, yet in spirit they serve a world-uniting movement greater than any organized part of it. Some of them as teachers, or directors of research, or superintendents of national forests, or agents of county farm bureaus, or engineers and other specialists in public service, no less than agricultural missionaries, have refused larger financial inducements because of a vision and motive that science alone does not supply.

Yet a combination of scientific knowledge and religious motive like theirs is needed everywhere if the people are to reap the benefits of science, if they are to be saved, for instance, from floods, dust storms, unemployment, inadequate housing, undernourishment, disease, and war. The devotion of the men and women just mentioned, and the ways in which their work is hindered, often unwittingly, by those who are indifferent, personally ambitious, or provincially minded, show clearly the necessity for a religiously motivated, far-seeing public spirit among citizens generally, whether they are producers, distributors, or consumers. For without the wide extension of an enlightened public spirit, which science alone does not create, science will fail in service to the people because it cannot control self-seeking and short-sighted aims throughout the body politic. Science is all too easily diverted to serve a narrowing nationalism, to support the status quo, or to empower political and industrial dictators. It may result in the suicide of civilization. It has even now supplied the means, and these may be wrongly used even when scientists protest.

If, then, the rank and file of citizens are to support the proper use of science for the general well-being, they must practice a socially minded way of living in local communities. If it is not practiced there, if self-seeking or underhand methods prevail in the simpler relations of neighbors, citizens will not be prepared to employ the creative and to avoid the destructive uses of science in national or international affairs. Our rural communities, therefore, illustrate a process of the utmost importance everywhere. For instance, where a farmer has limited his use of science to making more money for himself, he has made little if any contribution to society; he has in fact often pressed his own advantage to the detriment of less well-equipped neighbors. But where farmers have used science under truly religious motives in many-sided co-operation for neighborly living, whole communities have been rejuvenated and a new sense of civic responsibility has been gained.

In Rural Life It Helps Civilization to Survive

This union of scientific and religious resources in country life bears directly upon the survival of our civilization. In a

biological approach to this problem, two investigators discuss the need to retain or to recover on farms a sufficient
proportion of the public-spirited men and women of ability
who are best fitted to be the parents of leaders for a new day.
They stress this need, not only because the farm offers exceptional opportunities for growth of the initiative and re-
sourcefulness essential to leadership, but also because city
residents who possess these qualities do not have, on the
average, enough children to perpetuate their kind. Obviously there must be developed in country communities a
type of life that will retain or attract the right kind of potential parents, and thus perpetuate the needed leadership.

The more this kind of farm life, combining science and
religion, can be realized, the more it will attract to the country other families who earn a large part of their living elsewhere, but who desire to share in the advantages of a modern
farmstead way of living. The investigators just mentioned
devote a chapter to this supplemental or "satellite farmstead
way of life." They show its importance, formerly in this
country and for almost four centuries in England, as a factor
in providing the nation's leadership. They find, however,
that we cannot expect a sufficient increase of this supplemental kind of farming to make it the decisive factor in our
nation's life and leadership. It follows that farming as a livelihood by many families of the needed quality is necessary
to prevent a decline in the birth rate of such families, and
consequently in our future leadership. Here they find hope
for the saving of our American civilization.[18]

They find, however, that this saving influence of country
life will not prevail unless the rural churches co-operate to
foster community life in its completeness. "Our rural communities gape with need in the place that the church organization once filled." Yet many church members are so limited by sectarian or personal interests that they actually
hinder one of the chief tasks of religion, the creation of
community. Their lack of vision and fear of change have
often repelled essentially religious persons whose cultural

and scientific interests could help to recover the lost leadership of the church in this field. Nevertheless, many such possible helpers are learning from recent events that, without better co-operation of the churches among themselves and with other groups, there will be failure to cultivate sufficiently the kind of community life that is essential to a truly democratic and scientific civilization. When, therefore, many more public-spirited men and women of ability choose country living for its enriching family environment, these investigators conclude, the need for the rural church to present the good life in its completeness will be more widely felt. Then more families will demand larger co-operating parishes and more adequate leadership so that the church may offer better opportunities to serve its founder's ideal of community.

What can happen when country churches unite or federate to serve the entire community is shown in a fertile valley where not long ago were seven struggling churches within two miles. "Since then great changes have taken place in those churches. One has been closed and ceased to exist. Of the remaining six, five have formed themselves into one 'larger parish' with a staff of two ministers and a woman who is a trained director of religious education. They now operate with a unified program, and provide far more amply for their people as a whole. There are now a men's club, an active young people's group, a spring conference, a summer camp with special periods for mothers, for young people, and for children. There are a dramatic society and a daily vacation Bible School."[14]

This united larger parish makes possible also better co-operative arrangements for bringing students to Sunday School and for giving them weekday religious instruction at the request of their parents. What such training meant in the lives of the young people who came to Cornell University from communities where they enjoyed this advantage is stressed by Hugh Moran, who had years of intimate dealing with Cornell students. He is "profoundly convinced that, if

our free institutions are to endure, some such system of
teaching the principles of morality and religion must be
extended to the rest of the counties of these United States."[14]

The Christian Rural Fellowship, whose board of directors
represents major rural interests of the state, supports a field
secretary who helps churches to plan for united community
work and aids their religious education through bulletins,
radio programs, and institutes of rural church workers. This
Fellowship is a part of one of the most promising world-wide
movements of our time. Its members are active in twenty-
seven of the United States and in seventeen other countries.
Through the closely related Agricultural Missions Foundation, "the successful experiences and creative experiments in
all phases of rural reconstruction in any land are made
known to missionaries and others engaged in rural work all
over the world." This Foundation co-operates intimately
with the Food and Agriculture Organization of the United
Nations.

It Helps Adequate Diet Solve Economic Problems

A combination of scientific and religious resources in
both rural and urban life is needed also to insure an adequate and well-balanced diet for all families, and at the same
time to solve related economic problems. If all families in
this country had had the means, the knowledge, and the
disposition to use such a diet during the interval between
the world wars, there would have been no embarrassing surplus on the current average of production, and no occasion
to destroy surplus in order to maintain fair prices. It would
have been necessary, however, for producers and distributors
to work together in the public interest to supply the demand
for such a diet, and some readjustments of crops would have
had to be made. For instance, less wheat would have been
needed because many family diets contain too large a proportion of starch, which in its less expensive form is comparatively cheap. But this reduction in acreage of wheat
would have been made up by a larger demand for fruits and

vegetables, meat, eggs, and dairy products. The resultant growth of animal industry would have required in turn a larger production of other crops, including many more acres of grass and legumes to feed the increased flocks and herds. Under such conditions the nation would have had a more diversified, flexible, and soil conserving rotation of crops designed to meet emergencies.[15]

This effective demand by all families for proper food would require adequate, but not unreasonable or impossible, purchasing power. And to provide this for all families the principle and methods of co-operation would have to be carried far beyond the limits of this chapter even to consider. To be ready, however, to consider later some of the necessary steps, we should keep in mind these facts: that now for the first time the means to determine, to produce, and to distribute an adequate diet for all are within our reach; that through various agencies the general knowledge of nutritive values (though now spreading among housewives even in poorer sections of cities) could be carried much further in the interests of general good health; that, notwithstanding these possibilities, at least one-third of our population is undernourished, and many others who have sufficient means are so careless or ignorant of essentials as to go through life with a lowered vitality that makes them a handicap or even a danger to the general well-being. For instance, it is estimated that fifty per cent of the people of the United States do not get enough in the way of dairy products, fruit, and vegetables to enable them to enjoy full vigor and health. Here then is a challenge for all of us to help create an effective demand for an adequate diet and other conditions of health for everyone throughout this land of possible plenty, without neglecting what might be done to help other countries. Foreward looking experts hope that an adequate personal and family policy for nutrition, combined with a sound public policy, may be a large factor in helping the world to think in terms of a good life for all its people.

The Partnership Exemplified by a Great Scientist

How a thoroughly Christian application of science may advance the good life for all people is impressively illustrated in the character and work of a great Christian scientist, George Washington Carver. This is seen in the increasing response to his ideas and ideals coming from farmers, scientists, businessmen, and legislators of different races in many lands where his influence is still mounting. The story of how he overcame difficulties in his struggle upward from slavery, how he taught thousands of ignorant would-be farmers to find undreamed-of possibilities in Mother Earth—this story (written at Tuskegee with details that impart much of the faith, charm, and purpose of the man himself) is a sound prophecy of the better living that now awaits the co-operation of men everywhere. The way in which Dr. Carver developed from the plants and the earth about him so many new and useful products (three hundred, for instance, from the neglected, though leguminous, soil-enriching peanut) helped him to appreciate what he called "a fourth Kingdom of Nature, entirely within the control of man." He predicted that "a new world is about to come into existence. It will be the synthetic world. What has been done is nothing to what will be done in the years to come." He anticipated the judgment of other experts that the so-called substitutes, such as synthetic resins in paint, nylon for silk, or moulded plastics for steel, could be made an improvement upon what had been considered the real thing. He foresaw also that "the substitution of cellulose for steel could re-establish the farmer's place as a producer of the renewable raw materials of industry without cutting down the numbers of people employed in industry. And the risks to both farmer and industrialist would be reduced because the rate of production and demand could be more accurately gauged. As Dr. Carver had so often said, "agriculture could aid industry, and industry could help agriculture solve its economic and social problems. Both being basically chemical, they had a natural affinity for each other."[16]

Long before the National Farm Chemurgic Council, deeply influenced by Dr. Carver, was organized, he had shown that the application of chemistry to the manufacture of synthetic farm products might not only conserve mineral resources, which were being rapidly exhausted, but also save much impoverished or disappearing soil. This saving of the world's soil through proper tillage, rotation of crops, and so forth, he had taught for years as absolutely essential. He had taken to heart the warning of James G. Wilson, one of his early teachers: "Nations last as long as their top-soil lasts."

By his actual practice of enriching the soil and raising better plants and animals, Carver illustrated the interrelationship between the soil, the plants growing from it, and the men and animals dependent on the produce. In ways that everyone could understand he showed how the advance of men and nature requires teachable and brotherly co-operation. And by his invincible, Christlike attitudes toward nature, men, and God, he convinced all sorts of people that the needed co-operation can be realized decisively when enough members of many races seek their common destiny as children of a Christlike Creator.

It Can Co-ordinate Agriculture and Industry

Many practical scientists, working with statesmen, publicists, and others seeking solutions of world problems, are now needed to help co-ordinate agricultural and industrial resources throughout the world. They are needed also to help in well-directed sharing of scientific knowledge and techniques; for the conditions of agriculture in the various countries show how science could and must be used to increase food production, not only for neighbors but also for distant industrial people who are dependent upon imported food.

These intricate problems and possible solutions, requiring both science and religion at their best, are treated in a vitally important book by Arthur P. Chew, of the U. S. Department of Agriculture, with the help of other specialists.[17] In an impressive Foreword, Henry C. Taylor[18] endorses

certain conclusions of this book: "that wars are caused by
economic conflicts, and particularly by the conflicts between
industrial nations striving to maintain connection with
enough farms to balance their factories, is supported by historical fact. . . . Chew would have the agricultural countries
move but slowly toward industrialization, and make those
movements the most natural and profitable ones rather than
forced or subsidized developments. He would also have the
over-industrialized nations adopt a policy of gradually reducing their unbalanced position through emigration. This
would not mean that the manufacturing of the world would
be evenly distributed between countries any more than it
is evenly distributed within countries, but it would mean
a balanced world which would at any given time be satisfying to all countries and thus avoid the conflicts which lead
to war. When worked out equitably as a world economy on
the basis of the natural resources, populations, skills, and
managerial ability, the standards of living of all participating
peoples can be higher than on the more nationalistic pattern.
In the new pattern Chew sees the foundations of peace."

We are summarizing some conclusions of this book in
order to suggest, not any rigid solution of a constantly changing problem but rather certain possibilities toward which
many peoples, notably those in our own democracy, can co-
operate more extensively in various ways. The possibilities
are now multiplied everywhere to co-operate for better nutrition, health, and other factors of security through the
United Nations specialized agencies, whose operations are
not subject to veto by any uninterested or fearful nation. To
make the most of such opportunities there is instant need for
much wider public support in this country and elsewhere to
extend the work of the Food and Agriculture Organization
(FAO), the World Health Organization (WHO), the International Bank for Reconstruction and Development, the
International Trade Organization (ITO), the International
Labor Organization (ILO), and other UN specialized agencies. Enough has now been done through these agencies,

and through our own governmental and private enterprise, to suggest effective procedure for other areas. Illustrations outside the United Nations are found in TVA and similar projects, in the work of private corporations like those which apply science to safeguard and develop land, plants, and workers in Latin America, and in the democratic teamwork of farmers in their own co-operatives. All this should help in the more inclusive task—the international co-ordinating of agriculture and industry to promote world-wide security. And here the UN specialized agencies, including UNESCO, together with the Trusteeship Council and the International Court of Justice, may be made more effective means to reconcile national rivalries and to promote safe democratic world government.

Mr. Chew explains that "our own contribution to a good international farm and factory balance through vastly freer trade might cost us something. But we should have an important offset. Taking goods for goods, by lessening the necessity to give away our products, would save the taxpayers billions annually. It would benefit the treasury in two ways: first, in a reduction of the foreign relief bill, and secondly, in a reduction of our military outlay. Foreign countries thus helped to be self-supporting would be more peaceable. Expensive, yes; but not as expensive as another war; and perhaps not as expensive as the present relief system. . . . The United States may not feel nervous over the possibility of having to meet increased industrial competition. It has immense farm resources, and risks only a loss of trade—not a loss of food security. Other industrial countries risk life as well as trade: they must have a reciprocal relationship with agricultural countries or die."

Moreover, all possible agricultural countries, and many others largely industrial, need help of various kinds in order to stop the ravages discussed in *Our Plundered Planet,* to develop the possibilities suggested in *New Worlds Emerging,* and to provide more adequate food for the world.[19] For example, *New Worlds Emerging* shows that "throughout the empty Amazonian empire, the UNESCO's Hylean Institute represents the eyes and the hopes of the world. The institute will observe progress, study problems, and further active work from the scientific point of view. If the results are one-tenth as favorable as they now promise to be, a vast new frontier will indeed be opened for those surplus populations that now exist barely on the fringes of our economy, and that may, by being pulled into that economy, enrich and strengthen it many times over. Nobody can say what will become of all that in the near future, not because the possibilities are not there, but because nobody can predict the future complex shifts of international relations. . . . If the Latin American nations can continue on their present course [of agricultural development and gradual and diverse industrial growth] they will not only come to add materially to the store of foods by which the world can feed its surplus populations, but will also come to make room, within their expanding economies, for many millions from that surplus."[19]

Writing from his inside knowledge of the possibilities for peace in the specialized agencies of the UN, Lord Boyd Orr says: "If the sixty governments represented on them would agree to devote to them one unit of their currency for every hundred they are spending for war, and allow them freedom of action, I venture to predict that within a few years the political issues which divide nations would become meaningless and the obstacles to peace disappear. Permanent peace cannot be attained merely by efforts to prevent war. We shall be on the road to world unity and peace when the nations of the world jointly begin to apply science to develop the world's resources for the benefit of all. The means of co-operation are ready and waiting in the specialized agencies of the United Nations. The difficulty is to get a real beginning. . . . The government which is strongest and surest of itself is the one which should take the lead in this move for peace. The way other governments received such an offer would be an acid test of their intentions."[20]

In the wider co-operation for better food and health throughout the world, which Lord Orr finds essential, our own country has demonstrated the possibilities of vast and varied contributions, not primarily financial. We refer to achievements of our agricultural extension service, which unites national, state, county, and farmer co-operation, and to our educational, medical, and agricultural missions in China, India, and other needy lands—all sharing freely the best technical experience about better tools, soil conservation, irrigation, improvement of plants and animals for special purposes, and control of pests and diseases. Here we find tested ways to share with other countries, in various stages of development, not only the agricultural but also the industrial, medical, and democratic know-how.

It is especially this kind of sharing that Norris E. Dodd, successor to Lord Orr as director general of the UN Food and Agriculture Organization, stresses in the light of his visits to most of the undernourished peoples of the world. He found that "in more than half the world, the scythe has not yet supplanted the sickle. Simple tools are what the underdeveloped countries need to begin with—scythes, better hoes and plows, simple threshing implements, farm wagons. Most of them could be made in the countries where they are needed."[21]

Another primary need of the underdeveloped areas Mr. Dodd found to be the knowledge of how to restore and improve soil by crop rotation and by cover crops to be plowed under after the food crop has been harvested. In India, for instance, he suggested to government officials that "a small loan to farmers, enabling them to plant legumes, might be repaid many times in humus and nitrogen thus added to the soil."

In all this, a main function of FAO, as Mr. Dodd puts it, is to "bridge the gap between knowledge and practice." And this, he found, requires, not so much expensive machinery, as help and encouragement "to train native instructors, and to establish services which in turn will do what our extension

services and county agents do. Most underdeveloped countries have, in fact, asked to be taught. Many of them want the
answers to specific problems."[21]

Many of the problems, however, reach beyond the realm
of agriculture. Some have to do with sanitation and other
conditions of health, some with better industrial relations
and business management. Most of them relate to true democratic community. In fact, the needs are so vast and varied
that every man or woman going from nations that honestly
profess democracy to less developed lands should have some
training to help him represent the kind of democratic life
on which freedom and peace depend.

Toward meeting these various needs, a nonprofit corpora-
tion, called Koinonia, has been formed. Its purpose is to help
co-ordinate other organizations working for these ends, and,
where desirable, supplement them for the largest and truest
development of community everywhere. For example, this
voluntary Koinonia is working in close collaboration with
Frank Laubach in his work for world literacy, which wins
its way on the principle, "each one teach one," and which
seeks also to develop a better Christian literature for the
awakening millions who are learning to read. Movements
like these will demand further attention at later stages of
our inquiry.

Moreover, to be most effective anywhere in the world, the
sharing of worth-while knowledge or technique must be
done in a spirit of democratic fellowship and concern for all
workers. Nothing less than this will release the wholehearted
co-operation and energy that are needed. For these essentials
cannot possibly be released through mere mechanical technique enforced upon the workers. When the spirit of truth
and love is lacking in either giver or recipient, any so-called
sharing becomes perfunctory; it fails to engender eagerness
to learn as well as to give. Therefore the most creative sharing with others of either physical resources or personal experience requires religious motive, purpose, and attitudes,
as well as scientific method and results.

So, all that we have considered in this chapter, and much that is to follow, confirm the conclusion of a leading scientist, Robert A. Milliken: "The saving of the world rests upon the union of the attitude of religion with the method and results of science."[22]

Questions for Further Thought and Discussion

What are some ways in which religion and science (however much each is caricatured) and still in urgent opposition?

Is the real battleground mysticism vs. mechanism, traditionalism vs. change, theism vs. atheism, humanism vs. Christianity, psychology vs. theology— or what?

What role can religion play in such world organizations as the United Nations Organization and its specialized agencies?

7

APPRAISALS BY SCIENTISTS
AND PHILOSOPHERS

Testimony of Einstein, Planck, Kelvin, Cairns

THE TRULY SCIENTIFIC method has always implied certain
moral and spiritual attitudes, such as devotion to truth, and
faith in the essential unity and order of the universe. And
now we learn increasingly from the scientists themselves that
intuition is no less an organic part of the scientific process,
and that in this process at its best religious attitudes play a
decisive part. All this is seen in the character and spiritual
experience of the authors of two of the most fruitful scientific theories of our time. Albert Einstein, speaking of the
character and experience of Max Planck as leading to the
quantum theory and as giving promise of even greater
achievements, used words that apply no less to his own attitudes. At a gathering of scientists on Planck's sixtieth birth-
day, Einstein explained his friend's pre-eminence among
those who were trying to arrive at the universal elementary
laws from which a theory of the universe can be built up.
"There is no logical path to these laws," Einstein said; "only
intuition, resting on sympathetic understanding of experience, can reach them. . . . The longing to behold this pre-
established harmony is the source of the inexhaustible patience and endurance with which Planck has devoted him-

self, as we see, to the most general problems of our science, refusing to let himself be diverted to more grateful and more easily attained ends. I have often heard colleagues try to attribute this attitude of his to extraordinary will-power and discipline—wrongly in my opinion. The state of mind which enables a man to do work of this kind is akin to that of the religious worshipper or the lover; the daily effort comes from no deliberate intention or programme, but straight from the heart." And without this type of mind and heart serving in the temple of science, Einstein continued, "the temple would never have existed."[1] As he says in another connection, "the intuitive and constructive spiritual faculties must come into play wherever a body of scientific truth is concerned." Admitting that some scientific truth may be built up from its own teachings, logically arranged, he goes on to say that, for the best understanding and building, one must bring into play the constructive faculties of the artist. And, of the moral and religious qualities also, he adds: "I mean that our moral leanings and tastes, our sense of beauty and religious instincts, are all contributory forces in helping the reasoning faculty toward its highest achievements."[2]

Of the religious element in the best thinking, Planck himself remarked: "Every serious and reflective person realizes, I think, that the religious element in his nature must be recognized and cultivated if all the powers of the human soul are to act together in perfect balance and harmony." He thought it not by accident that the greatest thinkers of all time were also deeply religious souls, even though they did not make a public show of their religious feelings.[3]

In explaining similarities beyond the range of mere logic in the processes of both science and religion, D. S. Cairns shows the power of imagination, courage, and a sense of need in leading to the most promising hypotheses, as well as in testing them. He cites evidence of these qualities in great discoverers, Newton, Darwin, Wallace, Poincare, and Mayer. For instance, Mayer, the joint discoverer with Joule of the principle of the conservation of energy, said "I discovered the new theory for the sufficient reason that I felt the need of it."[4]

Dr. Cairns illustrated the importance of both intuition and co-operation in scientific discovery by the experience of Lord Kelvin. "This noted scientist once said that he had never reasoned his way quite up to any one of his great discoveries. He brooded over all the facts which seemed to him relevant to his problem, until there came a moment when his mind took a life-or-death leap away out into the unknown. He felt in the very marrow of his being the conviction that the solution lay just *there*. . . . I [Cairns] told this incident to two very distinguished men of science. Both of them at once agreed in the view that that is how discoveries in science are always made. 'The end,' they said, 'is seen before the means.' But there were two further points in the story. The first was that Lord Kelvin was never able to put in the intervening stepping-stones of demonstration between his old position and the new to which his life-and-death spring had brought him. The other was that he was not content to leave it there, but before he published his discoveries, got his two friends, Tait and Clerk Maxwell, to work out the missing deductions."[5] What a fine illustration such co-operation gives of faith working in fellowship, of the very way in which we may expect to make further advance in all that concerns our common life!

There is a further step in which Dr. Cairns shows "a deep underlying unity beneath the processes of scientific reason and religious faith. The final step in the demonstration of a new fact or law is verification. We assume the truth of the scientific intuition. If it is true, certain consequences will follow when we subject the intuition or hypothesis to experiment. If these consequences actually do follow, the intuition passes into accepted knowledge, and a new base of operations is ready for a new advance into the regions still unknown. Verification is perfected when we can prove the unity of the new fact or law with the whole of human knowledge, but that process is necessarily incomplete so long as human knowledge is incomplete. That a fact or law works out as true in experience is its primary verification. . . . Science gives the power to verify the intuitions of genius; otherwise the most brilliant intuitions of its creative minds would be only guesses at truth. Is there anything like this in religion? What is religion worth unless you can verify it? Christianity would have died out ages ago if it had not been for the verifications of Christian experience. One of the inner secrets of its endurance is the fact that it is constantly verifying itself in the experience of those who believe in it."[5]

Differences in Methods of Verification

There is, however, a difference of range and of requirements in the verifications of science and of religion; and this difference helps to explain the frequently slower progress of religion. It helps to explain also why science needs to be permeated by religion with its wider range and in its highest form.

Why has science, when pursuing its true method, as Dr. Cairns said, "been so steady in its discoveries and so victorious in their verifications, whereas religion has had so confused and often so disastrous a history?" Is it not, he suggests, because religion is at work on a vaster problem than any problem of science and makes greater demands on the entire man? In science the mind is concentrated on details, whereas in true religion, the whole mind and nature of man is concerned primarily with the universal. It is always trying to get the events of life into true relation to "the Creator Spirit." Therefore, it requires that men shall respond progressively to all that they can apprehend of the nature and purpose of God. "The true reason why Christian faith is still so hard for many today is that man, in general, has never quite had the courage to make the wholly decisive experiment of casting himself absolutely upon God. We hesitate, as our fathers and their fathers hesitated, to stake life absolutely on the moral imperative."[5]

And yet no easier solution is possible. Issues so vast require commitment of life. An intuition like that of Jesus that there is a father-like Spirit ready to help men live together as a harmonious family cannot be tested solely by means of the intellect. "We must verify such intuitions by a decision and habit of the will. Faith, in fact, is an act of the whole nature, it is the whole man, intellect, affections, imagination, conscience, and will, seeking the whole truth, and throwing everything into the hazard. If we would increase our faith, we must give the Eternal World the opportunity to verify itself in our experience. It is by such continual and increasing experiment and verification that the knowledge of God in Christ increases in the world, and that the truth about his nature and purpose is in process of demonstration."[5]

Thus we learn an important difference between the purpose of science and the purpose of religion. "Science," says Professor Harkness, "analyzes events and entities into their elements and tries to find causal relations among them. Religion tries to 'see life steadily and see it whole.' The result is that science, by virtue of its purpose, is always an abstraction—a statement of truth 'drawn away from' all that does not directly pertain to it. Religion exists to overcome such exclusion—to relate the whole life of the individual to the whole of his world."[6]

The nature and need of this unifying work of religion are stated by another philosopher, who was also a great mathematician and physicist. Alfred North Whitehead said: "Religion is the vision of something which stands beyond, behind, and within the passing flux of immediate things; something which is real, and yet waiting to be realized; . . . something that gives meaning to all that passes. . . . Religion has emerged into human experience mixed with the crudest fancies of barbaric imagination. Gradually, slowly, steadily the vision recurs in history under nobler form and with clearer expression. It is the one element in human experience which persistently shows an upward trend. It fades and then recurs. But when it renews its force, it recurs with an added richness and purity of content. The fact of the religious vision, and its history of persistent expansion, is our one ground for optimism. Apart from it, human life is a flash of occasional enjoyments lighting up a mass of pain and misery, a bagatelle of transient experience." "The final principle of religion is that there is a wisdom in the nature of things. . . . Religion insists that the world is a mutually adjusted disposition of things, issuing in value for its own sake. This is the very point that science is always forgetting."[7]

Some who are thus forgetful even go so far as to assert that the religion of the future will be nothing more than an echo or servant of science. They underestimate the insight and motive which religion at its best provides, and they overestimate the ability of science to provide guidance for life. Science alone never gives us ethical or esthetic distinctions. In fact, as Walter Horton shows, "Science never speaks in the imperative, but only in the future conditional. 'If you wish to do so and so,' she says, 'you must fulfill precisely certain conditions: and the results will be thus and thus.' That helps to guide us; it keeps us from running blindly and heedlessly into paths that do not lead to the desired results. But science cannot tell us what results are desirable; in all matters of value she remains coolly neutral. Good and evil, beauty, and ugliness, are all the same to her."[8] Many an extreme protagonist of science does not recognize that science has this limitation. So he fails to distinguish between wisdom and science, and is inclined to take an absurdly patronizing attitude toward the seers of earlier times. Is our age with all its technical skill so noted for wisdom that it is entitled to disparage the age of Socrates and the wisdom of Jesus? "Granted that the modern schoolboy knows more about the earth and the stars than did the ancient Hebrew prophets; does it follow that he is better able than they to solve the eternal problem of religion? How, in the present imperfect state of human knowledge, should man think about ultimate reality, and how should he guide his steps, in order to escape life's pitfalls, and attain the utmost fullness of life of

which humanity is capable? Some answer to this question
man must have. He cannot get it from all the sciences put
together"—unless he stretches the boundaries of science to
include values and ways of appraising them that are not
usually recognized from a strictly scientific point of view.
Yet, even as usually defined, "science has as much the duty
to point out the vagaries and fanaticisms of religion as religion has the duty to point out the limitations of science.
At its best, religious experience gives insight into life as it
really might be, and some day will be, if the right conditions
are met; and science may aid enormously in making religion's dreams come true, by defining the conditions which
must be met if they are to be realized."[8] Thus science and
religion may advance together, not in the sense that either
dominates the other, but in such a spirit that each profits
from the distinctive contributions of the other.

Increasing Agreement about Procedure

With regard to procedure and common hindrances, as
well as in general outlook and purpose, we find that there
is increasing agreement among leading thinkers in the fields
of science, philosophy, and religion. For instance, a great
British scientist, J. S. Haldane, said: "The conclusion forced
upon me in the course of a life devoted to natural science
is that the universe as it is assumed to be in physical science
is only an idealized world, while the real universe is the
spiritual universe in which spiritual values count for everything. . . . We live, if we will only realize it, in the presence
of and through the power of, this spiritual reality. It is the
inspiration of all the splendid and painstaking effort which
has built up our language, our literature and art, our science,
our institutions, our machinery of all sorts, our loyalty to
one another, and all that we call civilization. . . . It often
happens that scientific men are hostile to religious belief
and disclaim any connection with it. In actual scientific
work, however, they behave just as if they were actuated by
faith in the reality and unity of the highest spiritual values.

Belief in the reality and self-consistency of truth, combined with the conviction that truth will help in the realization of everything that is called good, differs only in name from religious faith."[9]

Here we are on common ground with a comprehensive study of the philosophy of religion by the late Eugene Lyman. He shows that "religious faith, when its various elements are rightly adjusted to each other, has a genuine kinship to scientific inquiry. It is not a blind trust, nor an arbitrary will to believe, but presupposes experience and judgments based on experience—judgments which have their own testing, as the following chapters will bring out. And it has its own experimental quality, namely, the moral faithfulness which puts conviction to the test of action. . . . Of course there are types of faithfulness, apparently religious, which are decidedly unexperimental—faithfulness to creeds, for example. But such faithfulness is only formally religious. Religious faithfulness in the deeper sense of the term is faithfulness to truth and reality in the conviction that thereby the greater values will be possessed or achieved."[10]

This need for more inclusive experiences receives increasing emphasis from men of science. Albert Einstein cites the history of science to show our need for "the totality of the data of experience." Although he grants that in Euclid's geometry ancient Greece created for the first time the intellectual miracle of a logical system, he concludes that the time was not ripe for a science that could comprehend reality until a second elementary truth had been realized about the essential function of experience. "Pure logical thinking can give us no knowledge whatsoever of the world of experience; all knowledge about reality begins with experience and terminates in it. Conclusions obtained by purely rational processes are, so far as Reality is concerned, entirely empty."[11] Einstein saw that Galileo recognized this, and impressed it upon the scientific world; and that he thus became the father of modern physics and of the whole modern natural science.

Accordingly, as du Noüy's scientific inquiry shows, "excessive intelligence, which creates an Archimedes or a Descartes, anesthetizes the more subtle qualities of the brain. . . . Intuition disposes of a much greater field of action than does reason, and purely intuitive, religious faith is a much more efficacious human lever than science or philosophy. Action follows conviction, not knowledge. The history of human thought furnishes a thousand proofs of our ignorance of the true value of men." For instance, "the Roman patricians of the year 33, the philosophers, and the intellectuals would have been highly amused if they had been told that the unknown young Jew, tried by the procurator of a distant colony . . . would play an infinitely greater role than Caesar, would dominate the history of the Occident, and become the purest symbol of all humanity. . . ."[12]

Accordingly, W. R. Matthews finds: "The more philosophical men of science have readily confessed that religion as a phenomenon cannot be omitted from among the facts of the world, and that it may serve as the starting point of a theory of Reality. . . . The modern mind, with its training in the method of science, is prepared for a new beginning in theology, and can have no reasonable objection to our procedure if we start from the facts of religious experience and attempt to understand them."[13]

In any attempt to understand the facts of religious experience, the Old and New Testaments may take "a place of supreme importance among the data of our thought just because they contain the record of a religious experience unique in its continuity and its sustained elevation." This use of the Bible should become increasingly congenial to those schooled in the modern scientific method, since this method "begins not with first principles but with observed fact."[13]

Fortunately, more leaders in science, religion, and practical affairs are coming to realize an urgent necessity to square their theory and practice to the data of experience even beyond the limits of their own specialties, and to include values beyond the range of physical measurement, as J. S. Haldane has emphasized. This wider inquiry now seems more promising because, for one thing, the materialistic conception of the universe, which kept many of the last generation from taking the intuition of Jesus as a working hypothesis, is now found inadequate by more and more scientists and philosophers. Unfortunately, its benumbing influence still persists in the world of affairs, and survives under modified forms among some scientists. Nevertheless the old materialism, which tried to explain everything in terms of matter and mechanism in a rigid kind of time and space, is more than ever discredited by thinkers who cannot be suspected of any theological bias against it. Bertrand Russell, for instance, has shown why the old idea of matter as something which persists in time and moves in space is no longer tenable for modern relativity physics. "A piece of matter has become, not a persistent thing with varying states, but a system of inter-related events. The old solidity is gone, and with it the characteristics that, to the materialist, made matter seem more real than fleeting thoughts." "What we know about the physical world is much more abstract than was formerly supposed."[14]

It is so abstract, in fact, that much of what we know about the physical world can be expressed as yet only by mathematical symbols. In this way, for instance, Einstein has been able to go much further than any concrete observable facts would at first warrant by his use of abstract mathematical processes to express and test his intuitions; and yet he has persevered in testing them even when they seemed to contradict the most generally accepted scientific views.

In the very nature, then, of the abstract conceptions with which both science and religion have to deal, we find it necessary to use symbolic terms for things not seen and only imperfectly understood. Eddington illustrates this necessity for symbolism in science and in religion by taking a common table, apparently substantial, yet now recognized by science as "mostly emptiness with sparsely scattered electric charges rushing around at great speed." He concludes: "Our conception of the familiar table was an illusion. But, if some prophetic voice had warned us that it was an illusion, and therefore we had not troubled to investigate further, we should never have found the scientific table. To reach the reality of the table we need to be endowed with sense-organs to weave images and illusions about it. And so it seems to me that the first step in a broader revelation to man must be the awakening of image-building in connection with the higher faculties of his nature, so that these are no longer blind alleys but open into a spiritual world—a world partly of illusion, no doubt, but in which he lives no less than in the world, also of illusion, revealed by the senses."[15]

Many who are learning to use such image-building in the inquiries of both science and religion find new suggestiveness in the way Jesus used figurative or symbolic pictures to illustrate how to live as members of the family of God. A good instance is the parable which contrasts the readiness for fellowship in the repentant prodigal, who was eager to come back to the life of his family, with the churlishness in the complacent elder brother, who made the best family life impossible.[a] Beyond the usual application of this parable to the possibilities of repentance and forgiveness for prodigals, the acts and attitudes of its symbolic father represent God as eager to establish the relations of a true family in the use of common resources. They suggest that God is much more concerned to restore and to enlarge these relations among men than to apportion blame or punishment for past delinquencies—and that he is thwarted in this endeavor less by the prodigal son who comes to his better self and is eager to renew the family relationship than by the practical elder brother who is bent upon saving the family heritage for himself, and so is angry and will not go into the feast that welcomes his returning brother. Surely these symbolic characters were never more suggestive of man's need and possibility of fellowship in the use of physical as well as spiritual resources than they are now.

Why Each One Needs Both Science and Religion

All who would increase the fruits of such fellowship in the related fields of science, religion, and the arts may find the haughtily jealous elder brother a timeless example of what to avoid, a warning against the disguises of pride and self-centeredness. If scientists, philosophers, artists, and all who take part in the serious work of the world would heed this warning, and work with the common things of life to interpret and to share their full significance, what heightened possibilities might emerge for all arts and services, as well as for science and religion. Each would bring greater aid to the others.

The need that everyone should work for the greatest mutual aid between science and religion is intensified by the emergence of atomic energy in a usable form. In this crisis, "both our fears and our hopes are centered not about the material forces of the universe, but about ourselves. The explosive energies of the human personality are far greater than those of the atom, and can have a more devastating effect if released in the wrong way."[16] Moreover, what is done through science with atomic energy, as with other material forces, depends upon the motives and actions of men, and these in turn depend in large measure upon the quality and influence of their religion, or upon their distortion or rejection of religion. For in religion and science, as Whitehead has said, "we have the two strongest general forces (apart from the mere impulse of the various senses) which influence men."

Another of our far-seeing scientists, Kirtley Mather of Harvard, though recognizing that much disastrous conflict has come from confusing the respective fields of science and religion, nevertheless points out that there is a broad, overlapping area in which they must be practiced together so that men may understand and share the abundant life now within their reach. How, he asks, can one tell what is the most abundant life, and "how can one get a satisfactory religious

motive and outlook for life in a physical world without understanding the nature of that physical world? Somehow religion must be related to the life which we know through
observation and experience: and this life is certainly part of
the field of natural science. We must discover how the mind
of man operates in order to learn how the soul of man may
grow. We must know the regulations of physical life in order
to reach out and upward into the realm of psychical life.
Science and religion are too intimately related to permit any
barrier to be erected between them."[17]

Because this intimate relation, whether in the breach or
in the observance, affects so profoundly every human life,
it is not enough (though many seem to think it is enough)
that some persons cultivate science, others art, and still others
religion, as if these could be separable pursuits. On the contrary, science and religion can attain the best results only
as they both become effective in the life and work of many
individuals. What Einstein says about the results of scientific
research applies no less to religious experience: "It is not
sufficient that each result be taken up, elaborated, and applied by a few specialists in the field. Restricting the body
of knowledge to a small group deadens the philosophical
spirit of a people and leads to spiritual poverty."[18] Every
person, therefore, is needed to take his part in the interplay
of science and religion in order to develop sound procedure,
not only in personal habits and business life but also in
local, national, and world affairs. Those who seek such opportunities share a growing experience of religion and science working together in their own lives. Obviously this
experience should begin as early in life as possible, and be
an incentive to lifelong education. Only in some such way
can one realize in practice that "the saving of the world rests
upon the union of the attitude of religion with the method
and results of science."[19]

Questions for Further Thought and Discussion

Although quotations and attitudes of scientists given here are largely favorable to religion, would the same be true of most scientists, or just "science," as it appears in typical formal scientism?

Does the friendliness of scientists for religion usually involve their insisting that they be allowed to define what, for them, "religion" is?

Is the variety of testimony given here—whatever may be the attitudes of those scientists who are hostile to faith—impressive evidence for the validity of Christian claims?

If most Americans had to get along without either religion or science, which would they choose to discard? What could change that trend?

8

RELEASE OF ENERGY THROUGH THE
INFLUENCE OF JESUS

Hindrances to Release of Energy

CAN WE RECAPTURE for our day the secret of that spontaneous outburst of energy which transformed discouraged
disciples of a crucified teacher into a force which the Roman
Empire could not subdue? Can we discover what made them
such an influence that Constantine, though he little understood the secret of their power, turned to them as the last
hope of his crumbling empire? At least we can examine the
experience of some of this early group who found spontaneous energy coursing through themselves and making
possible new levels of creative living. We can compare their
experience with later insights and achievements. We can
explore the conditions for releasing such energy in similar
ventures of our own.

Until after the crucifixion of Jesus his disciples had been
so preoccupied with hopes of temporal rewards and political
changes, which they expected from him, that they did not
realize their own need to be energized and directed by the
Spirit that animated him. Similarly, many of us today are
so preoccupied with external affairs that we do not realize
what we need in ourselves in order to become a creative
community. Because the early disciples also were absorbed

104

by worldly aims when commissioned by Jesus to carry on his work for the world, they little understood why he asked them to wait together in Jerusalem until they knew that the Spirit dwelling in him had taken possession of them.

But while they waited in the quiet of an upper room, facing the perils of their new task without the visible leadership of Jesus, and contrasting their past failures with his mastery, they became more keenly aware of why they had failed. Some of them doubtless recalled his exclamation—"O faithless and perverse generation!"—uttered after they had failed to help a boy in convulsions. When they asked him why they had failed, he answered, "Because of your little faith."[a] Then they saw that Jesus had not attributed their failure to insurmountable limitations in themselves or in circumstances, but to lack of fearless confidence to commit themselves to the Spirit manifest in him, and thus to learn the art of living to the full.[b]

Moreover, this exclamation about a faithless generation implies that energy like that of Jesus may be curtailed also by an unbelieving and fearful attitude of an entire people. For earlier in his work, when surrounded by his skeptical fellow townsmen in Nazareth, "he performed but few mighty deeds there because of their want of faith."[c] So in the case of the afflicted boy, Jesus' exclamation suggests that the energies, which otherwise might find expression through men of good intention, may be restricted by a general lack of confidence affecting an entire community, or even a generation..

The subtle influence of such distrust can be seen now, as then, in the spread of enervating fears. Such fears have always been highly contagious, and are often unrecognized by their victims. They are especially prevalent under conditions of insecurity, agitation, and anxiety. Medical science finds that such conditions "create states of consciousness which bring about nervous and organic disorders," and lead to diseases that "are almost unknown in social groups where life is simpler and not so agitated, where anxiety is less constant."[1] In much disease today "emotional states show themselves to be a complicating, often a controlling influence. Anxiety becomes a biochemical factor. Through its stimulation of secretions from nerve endings and from glands it may release materials as upsetting as the poisons of bacteria. Indeed bacterial invasions themselves seem to be aided by mental tensions. Even the common cold seems to strike with maximum virulence when its victim is in a state of anxiety."

Moreover, it is said on good authority that if we could banish fear from modern life, we would free men from half their mental ills. Fear, too, in one form or another, is at the bottom of half man's moral weakness. Much temptation is intensified by the fact that we are afraid of it. Especially does the adolescent often feel a real sense of terror because he faces forces he does not understand. To explain to him, therefore, the operation of the forces surging through him, "to translate him out of darkness into light," is one of the best ways to give him moral courage. And far beyond the years of adolescence there are men and women everywhere who are fettered and their energies limited by an undefined but haunting fear. "They are afraid of life and afraid of death: they are even half afraid of themselves." At the heart of this fear is uncertainty about the character of God, and about the real nature of the universe.[2]

Jesus Shows the Way of Release

What a different attitude came through the liberating faith that Jesus ultimately inspired in his early disciples! Instead of hopeless struggle and dread of defeat, came invigorating confidence in the Creator of a friendly world. The fears and perversions that had defeated the earlier efforts of the disciples gave way to a sense of partnership with the Spirit of life that they were coming to know through Jesus. They remembered that when he gave his instructions to those whom he had sent two by two into the towns and villages he had taken for granted that they could do the same kind of work they had seen him doing. As they understood him, he claimed to act by virtue of powers that men everywhere

should possess and exercise if they live as God intends them
to live and exercise those powers which God places at their
disposal.[3]

Their own scriptures had led the disciples to expect that
God might at times draw very near and speak to them, but
that he would remain, as it were, on the outside and would
be always more or less detached, as one apart from them.
But in Jesus they had seen what they had never learned before, that God works from within, that his Spirit can so
penetrate and possess the human body as to look with his
love through its eyes, speak with the accent of his own tenderness upon its lips, and put the healing touch of his confidence into its hands. So it began to dawn upon them that
what God, through Jesus, had done for them he desired,
through them, to do for others; in fact, he was calling them
to "be filled with the same spirit," and to speak and work
"in demonstration of this power."[d]

The disciples remembered that a look or a word or a
touch from Jesus had often opened the way to man's recovery. Thus he had dispelled the nameless fears that were
paralyzing an impotent man, and had convinced a raving
demoniac that there was a Spirit of love stronger than any
spirit of evil by which he thought himself possessed. When
Peter and John, now filled with the sympathy and energy of
the same Spirit, suddenly met a paralytic who asked for alms,
they naturally tried to do what Jesus would have done—
what, in fact, they believed he intended them to do as his
representatives. When, therefore, they took the helpless beg-
gar by the hand, the love of God was shown through them
with like freedom and effect: the hopeless man was set free
from paralyzing fears and responded to the healing Spirit
that worked through Peter and John. From Jesus they had
learned that it was not a magic look or touch which had
wrought the change in those whom he had healed; it was
the confidence he inspired in a God of love and in the power
of that God to help them. So Peter exclaimed to the awe-
struck crowd that rushed upon them while the paralytic

walked with them into the temple. "Why are you surprised at this? Why do you stare at us, as if we had made him walk by any power or piety of ours? . . . The God of our fathers has glorified Jesus his servant. . . . It is the faith he inspires which has made the man thus hale and whole before you all."[e]

Similarly, though using somewhat different terms, a survey of advance in medicine shows the remedial influence of religious faith upon physical and mental ills. After explaining how the victim of fear, anxiety, or resentment is poisoned by the secretions released into his blood stream by an excited nervous system, the survey contrasts this condition with that of the man who is neither frightened, anxious, nor resentful, even though he encounters the same difficulty: "Suppose he has faith in his destiny, confidence that 'the universe is friendly,' that the supreme power is interested in his welfare —then the chemicals which go with fear and uncertainty and resentment are not released by his nerves, and his blood is not saturated with these overactive secretions."[4]

In reporting a prolonged study of 275 rheumatoid arthritics who "had no vital faith and were therefore fearfully facing life's responsibilities alone," the physicians said of these patients: "We found that the solution begins in an honest facing of themselves with the doctor, and with his aid ends in the development of a vital faith. A deep religious faith is the most effective faith, provided the doctor himself has such a vital faith to give. . . . Five years of observation convinced us that just facing the negative attitudes is not enough to overcome them; but, with the development of a faith (and its positive philosophy for living) fear goes, improved health follows, and most important of all for the future welfare of the patient, personality changes take place."[4]

Influence of the Body upon Mind and Spirit

While early disciples of Jesus learned that the functions of the body are profoundly influenced by states of mind and feeling, they learned, on the other hand, that thoughts, emotions, and even character itself are decisively affected by one's physical habits and condition. This truth, which received fresh emphasis in the New Testament, was soon overlooked, as it has been ever since, to the disparagement or neglect of the body. So far as we can tell from the records, however, the earliest Christians did not go to the extremes of later asceticism or other disregard of the body. What they had seen in Jesus as he ministered to various human needs must have impressed them with the powers of the body as a means of expression for the Spirit of God. Similarly Paul found personal capacity enhanced when body and mind worked harmoniously in the service of "the Lord, the Spirit." He wrote to new converts in dissolute Corinth: "The body is not meant for immorality, but for the service of the Lord. . . . Do you not know that your body is a temple of the Holy Spirit that is within you—the Spirit you have received from God? Therefore honor God with your bodies."[f]

Yet thousands of earnest, public-spirited men and women in our day, who would be the last to deny this obligation, are drifting into such disregard of their bodies as will later make havoc of their usefulness when it should be at the peak. Because the writer and not a few of his sanest advisers have seen this happen through the years to many potentially effective public servants, we feel compelled to consider this problem in some detail. The problem deserves close attention from young people also. Studies by experts of the habits of boys and girls throughout the whole period of student life, including postgraduate days, show that "the longer the student is in school and college the more faulty his health habits and therefore the poorer his health. The cause of this situation is that in school life the essentials of health are habitually disregarded."[5]

Yet the influence of physical condition upon one's disposition and work is increasingly emphasized by medical science and psychotherapy. In a volume based on the combined experience of many specialists, they explain that "discontent is undoubtedly very often the consequence of wrong conditions in the body. Though melancholy, worry, peevishness, and fear generally appear as arising from outward conditions, there are usually real physical sources, existing within the body itself. These are at times most difficult of recognition. A person who is physically ill (even when he does not know it) is likely to be ill-satisfied with everything, without suspecting the fundamental cause of the discontent." For example, the supposed "cause" of ill temper or depression in a man who is ill may be the mistake of a fellow-worker or the impatient word of a friend. Yet, when the same man is in good health, the same apparent cause may be without any unfortunate result, and may even be the occasion of better understanding. This was evident on a surveying trip in the mountains of Colorado, where the whole party enjoyed an ideal, healthful, out-of-door life. One of the party said, "I never saw so good-natured a crowd of rough men. Nothing ever seemed to make them angry. They were too full of exultant health."[6]

The real, though often hidden, cause of mental or emotional disturbance and lack of energy "may be constipation, eyestrain, the effects of alcohol or other drugs, a sedentary life, a bad posture or weak abdominal muscles." The trouble often begins without warning when infection gathers around teeth, tonsils, or some other part of the body, and painlessly spreads poison through the blood.[6]

These often neglected causes of poor health and lethargy point to the need for regular and thorough physical examination by competent diagnosticians. Those consulted should be able and alert to discover any glandular or nutritional deficiencies, as well as any injurious physical or emotional habits. Such causes of low vitality are more readily detected before some acute trouble complicates the situation. They may be more difficult to detect and to cure than is serious illness. For they often become silently habitual and require drastic correction of physical habits and mental attitudes. Even when these are not among the commonly called "bad habits," they may be as tenacious in resisting correction and in undermining health.

For instance, failure to overcome habits of nervous tension and to practice right habits of relaxation often causes poor health and inefficiency. "Many people waste more energy than they use when they work. They use muscles that are not needed for the job in hand, unaware that they are tense. After learning to relax, they become conscious of tensions hitherto unfelt and, naturally, let go of them. If you do that, the quality of your work will improve. You will be able to give more thought and attention to your job when your own muscle tensions are not tripping you up and turning your thoughts inward." Dr. David Fink, on whose wide experience we have just drawn, considers relaxation so important that he says: "A short vacation or leave of absence from work can be put to greatest advantage by using the time to acquire the simple skills of progressive relaxation. Two weeks so spent will be an excellent investment. . . . You may be able to learn during your spare time. If you do, you must carry your habits of relaxation over into your work."[7]

To carry relaxation into both work and play we must cultivate correct habits of posture in sitting, standing, and walking, as well as the habit of deep breathing; for tense and strenuous play, unsuited to one's age and physical condition, may do more harm than good. And the value of suitable play may be lost through tension during other hours of the day, hence the need of at least one period for rest during the day in order to correct the tension and tempo of prolonged activity and to help maintain relaxation during working hours. "Sitting, driving, reading, and writing are all opportunities for the practice of relaxation. You can make driving far less dangerous, and indeed pleasurable, by learning to relax in the driver's seat. And the practice of relaxation at mealtimes will help your digestion. It's really fun, once you get started, to see just how much tension you can eliminate, how progressive your relaxation can be."[7] The more progressive it becomes, the more likely you are to forestall serious illness and to prolong a well-balanced, productive life.

A ripe old age, however, and also the best middle years
are not likely to be enjoyed unless the other habits of right
living are cultivated continuously. What you eat and how
you eat it, when and how you exercise and rest, what you
do with your spare time—these also are among the factors
that determine the length and value of your life's work. Dr.
William Emerson says that "fast eating has become a national bad habit; 70 per cent of all Americans eat with
nervous rapidity." He shows also the widespread damage
caused "by unchewed food feverishly washed down with
various drinks," and the danger of eating when overtired
or tense.[5] To change our faulty health habits we must co-
operate with the doctor in discovery as well as in cure. He
cannot observe us during all our hours of work and play;
nor can he change our habits for us, or even, perhaps, convince us of their danger, especially if he has failed to correct
such habits in himself. Yet if young and old are to be prepared to deal with the inevitable emergencies of our un-
stable civilization, habits that sap physical and spiritual energy must be supplanted by habits that make for abundant
life. This was learned by a noted sculptor who was supposed
to be "down and out" in the artistic world. Some years later,
however, he "came back" with a masterpiece, after he had
adopted a new purpose and way of living that gave better
scope for all his faculties.

Need of a Purpose Giving Scope for All Our Powers

To gain these conditions for the release of energy, we must
overcome undue absorption with the body and be set free
from empty fears, enervating conflicts, and debasing motives.
To this end, we need to be moved and mastered by some
purpose great enough to give full scope to all our powers
and lasting satisfaction to our better total selves. For, as
Robert Woodworth explains, "it is the individual that must
be satisfied, rather than any specified one of his tendencies."
Certain tendencies or motives may have to be rejected, even

though they have some survival value; and "the most adequate way of handling rejected motives is to co-ordinate
them with accepted motives—to harness them into teams
and set them to work. . . . When the boastful boy becomes a
loyal and enthusiastic member of a school, his self-assertive
motive is combined with social motives into an effective
team. Probably a motive can be sublimated only by combining it with other motives."[8]

In dealing with this question of how to liberate latent
energies, Professor Woodworth says: "A definite purpose is
the first requirement; without that, one merely drifts, with
no persistency and no great energy. The goal should be
something that appeals vitally to you, and something which
you can attain. . . . If the ultimate goal is distant, there must
be landmarks along the way which you can take as more
immediate goals, for a goal that can be reached by immediate
action enlists more present effort. The student puts more
energy into his study when the examination is close at hand;
and although this is regrettable, it reveals a side of human
nature that can be utilized in the management of yourself
and others. A well defined and clearly visible goal is a much
better energy-releaser than vague 'good intentions.' "[8]

Where, then, can we find a goal so evocative of all creative
energies, so satisfying for all concerned, as that for which
Jesus called his disciples, and which they found in accord
with the purpose of God for the world, as well as with the
deepest needs and longing of his creatures.[g] Under the influence of Jesus the disciples were roused to larger use of their
powers in the endeavor to realize a true community of men
with God and nature; and they bent their energies to daily
tasks which, they believed, had a part in this reconciling work
of a Christlike God. The first disciples could better understand this release of energy by "working together with God"
in the common tasks of community because their Master,
himself, had worked with his hands, and because they, like
him, had been reared in a tradition that encouraged every
boy to learn a trade and honored manual labor as an ex-

pression of the will of God. They were in the succession of
those who prayed "establish thou the work of our hands
upon us," who believed that "except the Lord build the
house, they labor in vain that build it." This idea that the
day's work should express the purpose and power of God,
they found also in their nation's history. They saw it illustrated in the restoration of Jerusalem, when both priests
and people braved the danger of rebuilding the city wall
because of their confidence that "the God of heaven he will
prosper us, therefore we his servants will arise and build."[h]

This background of the early Jewish Christians helped
them, as it should help us, to cultivate a sense of personal
vocation in the stream of history. Everyone is expected to
respond to some high calling of God, whether layman or
clergyman. The Jewish pioneers of faith, Abraham, Moses,
and others, show how men and women in various walks of
life may gain courage, foresight, and energy when they respond to some definite part in the work of God for the
world.[i] "By suitable work man can fit into the overall purpose that God has set in motion in the world, but not by
irresponsible activity. The work that spells out the content
of God's vocation for men must meet genuine need, must
call forth all the worker's capacities, and must contribute
toward the common good. These standards are not easy to
maintain. Besides work there is needed a continual renewal
through face-to-face worship of God. Through such renewal
—through the hearty love, the humility, and the stability it
brings—fresh starts can be continually made and new insights come. Herein lies our main hope."[9]

The early disciples remembered what seventy men like
themselves had dared to undertake when they had been
called and trained by Jesus to go on special missions to the
places where he was about to come.[j] So in various ways they
learned by deed that the Spirit of God was working in them
also to co-ordinate their various gifts for the development of
a true community, as well as for their own growth in Christlike character. And they gained a new sense of peace and

power from the assurance of their own vocation as a part of the purpose of God. Sharing like confidence, Paul could declare: "There are varieties of talents, but the same Spirit; varieties of service, but the same Lord; varieties of effects, but the same God who effects everything in everyone. Each received his manifestation of the Spirit for the common good."[k]

Such Purpose Needed in All Our Institutions

The most discerning of the early disciples tried to help others find ways to express the common purpose in the day's work. The early Church soon began to recognize an obligation, which the Church today needs more than ever to fulfill—an obligation to help its members find needed work in which each can best contribute to the general well-being through the best use of all his powers. This obligation to help make the layman's vocation a reality must be fulfilled now, if the increase of lay initiative, which holds great promise for the future, is to come to fruition before it is too late.

Only the exceptional church or school has begun to give the needed help through adequate vocational guidance and the wider range of personal counseling about family life and other problems. Present emergencies, therefore, call insistently for a great advance in the training of competent counselors for churches and schools everywhere. Moreover, the variety of problems with which they have to deal shows the need for consultation with those in different professions. For example, some problems of health and consequent vocational adjustment may involve medical, psychological, or economic questions. The right diagnosis and treatment may be decisive for the future energy and usefulness of many a student or church member who needs expert help. This need for a well-balanced staff or group of advisers is additional reason for close co-operation between churches and schools, and between neighboring churches, especially in rural areas, where no single church or school can provide the needed guidance in all cases.[10] What the Young Men's and Young Women's Christian Associations have done in personal counseling and the awakening of laymen suggests how much more needs to be done.

Underlying these specialized skills are certain qualities which multiply the usefulness of any counselor and help to call out unreleased energies from others. These qualities correspond in general with those which the first disciples discerned in Jesus. In him they saw such unifying purpose and spontaneous, outgoing love as could rouse new aspirations in all kinds of people, establish their confidence in a co-operating Spirit of love, and so deliver them from fear and self-seeking. Such love quickens a counselor's discernment of hidden aspirations in others and discovers ways in which such aspirations may be realized. Jesus, for instance, was quick to see what no one else discerned in the unpopular tax collector, Zaccheus, and took instant steps to help him become a good citizen in the new society.[1] So the disciples came to understand why the indifferent, the rebellious, and the outcast of their day, repelled by such a God as their religious leaders claimed to represent, had yet come freely to Jesus and found through him a father-like God who was already seeking them. Eventually all sorts of people were shown the way to release the energies of love in a world-wide society of brothers. This, in part, is what the early Church set out to do, and what the new World Council of Churches now seeks to encourage through an indigenous church in every land, each bound to the others in brotherly concern.

The work of this Council, and the way it co-operates with the United Nations and other agencies for the relief of human need in many lands, now gives the Church exceptional opportunities to pioneer in the work of bringing our world together.[11] (At various stages of our inquiry we will go further into essential conditions and new developments of this work.) To take at the flood the present tide of world-uniting opportunities, church members everywhere must press far beyond comfortable and complacent relations with one another in any form of exclusive association. Racial and class pride, with embittering segregation, should no longer be allowed to wreck mankind's development. Only in so far as there is increasing sensitiveness and response to human need and high aspiration, does the Spirit have free course to develop a new humanity and to release through it the divine-human energies.

Questions for Further Thought and Discussion

What proportion of religious people today, would you judge, know personally the release from nervous tension found through Christian vocation?

Why do people seek out a psychiatrist often these days instead of a minister: are the clergy ineffective, or hard to reach, or too busy with others, or what?

What proportion of Americans, so far as you can judge, are released nervously by their everyday jobs?

How can the Church, and medical men, properly use religious means for curing bodily ills today?

9

THE AVAILABILITY OF ENERGY

Two Theories of Available Energy

THE VIEW of man's enlarging capacities, which we have been considering, corresponds with the psychological theory that we may tap unplumbed sources of energy. This theory may be clarified by contrasting it with a commonly held physical theory, which states that "in each of us there is a certain supply of energy derived from the food we eat and the air we breathe, and, therefore, strictly limited in amount. . . . The natural consequence of this belief in the physical character and the limited supply of our energy is that we are careful to economize our little store of strength, to husband our resources, lest by excess of expenditure we find the springs of our life running dry."[1] If we live under the shadow of these supposedly rigid limits, we are more likely to suffer from needless fears or fatigue, or from a sense of frustration.

In contrast to this physical theory of fixed limitations, Dr. A. J. Hadfield, like many other psychologists, supports a theory of expanding capacities: "If our powers seem to fail, it is not because all the energy available is used up, but because its flow is checked, either by the channel being blocked up or by our inability to use it aright. The chief cause of fatigue is not exhaustion but stagnation. The way to power, therefore, is not to harbor our resources and store up our strength by inactivity, but to find the way to tap the resources of power at our disposal, so that they may flood our life and fill us with energy. . . . The fact that whatever their ultimate origin there are resources of power whose existence we do not ordinarily recognize, but which can be made available for the purpose of our daily life, is one which has been firmly established by the scientific researches of recent years."[1]

Dr. Hadfield finds evidence in many experiments that the limits of possibility in our daily lives are defined less by the body than by the mind, and that the resources of power are psychic rather than physical in character. He finds this evidence corroborated by the fact that usually the mind is exhausted before the body. This may be explained in part by the fact that the mind is the latest part of the human organism to have developed in evolution, and is therefore the least completely adapted to its environment. It may be explained also by the fact that "the susceptibility of the mind to fatigue is valuable in warning the body of its approach to the danger zone, and so preventing the body from going too far. But in the majority of men such mental fatigue occurs long before we get anywhere near the danger zone of bodily fatigue, and the body is rarely given the opportunity of showing the extent of its endurance."[1]

If, however, we would go safely beyond the beginning of mental fatigue, we must attend to the conditions explained in the previous chapter for keeping the body at its best. It is easy to become so absorbed in work or pleasure or even in a good cause that the devotee drifts into habits or conditions that impair his physical and spiritual life, as well as sap his energy. Consequently, he may be unprepared to draw safely upon the reserves which otherwise could multiply and prolong his efficiency.

On the other hand, the possibility of overcoming weakness or apparent fatigue by tapping unknown reserves of energy deserves continued scrutiny. It was so engrossing an object of investigation to William James that for many years he mused on the phenomena, which he found hard to explain, and then wrote his most widely read essay, *The Energies of Men*. In it he said: "Conversions, whether they may be political, scientific, philosophic, or religious, form one way in which bound energies are let loose. They unify us, and put a stop to ancient mental interferences. . . . In religious conversions we have so fine an adjustment that the idea may be in the mind years before it exerts effects. . . . Whatever it is, it may be a high water mark of energy, in which 'noes' once impossible are easy and in which a new range of 'yesses' gains the right of way."

Prayer as a Way to Release Energy

In the same essay prayer is emphasized, on the basis of expert medical opinion, as a way of making conditions favorable for releasing inhibited energies. Regretting that there are not more scientific men who "can carry on any living commerce with 'God,'" William James continues: "Yet many of us are well aware of how much freer and abler our lives would be, were such important forms of energizing not sealed up by the critical atmosphere in which we have been reared. There are in every one potential forms of activity that actually are shunted out from use. Part of the imperfect vitality under which we labor can thus be easily explained. One part of our mind dams up—even damns up!—the other parts."[2]

In discussing "The Gospel of Relaxation," William James shows the relevance of religion and especially of prayer in connection with "a law of very deep and widespread importance in the conduct of our lives—a law which we Americans most grievously neglect. Stated technically, the law is this: that *strong feeling about one's self tends to arrest the free association of one's objective ideas and motor processes.*" The result of this undue preoccupation with self is a more or less unconscious benumbing of one's faculties. The victim is scarcely aware of the way in which this absorption in himself has unfitted him for the usual duties, as well as for the exigencies of life. The remedy is the same that William James prescribes for worry. "The sovereign cure for worry is religious faith. The turbulent billows of the fretful surface leave the deep parts of the ocean undisturbed, and to him who has a hold on vaster and more permanent realities the hourly vicissitudes of his personal destiny seem relatively insignificant things. The really religious person is accordingly unshakable and full of equanimity, and calmly ready for any duty that the day may bring forth. This is charmingly illustrated by a little work, *The Practice of the Presence of God, The Best Rule of a Holy Life,* by Brother Lawrence, being Conversations and Letters of Nicholas Herman of Lorraine."[3] Brother Lawrence, a Carmelite friar, occupied chiefly in the kitchen or on purchasing journeys for the monastery, had so mastered the art of living, including the relaxation of all unnecessary solicitudes and anxieties, that men of learning and high position came long distances to talk with him. He said that when he was a footman in Paris, he had been a great awkward fellow who broke everything. Yet he had learned through the practice of the presence of God so to meet difficulties, and to make right adjustments with men and things, as to bring the disconnected, everyday concerns, which often distract or defeat a man, into fruitful relation with the whole of life.

For lack of some such way either to assimilate or to exclude these wasters of energy, innumerable lives are frittered away without knowing what is the matter with them. "The thousand little things that enter into our lives every day will weaken and eat away our strength unless they are assimilated into some integrating purpose of living. If they are not so assimilated they are like so much waste material clogging and poisoning the process of life."[4]

How the multiple details of an executive position can be assimilated into the larger purpose, Henry Wieman has demonstrated in his own experience. He tells how he found himself, an absent-minded college professor, suddenly involved in many new and complicated responsibilities. "I had stepped out into the jam of modern life. I was overwhelmed. I was lost unless I could remember innumerable details and keep a great number of things systematically in my mind. It was then that I discovered what great things can be accomplished by the exposure, diagnosis, and reconstruction of prayer. I rose in a week to mastery of the total situation." In explaining this experience he shows that the kind of prayer he is describing is more than autosuggestion: "The prayer is in the attitude, not in the words, and this attitude is not prayer to self, because it is an adaptation to that phase of our environment which will do our remembering for us, as air does our breathing for us. The courage, the community, the love, the memory, the mastery, these are not in ourselves alone, but are brought to us by something in the environment. The problem is to find and establish that adjustment through which God can do this for us." In the case of a group of workers in an office, for instance, the needed adjustment may involve the attitude of meekness, sympathy, and good will through which the order of God may enter into this group. "If my attitude is the needed attitude, the order of God will become more potent and pervasive in that office. By order of God we mean the order of community which leads to the highest values. Prayer at its best is the deliberate establishment of those attitudes of personality through which the order of God can possess the world."[5]

We shall consider later how these attitudes may be fostered by the exposure, diagnosis, and reconstruction that prayer makes possible.

Early Christian Experience Effective Today

Experiences like those just cited, and investigations like those of Dr. Hadfield and William James, show how applicable today are the conditions observed by the early Christians for the release of energy. It was in giving to others that they received. Powers like those of Jesus flowed through their work so far as they lived in the spirit of his life and teaching, "freely ye received, freely give."[a] In terms of the psychology of power, Dr. Hadfield states the same condition: "Nature is lavish in her gifts to those who will use them, and especially to those who devote them to nature's altruistic ends, for such ends harmonize the soul. How wonderful is the way in which with quite ordinary folk, power leaps to our aid in any time of emergency. When great demands are made upon us, if only we fearlessly accept the challenge and confidently expend our strength, every danger or difficulty brings its own strength. Several of the greatest psychologists have tended towards the view that the source of power is to be regarded as some impulse that works through us, and is not of our own making. Their views suggest that we are not merely receptacles but *channels* of energy. Life and power are not so much contained in us, they *course* through us."[1]

In any case, confidence or lack of confidence that adequate energy is available has been found by careful experiments to determine in large measure whether such energy will course through men when needed. Some who failed in Dr. Hadfield's experiments could say "I will" *but they had not learned to say "I can."* They were in the plight confessed by Paul: "To will is present with me, but how to perform I know not." Such cases show that the will alone does not assure success. "Want of belief in its possibility is always the main obstacle to the performing of any mighty work. Faith in its possibility—a faith not necessarily founded on evidence, but one that dares to take the risk—is the greatest asset to success in any task. 'If thou canst.' 'All things are possible to them that believe.' "[1, b]

Confidence like this was intended by Jesus to be the normal experience of his disciples. It was, in fact, characteristic of their life, as disclosed in the Epistles and The Acts of the Apostles: "I can do all things"—"You will receive power."[c] The disciples ascribed this enhancement of power "to the operation in and through them of a divine energy to which the community gave the name of the 'Spirit.' Pentecost, the healing miracles of the Apostolic Age, the triumphant progress of the religion through the Roman Empire, the heroic

deeds of saints and martyrs—all these point to the sense of
a power newly discovered."[1]

A comparison between conditions in the first century and
the twentieth has been made by a representative international commission investigating the situation in many lands.
Changing conditions now make their conclusions even more
impressive: "The Apostles were driven back on their mem-
ories of the Lord, they were driven into closer fellowship
with him, they were cast upon the undiscovered riches of
the divine power and wisdom and love, because the opportunities and the dangers of their task taught them the insufficiency of all their past discoveries of him. New faith is
always born out of new emergencies, and it was simply because the Apostles faced the great emergency, and were
driven back by it upon the undiscovered in God, that we
have their great discoveries of God in Christ." The Church
in later ages, as the commission shows, took a more limited
view of God and of the obligation of Christians to all races.
It flinched from facing the emergency of a whole world's
need. It failed, therefore, to experience the power which
comes through facing an obligation utterly beyond the ability of the Church in herself to fulfill. The failure to face this
obligation kept the Church "from the' pressure of that extremity of need which is God's opportunity of revelation.
Today we stand in that extremity once more. . . . History
tells us how the ancient emergency was faced, and how in
new discoveries of God, the Church rose above its impotence,
and laid the foundations of Christendom. So only can the
Church of today rise out of its divisions and comparative
impotence. There is assuredly more in God and in that Gospel which is the truth of God, than we have yet attained.
We still wait for any thorough understanding of the place
of the Spirit in the life of man."[6]

Better Conditions for the Release of Energy

If, therefore, as the commission just quoted maintains, the
Church is to lead toward so thorough an understanding of

the place of the Spirit in the life of men that, through the Church, the Spirit may have free course to fashion a new humanity, then surely the Church must be alert to all that affects the creative energies of men. The Church and all forward-looking groups must consider why creative energies are so often checked in modern life. They must deal with the social conditions that make much productive work uninteresting and toilsome. "Why," John Dewey asks, "is the psychology of the industrialist so different from that of inventor, explorer, artist, sportsman, scientific investigator, physician, teacher? For the latter we do not assert that activity is such a burdensome sacrifice that it is engaged in only because men are bribed to act by hope of reward or are coerced by fear of loss."[7] If productive activity has become such a burden this fact is ample proof that the conditions under which work is carried on irritate and frustrate natural tendencies instead of carrying them forward to fruition. So the ailments of the industrial order and their counterpart in the world of nations, like all occasions of conflict and disunion which impede the free working of the Spirit of God, are part of the emergency which must be faced, because they decisively affect the energies and even the destinies of men.

Moreover, no release of the balked energies of mankind can be complete unless better provision is made for that half of the race which in nearly all lands has been most repressed. Women, who have been so long under the restrictions of a man-made world must be given their full share in such reshaping of the social order as will call forth the best energies of all its members. Towards this enlargement of women's opportunities the Church undoubtedly should point the way with something of its Founder's far-seeing leadership.

So also the better relations which church, home, and school should foster between adults and youth are essential to the best expression of those thwarted impulses which now occasion so much confusion and unrest among the young.

Especially important for children and youth are relations of comradeship and confidence in the home.

It appears, therefore, that not only in our industrial and international affairs, but in all relations between men and women, adults and youth, members of different groups and races, there must be an increasing sense of our interdependence, a more inclusive unity of purpose, a more appropriate distribution of work and its products. Here is both an emergency and an opportunity: an emergency that threatens the disintegration of civilization, an opportunity for creative fellowship that is unparalleled in history.

When fellowship became a chief concern of the early Christians as they began to carry out the world-embracing purpose of their Master, they discovered complex needs in all sorts of people, and they saw the insufficiency of merely individualistic efforts to meet them. If we face similar emergencies with the same quality of fellowship, we too may see more clearly that our common purpose involves nothing less than a change of direction in civilization itself "from the quarrelsome work of exploiting the material world to the co-operative work of developing the spirit of man."[8]

Questions for Further Thought and Discussion

What examples can you cite of group solidarity releasing people's energies— worthily or unworthily?

If the millions who complain of brain-fag and mental erosion are really suffering from a disease of the will, what are some solutions for the difficulty?

How greatly do societal customs, economic patterns, and world trade practices affect the releasing of energies among the various world peoples?

Part III

AMPLER FELLOWSHIP WITH JESUS AND
THE GROWTH OF COMMUNITY

IO

HOW JESUS EXPANDS FELLOWSHIP

He Calls for Greater Purpose and Better Attitudes

IN SPITE OF opposing forces—political, economic, and ecclesiastical—Jesus brought a community governed by love within the range of daily experience. So we turn again to those short years of his public life, which the historian Lecky found the most significant in history.

Jesus began his public work in his native Galilee by proclaiming: "The time is fully come, and the Kingdom of God is close at hand; repent and believe this Good News."ª If, through familiarity, these words have lost their revolutionary significance, let us try to recover the original idea as embodied in the life and teaching of Jesus. It is as though he saw a new era already on the way, and said: "The times are ripe for it, God's realm of love is at the door: change your attitudes, stake your life on this Good News." Jesus meant that he was offering new possibilities of realizing an order of society controlled by love. He wanted men to be so sure of a Spirit of love at work in the world that they would commit themselves to this Spirit, in order that the new order of life might be embodied in them. Thus they would discover, as in fact many have since discovered, that "the true divine order is ever ready to break into the world, if men will only suffer it to break into their hearts."[1]

Though Jesus never overlooked the value of the individual, or the relation of the individual to God, he saw clearly that it is also in right relations with others that man must exercise those qualities that make him akin to God; for "by the love of the brethren alone, can we realize our place in the family of God."[2] So Jesus called everyone to seek first, not his own salvation, but a society in which all may realize their sonship to God. He even went so far as to say, "whoever is bent on securing his life will lose it."[b] In mistaken efforts to make their own lives secure, Jesus saw many apparently religious men of his time missing the true goal. Even reputedly religious leaders were wasting time by seeking first to win favor with God, and to enhance their own reputations with men. Knowing how ramified, though hidden, are these self-centering tendencies, Jesus called everyone to deny self in the quest of the great objective. He saw that nothing less than the pursuit of a universal order of truth, goodness, and mutual aid would lead men beyond self-interest and group prejudice and open all their faculties to the re-creating energies of love.

At the same time, Jesus saw that to work together in love for the common welfare requires not only a new objective but also a new disposition. "I tell you truly," he said, "unless you turn and become like children, you will never get into the Realm of Heaven at all."[c] The nature and influence of the childlike disposition will appear in the course of our inquiry. For the present we are concerned with the emphasis of Jesus that the new disposition and the new objective must be interacting. Neither can develop apart from the other. Only as men have a teachable, self-denying love can they co-operate fully to realize the new society. Yet only as they put first the interests of the new society can their love reach beyond the limiting attachments of family, class, or other special interest.

When men who were missing this two-fold approach asked Jesus when the Kingdom would come, he answered: "The Kingdom of God is not coming visibly, and people will not say 'Look! Here it is!' or 'There it is!' for the Kingdom of God is within you."[d] It can come in the outer world, therefore, only as its richer life develops in the individual. And it will come increasingly, Jesus taught, as the love of God in the hearts and minds of men is given free course to express itself in all human relations.

He Is Concerned for All Sorts of People

So Jesus began, not with abstractions, but in a warmly human way. One picture of how he began shows him spending the rest of the day with two disciples of John the Baptist, after John had called their attention to Jesus. The next morning, Andrew, one of the two, found his brother Peter and brought him to Jesus; and the day following, Jesus found Philip, who in turn brought Nathaniel.[e] Some time later Jesus came upon Andrew and Peter, James and John, as they were fishing by the Sea of Galilee. He asked them to become his pupils and also his partners in winning men to the great enterprise. They went with him soon after to the synagogue in Capernaum, and saw that everyone was astonished at the convincing reality of his words, so different from the puzzling legalism of the scribes. Even a so-called madman, obsessed by fearful delusions, felt the calming power of love in Jesus and was delivered from his madness. From the synagogue Jesus went to Peter's house where Peter's mother-in-law was ill with a fever. He was able to bring harmony to the troubled body, as before he had restored the disordered mind of the man in the synagogue. Then he went among the dense crowd of sufferers who were brought that evening to the door, "and he laid his hands on every one of them and healed them." The next day he started with his new friends on a tour of their own province of Galilee.[f] In all his crowded days he never made the mistake, so fatal to reformers, of becoming absorbed in a cause to the neglect of men, women, or children. Because he loved them for themselves, as well as because of what he said and did, "the common people heard him gladly."[g]

Those who continued with Jesus saw the ideal society illuminated by his constant concern for all sorts of people—in
sharp contrast to the aloofness of their "religious" leaders.
Wherever he went he made friends of those whom the world
despised; and by his faith in them and his love for them he
won them to himself. Even those who seemed to be possessed by evil spirits could feel that he cared for them. And
the lepers, who were kept from all contact with other people
by heavy penalties, came to him without fear. A woman,
called a sinner, to whom he had spoken words of forgiveness, stole in behind him as he reclined at supper, and wept
over his feet. The great mass of people found his concern
for them an entirely new experience; for the world as they
knew it was hard and pitiless. "The peasants were ground
down by the rich landowners, and could never be sure of
the next day's bread. Whole classes were pronounced unclean
by the grim Mosaic Law, and, under the sense that everyone
despised them, grew embittered and vicious. No provision
was made for those who could not fight their own battle.
The blind and crippled were left to beg by the wayside;
widows and orphans had no recourse but to sell themselves
into some kind of slavery. To this dumb, suffering multitude
the coming of Jesus was like a great light. As he moved
among them, healing and comforting and speaking of the
love of God, he seemed already to have brought in the
new age."[3]

This love of Jesus for men, women, and children, wherever he met them, revealed such insight and evoked such
response as could not come to the sect-bound religious leaders of his time. In men and women whom they considered
hopeless, Jesus could discern and encourage hidden longings.
They looked upon Zacchæus, for instance, as merely a despised tax-collector in league with the exploiting Romans.
When this little man climbed into a sycamore tree to get a
sight of Jesus, they saw only curiosity. Jesus, looking up,
saw suppressed aspirations and encouraged them. " 'Zacchæus,' he said, 'come down at once, for I must stay at your

house today.' He came down at once and welcomed him gladly. But when they saw this, everyone began to mutter that Jesus had gone to be the guest of a sinner. So Zacchæus stopped and said to the Lord, 'I will give the half of all I have, Lord, to the poor, and if I have cheated anybody, I will give him back four times as much.' And Jesus said, 'Today salvation has come to this house.' "[h]

Through experience like this Jesus trained the disciples who were to carry on his work. From among them "he appointed twelve that they might be with him" in a closer companionship than was possible for all his followers.[i] Even in the larger group it was by way of fellowship in a common cause that Jesus brought men and women to an aim and method like his own. It was such fellowship, we shall see, that ripened into the Church, and made it a means and a foreshadowing of the ultimate community.

Even in the early days, the training of disciples was not confined to pupilage. Jesus not only gave them opportunities of observing his own work among men, but before long he sent them out to do like work themselves. And, when they returned to him with their tale of success and failure, he helped them to effect better adjustments with God and with men.

To this end he guarded them from the deadening effects of publicity and overwork. When "many were coming and going, and they had no leisure even to eat," he took the Twelve with him into the quiet of a lonely place. By guiding them in such interplay of solitude and social experience, Jesus let them see the secret of his own power, and prepared them better than they knew for the enterprise he would soon entrust to them.[j]

He Explains the Beloved Community

All that Jesus did, as well as all that he taught, had practical meaning for the coming Kingdom. Because he conceived this Kingdom as the aim and essential environment for everyone, "we may learn about it not merely from what

Jesus said of it by name, but from all that he told us of the
order of life that he was establishing. All that he said about
the way in which men ought to live, that is, all his teaching
in ethics and religion, all his inspiration and his ideal of
life—goes to show what he meant by this great term. As his
whole work laid the foundations of the Kingdom, so his
whole utterance of truth shows us what it is."[4]

Yet in the record of all the vivid talk of Jesus about this
new order of life there is no definition of it which might
later limit the thought or action of those living under different times and circumstances. His way of speaking in parables,
with incisive warnings and searching questions, avoided the
perils of rigid system-building, yet stimulated the imagination, roused men to think for themselves, and encouraged
bold experiment. Like all teachers, he was limited by the
language of his day. When he used apocalyptic imagery familiar to his hearers, though strange to us, he gave it new and
vital bearing upon present conduct, and used it to emphasize
the need, not only for the initiative of God, but also for
radical change in the ways of men.

Though Jesus saw the Kingdom as an expression in history of the love and power of God, he taught that God's
acts are not arbitrary. In his own life, Jesus showed that the
coming of the Kingdom on earth depends also upon the
response of men to the whole order of life that God provides.
"This Kingdom is not 'spiritual' in the sense that it has
nothing to do with the physical universe, nor is it 'apocalyptic' in the sense that it is to be established by means of cosmic
catastrophes."[5] For Jesus, the physical and the spiritual are
elements of one system, organized by one God, the Father.
Jesus not only described events and processes in both elements; he experienced them and he dealt with them. His
healing of physical and mental disorders indicates that he
stood in more intimate relation to natural processes than
did other men. Moreover, "the religious and the ethical are
for him as completely one as the physical and the spiritual.
Conduct toward men and towards God is characterized by

the same fundamental principles of love and trust."[5] Jesus
held such conduct to be essential for realizing a divine order
of life on earth.

He urged his followers, therefore, to venturesome experiments on a basis of love and trust. He assumed that these
would be justified eventually, despite human failure, by the
fundamental nature of reality. Like some of his modern interpreters, he seemed to discern that "there are cosmic forces,
as for instance, the cosmic trend toward harmony, fellowship,
and mutual aid, which are relevant to all human activity."
Yet Jesus saw realistically what we have been but slowly
learning from the interdependent life of the world, that
"only as we experimentally develop mutual aid can we discover how much the universe lends itself to the support of
that effort." It follows that a response from the universe may
seem doubtful indeed to those who selfishly exploit it or
any person in it, or who otherwise violate the laws of growth
in God's creation. Jesus, however, believed that a response
would come eventually to those who act on the faith that
the world proceeds from a God who cares for his creation,
even to the fall of a sparrow. So Jesus taught that faith in
such a God, even though its beginning is small as a mustard
seed, if it is exercised in overcoming hindrances to love and
mutual aid, will become strong enough to remove mountains.[k]

He Confirms It by Life, Death, and Later Victory

The influence of Jesus does not come to men merely
through his separate acts and sayings. His whole life on earth,
his death, and his continuing presence with his disciples
help them to come into relations like his own with nature,
men, and God. Thus he leads disciples beyond unbalanced
emotions and speculative thought about God, which often
deflect men from brotherly relations with their fellows. Jesus
brought a father-like spirit so realistically into all daily living that his disciples found in their deepening love for the

Father, revealed by him, an incentive for brotherly relations among themselves and with others.

Thus a wise teacher of philosophy in India explains the influence of Jesus: "The faith of Christ, as soon as the effort is steadily made to reproduce it in one's own daily conduct, reveals itself as immeasurably above anything that any one else achieves—so elevated is it, so discriminating in what it expects of the Father, so unfaltering assured. All faith rests on knowledge, but Christ's faith in his Father evidently is the assured insight springing from the most immediate intimacy. And so he who seeks to imitate the faith of Christ soon learns to distrust his own ideas of the Father, and to put his faith in Christ as the Revealer—to believe in God through Christ."[6]

As Sholem Asch learned about Jesus: "No one before him and no one after him has bound our world with the fetters of law, of justice, and of love, and brought it to the feet of the one living Almighty God as effectively as did this personage who came to an Israelite house in Nazareth in Galilee —and this he did, not by the might of the sword, of fire and steel, like the lawgivers of other nations, but by the power of his mighty spirit and of his teachings. He, as no one else before him, raised our world from 'the void of nothingness' in which it kept losing its way, and bound it with strong ties of faith to the known goal, the predetermined commandment of an almighty throne so as to become a part of the great, complete, everlasting scheme of things."[7]

It is not, therefore, merely because Jesus is a great ethical teacher, or even a supreme example of what man may become, that he helps us to translate his ideal into conduct. "It is because he affords us a glimpse of ultimate Reality, because we see in him the character and disposition of God dwelling among men."[8] He shows us how to come by way of the common needs and aspirations of men into closer co-operation with a Reality that makes for brotherhood. He shows us also how to come to our fellowmen by way of a transforming communion with the God who loves his creation. In such commerce of the soul with God, therefore, no less than in other forms of co-operation, Jesus points the way to the fullest sharing in a great family of brothers. He shows us the secret of his own disposition, and he shares with us the very substance of the society which he inaugurated.

What this society requires and what it makes possible have come to men most persuasively through the way in which Jesus, to the very point of death, faced the opposition to a co-operating world and banished the unnecessary fear of death to which men had always been in bondage. Because he has been able to impart the secret of this victory, unnumbered men and women ever since have been able to face suffering and loss and death itself, without swerving from the purpose that he inspires. Thus they have learned to look on death as a release of the spirit for more effective living. This unfettered living is what the death of Jesus made possible for him and for his disciples. It set him free for fellowship with them so intimate and far-reaching that the cross, which had long been an instrument of the most shameful death, became a symbol of the sacrificial, life-giving intimacy of God with men. Ever since Jesus thus "tasted death for every one,"[1] and broke its power by his continuing fellowship with his disciples, his cross has transfigured life and death. Despite endless misunderstanding it remains the supreme evidence of the purpose and power of God to deliver men from self-seeking, and to unite them through a mutual enterprise of love. The Cross is still the way to know "the disposition of the central energy of the universe," a sure "clue in an often unintelligible world."[9] When men follow this clue in the giving of themselves for the Great Community, as we shall now consider Jesus doing, they find their own fulfillment through keeping his requirement for discipleship: "If anyone wishes to fellow me, let him deny himself, take up his cross, and so follow me."[m]

Questions for Further Thought and Discussion

If Jesus' idea of community was free-flowing, with no acknowledged barriers, how do we account for the modern fact that it is often "religious" people who are most clannish and prejudiced?

Could what Jesus left be called an "organization"?

Is the community of faith today expanding rapidly or slowly?

What are the chances for a world faith amassing and combining characteristics of various existing religions? Would such a plan be desirable?

II

HIS WAY TO RECONCILE LOYALTIES

He Shows the Folly of Divisive Loyalties

THE EXPECTATION of his disciples was so different from the purpose of Jesus for universal brotherhood that not until they had tried to share his purpose and method with members of other races did any of them understand his way of reconciling loyalties in comprehensive fellowship. His solution becomes reasonable for us, too, when we recognize the same ever-recurring divisive tendencies in our day and try, as he did, to overcome them.

Throughout his public work, the purpose of Jesus was beset by the divisive tendencies that lurk in racial and class feeling. The intense and narrow loyalties of family and of country came to him in an appealing guise. Those nearest to him had no conception of that universal brotherhood in which all true loyalties are harmonized.

He found, therefore, that startling words were sometimes necessary to rouse his friends from the narrowness of traditional and tribal ways of thinking. Once he had to use such words in the days when his family did not yet believe in him and tried to restrain his apparent fanaticism. "While he was still speaking to the crowds, his mother and brothers were standing outside, asking to speak to him. Some one told him this, and Jesus replied, 'Who is my mother? and

139

who are my brothers?' Then, stretching out his hand towards
his disciples, he said, 'Here are my mother and my brothers;
for any one who does the will of my Father in heaven is my
brother and sister and mother.' "[a]

At first the brothers of Jesus were confused about the real
issue by short-sighted fears and family pride. Their purpose
in trying to interrupt his work may have been both to rescue
him from threatening danger and to save themselves from
family disgrace. Not only had the local authorities become
hostile, but emissaries from Jerusalem had come into Galilee
to watch their suspected brother. True to a habit that still
persists among such inquisitors, they charged that he was in
league with evil powers.

He Sees What Is Wrong with the Parties of His Day

Jesus suffered no illusion about the nature of the opposition gathering against him. He saw that it increased among
the ruling classes the more he subordinated their national
traditions to universal love. They tried to convince the people that he was undermining a sacred institution when he
exposed the inhumanity of the man-made rules by which
they tried to prevent his healing on the Sabbath. The thinking of many was so limited by traditional practice that they
could not appreciate his appeal to human need as a way of
discovering the intention of God. Such men have always been
unconscious tools of designing politicians. In this case the
politicians held the most influential offices in the Church.
They played the old game of politics buttressed by religion.
They appealed to racial and religious prejudice to keep
themselves in power. Behind their accusation that he was
in league with sinister forces, Jesus detected their scheme
to discredit him in order to maintain their own prerogatives.

It is not strange that the wealthy and calculating Sadducees, or the partisans of Herod, could not recognize the
moral greatness of Jesus. They were absorbed in their own
prosperity, their own amusements, their own court influence. Some of them doubtless persuaded themselves that any

movement which even appeared to be revolutionary would be disturbing and injurious to the entire country. It is always easy to think of public welfare in terms of private interest. Moreover, the Sadducees were the aristocrats and the conservatives of their day. They were not interested in a religious movement among the lower classes. Not until it gained such headway that they feared its political effect upon their own fortunes, did they pay any attention to Jesus. Even then, they had no desire to understand him.

More discernment might have been expected from the Scribes and Pharisees. The Scribes were the copyists and interpreters of the Scriptures, the lawyers of the people. To them the Jewish legal code was the only recognized law. Most of the Scribes belonged to the Pharisaic party because the Pharisees were the devoted champions of the law. They were keenly interested in any religious movement among the people, for they aimed at popular influence for themselves. Besides, they were a more liberal and progressive party than were the Sadducees. They were eagerly looking for the expected Messiah to throw off the hated foreign yoke and to realize the destiny of their "chosen" race. "In relation to the rest of the community, they corresponded to our clergy and leading religious laymen, probably formed about the same proportion of the population, and exercised at least as great an influence as these do among us. They can not be accused of having neglected Jesus. They turned their earnest attention to him from the first."[1]

Here is an ominous feature of this national tragedy. Some of the men who rejected Jesus, and were responsible for his crucifixion, were reputed to be "the best citizens." They were the teachers and examples of the people, the champions of their Bible and of their cherished traditions. They thought that they were judging Jesus according to the Scriptures, and that they were obeying the dictates of conscience when they treated him as they did. "There can not fail sometimes to sweep across the mind of a reader of the gospels a strong feeling of pity for them, and a kind of sympathy with them.

Jesus was so unlike the Messiah whom they were looking for and their fathers had taught them to expect! There is the same sadness about the fate of those who are thrown upon any great crisis of the world's history, and, not understanding the signs of the times, make fatal mistakes."[1]

Why was it, then, that so many of these Scribes and Pharisees, devoted interpreters of the religion of their fathers, failed to accept the leadership of Jesus? First of all, they were prejudiced by his humble origin, by his upbringing in rude Galilee, where the line was not so sharply drawn against foreigners as in more exclusive Judea, and by the fact that he had not attended what they considered the orthodox schools of Jerusalem. They could not see the greatness of a man who would not conform to their ideas of culture and exclusiveness. Then, too, they did not like the company that he kept, nor the disciples who were attracted to him. Nothing, perhaps, scandalized them more than his choice of Matthew, a tax-gatherer for the unpopular Romans, to be in the inner circle of apostles. How could Jesus expect them, respectable and educated, to associate with disloyal riffraff? Besides, they were offended by his disregard of ritual observances, which had for them a national importance. He did not require his disciples to keep weekly fasts or to practice other religious ceremonies which, however laudable in origin, had become barriers to better relations with "foreigners." Many of these human inventions, for which the Pharisees claimed divine sanction, Jesus saw as intolerable burdens upon the people, as substitutes for a religion of love and as a refuge for pride. But to many zealous Pharisees his attitude toward their time-honored customs made him a menace to racial solidarity.

Many Pharisees were neither hardhearted nor hypocritical in their attitude toward Jesus. It was, in fact, the warmth of their espousal of certain fundamentals of religion, as they understood them, and the ardor of their patriotism, in addition to their control of the synagogues, which explain their influence upon public opinion and their share of responsibility for the death of Jesus. Many of the Pharisees probably took no active part in opposing him. Some failed to realize what was going on; others silently acquiesced in the policy of their leaders. Like many modern "Christians," they had more or less unwittingly identified nationalism with religion. They imagined that the only way true religion could triumph was through the ascendancy of their race. They were too absorbed in this expectation to understand the universal hope of their great prophets that Jesus had come to fulfill. To many an earnest Pharisee, therefore, Jesus was a dangerous innovator: he was weakening national morale and, whether designedly or not, was playing into the hands of the dominant Romans; he was jeopardizing the future of a superior race, chosen by God for leadership.

He Overcomes a Threefold Difficulty

The crisis was further complicated by the hope of the people that Jesus might be the long expected Messiah who would deliver them out of all their troubles. Even his most devoted disciples kept returning to the question, "Will you at this time restore the kingdom to Israel?"[b] The group that went with him for the last time to Jerusalem "supposed that the Kingdom of God was to appear immediately."[c] The attitude of the masses is shown in the picture of the undernourished multitude thinking of Jesus in terms of their own acute need, and trying to take him by force and make him a "bread king."[d] All through his public work he had to reckon with the exciting hopes of the people that he might deliver them from both economic and political oppression.

The political turmoil Jesus faced was due, not only to faulty administration of the Romans and to misled fanaticism of the Jews, but also to economic conditions. "Over-population, especially in the cities; a declining productivity of the soil; and a two-fold taxation, civil and religious, beyond the powers of utmost thrift to sustain: such were the outstanding features of the political-economic situation in the Palestine of Jesus' time." In the absence of exact figures, it has been estimated "that the total taxation of the Jewish people in the time of Jesus, civil and religious combined, must have approached the intolerable proportion of between thirty and forty per cent." And this burden, for the most part, fell upon a people with only meager income. The difficulties, internal and external, from which the people suffered were too widespread and deep to be overcome by any merely national or political deliverer.[2]

Jesus profoundly sympathized with the longing of the Jewish people for deliverance from oppression. Yet he knew that Rome was not the only oppressor. What would the masses gain by substituting for Roman government a local combination of religious autocrats, selfish landowners, and corrupt politicians? How could the people ever attain freedom unless they gave precedence in their own hearts to the spirit of brotherhood, and so prepared for the sway of the same spirit in their corporate life? Jesus, therefore, sought to lead them beyond all temporizing toward a universal order of life that would bring justice, peace, and joy to the world.

Jesus recognized the devotion of sincere patriots who, though differing from himself in method, were willing to give their lives for their idea of freedom. Whether or not his apostle, Simon the Zealot, was so called because he belonged to the revolutionary party of the Zealots or because of personal zeal, there were undoubtedly among the followers of Jesus some who hoped that he would one day assume the revolutionary role.[3] Jesus, however, saw the fatal limitations of their methods. He wanted to save the people, not merely from external oppression, but from their own shortsighted selves. He longed to give patriotic ardor an effective outlet for all mankind.

In the exciting and misleading expectations of all classes, Jesus saw the necessity for a gradual explanation of his own mission. "Any sudden and explicit announcement of that mission would have been more misleading than silence itself; for the various factions would have understood such an announcement in various ways, and none of them in the right way. Jesus therefore adopted a method of patient suggestion by parables."³ But also, by his spirit and way of service, he aimed to show the kind of leadership that was needed in a discordant and self-seeking world.

From the time, therefore, when the people began to acclaim him, and the rulers to oppose him, Jesus faced a task of three-fold difficulty. He had to prevent a rash uprising of the people, bent on making him a temporal Messiah. He had to prepare some, at least, of his disciples to understand the nature of the deliverer who was needed. And in order to gain time for this work of preparation, he had to thwart the plots of Jewish leaders who hoped either to misrepresent him completely before the people, or else to put him out of the way by stealth. They were determined to befog or to suppress his purpose. He was determined to make it clear and enduring.

Jesus had tried to show the ruling group, no less than the oppressed people, that to serve in love without discrimination was the way to solve the world's antagonisms. It was to a lawyer of the ruling class that Jesus told the parable of the good Samaritan, the story of a despised alien who showed tenderness to a wounded Jew after the priest and the Levite of his own race had passed him by disdainfully.ᵉ It was to this lawyer, seeking to justify himself, that Jesus put the question: "Which of these three men, in your opinion, proved a neighbor to the man who fell among the robbers?" It was to the lawyer, when he answered, "The man who took pity on him," that Jesus said "Then go and do the same." Jesus tried to help all sorts of men to understand the universal neighborliness that he believed essential to a peaceful world. From such God-inspired love as Jesus showed toward men in all conditions, he believed that the Pharisee, the Publican, the Samaritan, and the Roman might learn to love one another.

This vision of universal love, transcending the barriers of class, race, and tradition, which Jesus shared with the most statesmenlike prophets of his race, was too great for the Jew-

ish leaders of his time to entertain. They were blinded by
their practice of racial segregation, and by the self-centeredness of their own class. They could not understand one
greater than themselves, demonstrating in his own life the
power of unlimited good will; but they saw the people beginning to respond to the influence that springs from impartial service to all. Then the rulers began to realize that
the growing influence of Jesus would make their proud pretensions to leadership seem irrelevant. And many of them,
like ruling classes generally, preferred that such an influence
should not prevail; for what, then, would become of their
power and their perquisites? Without themselves in power,
what would become of the nation?

He Chooses a Forum Where the Issue Cannot Be Hid

They began, therefore, to consider means—the more
secret, the better for their purpose—to put Jesus out of the
way. It seems to have been Pharisees, watching religious
movements more closely, who roused Herodians to the menace of Jesus. Some of these supporters of Herod as a local
king belonged also to the Sadducean party, which included the
chief priests. These worldly-wise politicians were accustomed
to scheme with the partisans of Herod. Both wished to avoid
any commotion that might lead Rome to interfere with their
own plans for profit and pleasure. So a strange coalition was
formed: some of the most ardent of the orthodox and those
whom they counted indifferent skeptics, the most punctilious
about religious observances and the crafty lovers of pleasure
—Pharisees and Sadducees, Scribes and Herodians—combined to suppress or to destroy Jesus.

The conspirators would have preferred to silence Jesus
with a minimum of help from the Romans. But they were
driven at last to a humiliating extreme when their trumped-
up charge that he aimed to displace Caesar led their hench-
men to cry: "We have no king but Caesar." Any recognition
of Caesar was the very thing the rulers sought to minimize.
They hoped to preserve their own authority with a mini-

mum of interference from Rome. Therefore it would seem
to them more expedient to convict Jesus publicly of some
offense that would give them warrant for having him stoned
to death—a procedure Rome permitted under certain conditions. A little later, the Jews contrived this punishment
against Stephen. But in order to have a victim stoned, it
was necessary to have people to cast the stones. And repeated
attempts had failed to turn the people against Jesus. Even
in the last week at Jerusalem, when the Scribes and the high
priests wanted to lay hands on him, they were afraid of the
people. So they sent spies who were to act the part of honest
men. They tried to trap him with a question about tribute
to Caesar, hoping that his answer would either antagonize
the people who hated Roman taxation, or else provoke resentment from the government against Jesus. "But he saw
through their knavery." He dealt so wisely with this con-
troversial question that "there was nothing here that they
could lay hold of before the people, and marveling at his
answer, they said no more."*

If they could not put an end to Jesus and to his influence
by turning public opinion against him, his enemies would
have preferred to destroy him without attracting attention.
But here also they were balked by Jesus' sure grasp of the
situation. During a critical period before his last journey to
Jerusalem, he withdrew with some of his disciples into remote regions around Galilee, going at times beyond the
jurisdiction of Herod Antipas. Thus he foiled any attempt
to do with him what Herod had done with John the Baptist.
He kept the popular excitement from coming to premature
expression, and he gave his most discerning disciples an opportunity to understand him better.

During one of these withdrawals, near Caesarea Philippi,
Peter recognized that Jesus was indeed the expected Deliverer; but in spite of all that Jesus could say, none of the
disciples seemed to understand what his mission involved,
either for him or for themselves. Only loyalty to him, whom
they had come to love as they had never loved before, kept

them with him through the gathering storm. But no one
except Jesus himself seems to have realized the possible consequences if the conspirators should succeed in falsifying the
issue or in putting him secretly out of the way.

So Jesus decided, at whatever risk, to clarify the issue
openly at a time and place where it could not be hid. In
so doing he showed for all time how faithfulness to his ideal
of divine-human community may evoke, in spite of apparent
failure, that profound loyalty on which a society of free men
must depend.

Questions for Further Thought and Discussion

*Is more harm done in today's world by leaders who make iron demands of
people, or by those who make too small demands?*

*Where do we find the greatest friction point as we seek to reconcile loyalties
in this generation: State vs. Church, social custom vs. religious code, self-
interest in marriage vs. sacramental sharing, scientific truth vs. religious
truth, or some other?*

*At what age in the developing personality does loyalty seem to mean the
most? Are our teaching and program in democracy geared to such a fact?*

I2

THE LOYALTY THAT CREATES COMMUNITY

Jesus Faces Death for World Community

WHEN JESUS SAW that his idea of community must be put to
a decisive test before powerful leaders of the opposition had
confused all the people, "he steadfastly set his face to go to
Jerusalem." Again and again he tried to tell his intimate
disciples what might be expected if he pressed the issue to a
conclusion in that stronghold of his enemies. But even they
could not understand. As Jesus went before them, "they were
amazed, and they that followed were afraid."[a] Others came
to him with a warning to turn aside because Herod meant
to kill him. But he answered, "Go and say to that fox, Behold, I cast out demons and perform cures today and tomorrow, and the third day I end my course. Nevertheless, I
must go on my way today and tomorrow and the day following: for it cannot be that a prophet perish out of Jerusalem."[b]

There must be no mistake about the issue. It must be
faced in the capital of the nation where centered all the
vested interests, political, financial, and ecclesiastical, which
ran counter to his purpose of brotherhood. In this center
of Jewish life the motives and policy of his opponents must
be unmasked. By the way he met their machinations he
would show men for all time the greater power of love in
the service of all. He would evoke from at least some dis-

149

ciples through the years a similar loyalty to the universal Kingdom of God.

Jesus had longed to lead the Jewish people to the giving of themselves for the world in the spirit that their great prophets believed would finally prevail. But selfishness and pride were entrenched in high places, and the people were confused. Their secular hopes had obscured the larger vision. So when Jesus drew near for the last time to the Capital in which the prophetic visions and the baser passions of his race had long contended, "he beheld the city, and wept over it, saying, 'O that at this time thou hadst known—yes, even thou—what makes peace possible! But now it is hid from thine eyes.' "[c]

Because the people did not appreciate how much of the future was at stake, it was the more important, in the little while that remained, to lose no opportunity of keeping the real issue before them. So Jesus had arranged with masterful foresight for a public entry into Jerusalem. Those who think the so-called triumphal entry out of keeping with his character fail to see that its very publicity was his only protection against the enemies who were trying to dodge the issue and destroy him secretly, and that his manner, gentle and riding on an ass, would in the end be a preparation of his followers to understand the real nature of his mission. The acclaim of the people coming to the Passover is the more significant because those who later cried "Crucify him" at an unexpected hour before dawn were doubtless part of a crowd packed against him by the conspirators, not the pilgrims from the provinces who had welcomed his entry to the city and who had no way to learn of his sudden and secret arrest under cover of the night. To the very last, his enemies were afraid that Jesus might be rescued by the common people who still regarded him as their champion.[1]

That a champion of the people may be compelled to oppose injustice even in high places was shown further by Jesus on the day after his public entry into Jerusalem, when he drove out and exposed the temple profiteers who were exploiting the poor. By this considered act, taken after inspecting everything, and seeing again how the temple was failing in its mission, Jesus brought the issue more clearly than ever before the people. By so doing, he intensified the opposition, but also exposed the designs of those in authority who saw him jeopardizing their gains from the temple traffic. His indictment of all who took unfair advantage of a public opportunity left no doubt that he would go to the roots of whatever interfered with brotherhood. He said, "Is it not written, 'My house shall be called a house of prayer for all the nations'? But you have made it a den of robbers." "When the high priests and the scribes heard of this, they tried to contrive to put him out of the way, for they were afraid of him, because the people were deeply impressed by his teachings."[d]

Even after Jesus had been betrayed, as he said, "into the hands of sinners," he saw the rulers so blinded by their own self-seeking that he could pray for them in his last agony, "Father forgive them, for they know not what they do."[e] In the spirit of this prayer he persevered through death for the winning even of his enemies.

His Loyalty at All Costs Creates Community

By a change of emphasis, even late in his ministry, Jesus might have prolonged his life to preach for years a partial gospel. But he saw too clearly to be content with offering only personal comfort in affliction, and he had often shown the insufficiency, even the impossibility, of merely personal salvation. Such self-regarding religion easily gathers multitudes of shortsighted disciples. Jesus saw, however, that such disciples, despite their numbers, would be a deceptive support compared to the resolute group who finally gave themselves to the larger purpose in the spirit of his own self-sacrifice. The example of these uncompromising pioneers has encouraged others ever since to follow the highest loyalty when opposed by family pride, class interest, or misguided patriotism.

The contagion of such an example is evident in the way it became both more intelligible and more attractive to his first disciples after Jesus had persevered even to the giving of his life. It was after he had paid the utmost price of loyalty to his Father's purpose for the world that his disciples were inspired with similar loyalty to him and to the community called by him to carry on his mission. Then they found his influence prevailing with them over all that his enemies could say or do. Neither scourging, imprisonment, nor threat of death could deter them. After they had been flogged, and warned "not to speak about the name of Jesus, . . . the apostles left the Council, rejoicing that they had been thought worthy to suffer disgrace for that name; and never for a single day, either in the Temple Courts or in private houses, did they cease to teach, or to tell the Good News of Jesus, the Christ."[f]

They held themselves accountable only to God and to their conscience. When their rulers "charged them not to speak or teach at all in the name of Jesus," Peter and John replied, "Whether it is right in the sight of God to listen to you rather than to God, you must judge; for we cannot but speak of what we have seen and heard." When called again before the Council because they had filled Jerusalem with their teaching, they asserted their conception of the highest loyalty: "We must obey God rather than men."[g]

The theory of a deified state, still current in our day, did not obscure for them the real issue. Their appreciation of the larger loyalties is the more impressive because their national leaders were also the rulers of the Jewish Church. The disciples saw, however, that their rulers' rejection of Jesus was fraught with the gravest consequences to their nation. They discovered that the same temporizing spirit had prevailed at other times of crisis; that, in fact, the influential classes had usually combined against the far-seeing prophets of their race. These conclusions were reached by men like Stephen when events compelled them to consider history from other points of view than those of class interest or national pride. They were trying to profit from the mistakes of the past.[h] So they found it necessary to take their clue, not from counsels of expediency enforced by those in brief authority, but from the character and ways of God as disclosed by Jesus. In the light of his life they concluded that the surest way to serve their countrymen was to adhere to the loyalties learned from him. The way Stephen dealt with the reactionaries who were plotting to stone him shows how the Spirit manifest in the cleansing of the Temple and on Calvary continued to work through those who had become partakers of the same Spirit.[h]

The Cure for Divided Loyalties

Since the time of Jesus and the Apostles, we have become more confused in our thinking about the state. Narrow views of loyalty and tribal ideas of God have been blended in a medley that is neither true patriotism nor true religion. Many Christians who would refuse to subscribe to the doctrine, "my country right or wrong," are dangerously quiescent while this doctrine is preached with seductive euphemisms. However it is disguised, even under democratic forms, any doctrine of the absolute state which claims a religious quality of supreme devotion is the foe both of freedom and fellowship. It subordinates the Church to secular government in ways which hinder a world-wide brotherhood such as Jesus intended. The League of Nations, the one serious political effort to unite the world before the formation of the United Nations, was limited in large measure because it was in fact a league of national states, unwilling to subordinate any of their exclusive prerogatives.

Traditional reverence for an institution has often been used to gain popular support after the institution itself has been diverted from its true purpose. This has happened to national governments in our day, as it happened to the institution of the Sabbath in the time of Jesus. When tradition was used to support perversions of Sabbath observance, Jesus laid down a principle of universal validity: "The Sabbath was made for man, not man for the Sabbath."[1] What less can this mean for us than that all institutions, including government, should contribute to the highest development of all men, rather than that men should be exploited or coerced in conscience for the sake of any institution?

The bearing of this principle upon national and international life is clarified in a notable statement by the Bishops of the Anglican Communion: "Each of us belongs by his birth to some one of the many nations of the world. But every Christian belongs by his second birth to one holy nation which is God's own possession. When loyalty to his own nation comes into conflict with loyalty to that nation of which Christ is King, a Christian can have no doubt which loyalty must give way. 'He that loveth father and mother more than me,' said Jesus Christ, 'is not worthy of me!' National loyalty has often led men into exclusiveness, jealousy, and hatred, which are far from Christ's purpose. No selfishness in the world has been so persistent or so ruthless as national selfishness. It is to save men from such wickedness that Jesus Christ binds them together into one holy nation. In the fellowship of this great unity, nationality finds its redemption: while national characteristics are preserved for noble use and mutual benefit. But the love of God encompasses all and reconciles both men and nations in the brotherhood of redeemed humanity."[2]

The Larger Loyalties Must Be Nurtured at Home

This sense of brotherhood in a redeemed humanity seems impossible to realize unless it is nourished and disciplined in local communities where shortcomings can be detected and amended. We need a kind of community life in which a feeling of community responsibility and a feeling of failure if we do not act on that responsibility may be real experiences. A sense of mass interdependence is not enough. The people of our largest cities depend for their daily milk upon hundreds of thousands of farm workers. But such dependence alone lacks personal meaning. So long as it remains merely commercial dependence between masses, it falls short of human sympathy between persons; it evokes no loyalty and allows no breathing-space for love. Accordingly, Middleton Murry finds that "just as the creation of a new kind of simple community, in which men were truly members one of another, arose by inward necessity among the early converts to the Christian faith, so the only social context in which the reality of Christianity can be rediscovered is the simple community. In the modern world such community may take a variety of forms, demanding different degrees of self-dedication; but common to them all must be the replacement of the abstract, depersonalized, and unreal social relation by the direct, personal, and real one. We need to see our brothers in order to love them, and in order to love God whom we have not seen."[3]

Families, therefore, as well as churches, synagogues, and associations of many kinds, where personal relations are still possible, have a duty to cultivate the vision and habits of community. Such a group may unwittingly confine its members to the lesser loyalties of its own special interest. Rather, it should enlarge their outlook and help them to correct any indifference to the community as a whole. All of us need to recognize that family tradition, family selfishness, and family pride, as well as class interest and false patriotism, threaten the larger Christian loyalties. That danger is almost inevitable in any family where the supreme loyalty does not correspond in essence to the loyalty of Jesus to the Kingdom of God. The temptations to be lukewarm towards that universal community are intensified when the pride and social ambitions of the family, or the selfish interests of any of its members, take precedence over some call to unfashionable service that comes to one of its members. Even when little is said under such circumstances, a sensitive and affectionate nature may be frustrated by the mistaken idea of loyalty prevailing in such a family. Dynastic ambitions are not confined to royalty. They thrive in many a family and weaken in its members the desire to practice community with those of other races or conditions.

The way to live when these various loyalties seem to conflict becomes clearer in the light that the conduct of Jesus throws upon his purpose. Although in his youth he enjoyed questioning the doctors of the law in Jerusalem, he returned with his parents to the discipline of a Galilean home and to the educative opportunities of life in its environment. The more sophisticated training of the rabbis was not the best preparation for his daring experiment. Also, Jesus may have felt an obligation, after the death of Joseph, to be a breadwinner for younger brothers and sisters. Whatever factors influenced earlier choices, the time came when he had to leave the home and the carpenter shop in Nazareth for a great venture of faith. His family, as we have seen, could not understand him at the time. Yet he went his way patiently, without bitterness, still loving his kindred who tried to interrupt his lifework. His good will toward all sorts and conditions of men may have helped his mother and his brothers finally to believe that his mission was a fulfillment of the world-wide vision of their great prophets. Whatever led them at last to the same supreme loyalty, we know that after the Apostles had been commissioned for their world task, they "continued unitedly in prayer with Mary the Mother of Jesus and with his brothers."[j] They learned gradually to harmonize loyalties by seeking first that universal community to which the foremost leaders of their race had aspired.

Questions for Further Thought and Discussion

Could our Lord conceivably have trained fifty, or five hundred, or three, as effectively as the Twelve were trained?

What other world leaders have come nearest to saying, "Ye are my friends if ye do whatsoever things I command you"?

How does war clarify and complicate the concept of loyalty for the Christian?

In what sense and in what situations does national loyalty create genuine community among citizens?

13

THE AWAKENING TO SOLIDARITY

Early Christians Solve Class and Racial Issues

SOLIDARITY, the aversion of some preferring to keep themselves in a class apart, the rallying cry of many preaching violent revolution, the hope of others seeking peaceful unity —what shall we make of this idea? Will it be defeated by the persistence of conflicting interests, or can it be realized on an ever increasing scale through wise co-operation? The early influence of Jesus throws light on this question. After his death, even more than before, he brought a unifying sense of solidarity to those who had been separated by divergent interests or racial antipathies.

As Simon Peter and his fellow disciples reflected on the opposition of their rulers to Jesus, and on the acquiescence of many others in what their rulers had done, it dawned upon them that there was a collective responsibility for what had happened on calvary. They felt that there was something radically wrong with people who would not rally to support "the Pioneer of Life." So, on the day of Pentecost when the bewildered crowd first gathered about the Apostles in Jerusalem, Peter boldly charged his countrymen with a corporate responsibility for the death of Jesus. "When they heard this, it went straight to their hearts; they said to Peter and those with him, 'Brothers, what are we to do?' "[a]

Far more than we usually realize, this early preaching

157

stirred the conscience of the people by dealing explicitly with
social as well as personal implications of the gospel. Or
rather, this effective preaching never suggested the impossible division of man's life into personal and social compartments. Such attempts at division came in later centuries.
From the beginning, a unifying social influence pervaded the
relation of Jesus with his disciples; and after he had wholly
committed his work to them, they shared more and more
his concern for men of all classes and for the conditions of
their daily living. Consequently, they tried to tell the Good
News about Jesus in its relation to the whole of life. Their
opportunities for its wider application were limited by persecution and by political conditions. But these very limitations, together with their hope of Christ's early return, make
all the more impressive their insistence upon social responsibilities and consequences.

In spite of the persistent opposition of influential men,
this kind of preaching arrested the attention and changed
the conduct of many who heretofore had been indifferent or
hostile. In the second recorded instance of this courageous
speaking to the people about Jesus, Peter said, "Pilate had
decided to release him, but you repudiated the Holy and
Just One, you killed the pioneer of life."[b] Although Peter
and John were arrested by the Jewish authorities while they
were still speaking, "many of those who had listened to their
preaching believed."[c] Even though the unpopular facts of
national guilt, as Stephen preached them,[d] roused immediate
resentment, some of his hearers, notably Paul of Tarsus, acknowledged later the truth of the indictment.

Doubtless many whom Peter and Stephen called to account for the national tendency to persecute the prophets
were, like Paul, men of religious zeal and exemplary private
life. But, as every age can witness, a rigid personal morality
does not keep men from sharing more or less unconsciously
in great social sins. On the contrary, like many zealous Jews
in the first century, avowedly Christian people have often
become so preoccupied with the minutiae of personal con-

duct or of religious rites as to be lulled to quiescence about corporate wrongs or racial discrimination. In this way an earnest man, immersed in the concerns of his limited circle, may "participate in another man's sins"[e] in business, or in government, or even in the Church itself.

When the Jewish Christians became part of an enlarging Christian community in a world embittered by racial and social barriers, they were driven to a searching inquiry into their own exclusiveness. Thus Peter was prepared, as he prayed on the housetop, to learn that he must not call any man common or unclean. But the new truth did not become a positive part of his life until he had recognized it by accepting the invitation of the foreign messengers from Cornelius, had practiced it in the household of this Roman Centurion, and had defended it against the advocates of exclusiveness.[f] Even then Peter wavered in his adherence to this new attitude toward other races. He seems to have come to it more hesitatingly than did Philip, one of the seven deacons who preceded him in preaching to the Samaritans, and who did not hesitate to welcome, without any Jewish rites, an Ethiopian eunuch to membership in the new society.[g] It was, in fact, some unnamed pioneers from Cyprus and Cyrene who first shared the new interracial fellowship with Greeks in the Gentile city of Antioch, and thus opened this outpost for extending the fellowship into the Greek and Roman world.[h] Then, as now, the missionary work of the Church brought home to the conscience of its members the wrongs of racial discrimination and made more inclusive their sense of solidarity. The very necessity of working together deepened fellowship among those who had formerly emphasized their differences.

They Learn Whom the Divine Commonwealth Includes

What this growing sense of unity meant to these early pioneers is illustrated by the word which they chose to designate the new society. They called it the "Ecclesia." The English translation, church, and the adjective, ecclesiastical, are far from suggesting to most of us the intimate relations and social responsibilities that the early Christian use of the word implies. The Greek word, ecclesia, has a history overflowing with social significance. "It was used in the old free commonwealth of Greece for the general assembly of all free citizens, by which their common life was governed. When political liberty went, the name still survived in the restricted municipal self-government which the Roman State allowed. It was taken over by the brotherhoods and guilds which in some measure superseded the old political associations. Among the Jews who spoke Greek, this word seemed the appropriate one to describe the commonwealth of Israel as ruled by God—the historical Theocracy."[1]

The word received a larger meaning in the experience of the early Church. Paul expected that the fellowship into which Jesus drew men of all races would become a universal Ecclesia. Using the English word nearest to its original meaning, we may call it a universal Commonwealth. In principle, as Paul saw it, this Divine Commonwealth even now transcends all national and class antagonisms. "By seriously living out that which its association means, it is on the way to comprehending the whole race. Short of that its development can never stop. This is the revealing of the sons of God for which the whole creation is waiting."[1]

In Paul's usage, Ecclesia implies not only a wider, but also a more intimate fellowship. A company of people who are moved by rivalry or any divisive temper is not for Paul an Ecclesia at all. For him the true Commonwealth "is a community of loving persons who bear one another's burdens, who seek to build up one another in love, who have the same thoughts in relation to one another that they have in their communion with Christ. It is all this because it is the living embodiment of Christ's own Spirit."[2]

They Encourage Common Concern for One Another

How this continuing embodiment of the spirit of Jesus was to achieve unity through diversity is illustrated by the symbol early Christians used in thinking of their corporate life. They thought of themselves as the very Body of Christ, or as the Body of which Christ was the head, and of which all others were "members each in his part." This meant to them that "God has set people within the church, . . . apostles, prophets, teachers, healers, helpers, or administrators,"[i] so unitedly to work and to suffer as Jesus did that together they might "be to the eternal Spirit precisely what his manhood was in the days of his flesh."[3]

If this ideal of many members in one body seems too high for the compromising attitudes of modern life, we may take heart from the way it inspired even those who were rising from the depths of the pagan world. "Laying aside falsehood," they were told, "every one of you should speak the truth to his fellow-men: for we are, as it were, *parts of one another.* He who has been a thief must steal no more, but instead of that, should work with his own hands in honest industry, so that he may have something of which he can give the needy a share."[j] And because the members are parts of one body, they must "make every effort to maintain the unity of the Spirit in the bond of peace. For there is one Body and one Spirit, one Lord, one God and Father of all who is over us all, who pervades us all." Thus, all the various gifts allotted to men are shown to belong under the sway of the one Spirit for the upbuilding of the Body of Christ. And thus the members of the body come collectively, as they can not come separately, to "the full measure of development found in Christ," because "under him, as the entire Body is welded together, the due activity of each part enables the Body to grow and build itself up in love."[k]

So the ethics of these early Christians and the whole conception of their relations with one another were rooted in a consciousness of solidarity. They believed: "If one member suffers, all the members share its suffering; if one member is honored, all the members share its honor. . . . God has tempered the body together with a special dignity for the inferior parts, so that there may be no disunion in the body, but that the various members should have a common concern for one another."[1]

They Symbolize a Community of Nations under God

The wide range of this concern for the common life appears in all the records of the Apostolic Age. We shall see more of it later in the Acts of the Apostles and in letters to individuals and groups. Its corporate significance appears also in "The Revelation" that came to an isolated prisoner of Rome, who wrote in cryptic symbols to baffle persecutors, yet showed his social vision undimmed. Although he was confined on a desolate, fever-breeding island of the Aegean Sea, in one of the darkest hours of the Church's history, he saw more than redeemed individuals returning to God: "I saw the holy city . . . coming down out of heaven from God."[m] Even this doomed exile saw the ideal and aim of life, not in mere individual perfection, or in heavenly release, but in a corporate life. The city of his dreams is a community of truth, goodness, and beauty with freedom and unhindered fellowship among the nations. "Its gates shall never be shut by day—and there shall be no night there; they shall bring into it the glory and the honor of the nations."[m]

The light of this city, and the unifying principle of all its varied life, is found by this seer in the character of God, in the spirit of the divine self-sacrifice. This spirit he symbolized by a lamb, representing the self-sacrificing life of Jesus: "I saw no temple in the City, for its temple is the Lord God the Almighty and the Lamb. And the city has no need of sun or moon to shine upon it, for the glory of God is its light, and its lamp is the Lamb. By its light shall the nations walk."[n]

Now, if ever, is the time to remember that this seer on Patmos, looking into the future, saw a new heaven and a new earth. In view of the present need for this vision, which has often nerved persecuted or discouraged men to press on through suffering, surely no differences about the time and

manner of its fulfillment should any longer hinder the
Church from illustrating in itself a world-uniting community. How otherwise can the Church fulfill its mission and
help men to realize the consummation that the vision sym-
bolizes—a commonwealth of nations and peoples, inspired
by God?

They Seek the Classless Fellowship Begun by Jesus

The baneful results of a one-sided emphasis on either the
personal or the social aspects of the gospel will be forestalled
in so far as men practice its unity in fellowship with Jesus
himself. From the first he appears as the discoverer of the
individual. Nothing is in more striking contrast to the practice of those who preceded him than the way in which he
gave so much of his brief public ministry to dealing one by
one with all kinds of men, women, and children. Even more
significant than the time that he gave to these individuals
are the results he accomplished by this personal method.
What personal quickening, for instance, is suggested by the
story of Jesus inviting Andrew and, later, Philip to spend
the day with him and, through them, adding Peter and
Nathaniel to the growing company of his friends.° Yet the
effect of these personal relations of Jesus with individuals
was also to enlarge and to enrich their fellowship.

The same emphasis upon the importance of the individual
comes out in the teaching of Jesus, but never to the neglect
of man's social relations. In a parable illustrating the worth
of a single person in the sight of God, Jesus represents God
as a good shepherd leaving all his other sheep while he goes
in search of one that is lost. But the central idea of the shepherd in leaving the ninety and nine for the one is to complete
the fellowship. What a forced inference it is from this picture of the search for one lost sheep to suppose that the
Good Shepherd is not deeply concerned also for the correction of such conditions around and within the sheepfold as
expose any of his sheep to the beasts of prey! A related parable, which gives a timeless picture of the father's longing for

his prodigal son, we have seen to be also a warning against
the antisocial disposition of the elder brother who considered himself a model of rectitude.ᴰ "The climax of the
story of the prodigal son is the restoration of fellowship; and
the damning sin of the elder brother is that he refuses to
join in it."[4]

Jesus believed that fellowship, such as he portrayed in
these parables, proceeds not from the loneliness or insufficiency of man, but from the initiative of God. Jesus felt the
yearning of God for fellowship with his children, the desire
to share his life and purpose with them. At the heart of the
self-giving of Jesus was his desire to overcome the estrangement of men and to reconcile them to his Father. In a word,
his aim was fellowship. He was constantly seeking to train
those who were slowly learning what it means to be members
of the family of God.[4]

Evangelism (and missionary work), therefore, should be no
less comprehensive than was the work of Jesus. It needs
concern like his for individuals, and fellowship like his with
them, in order to enlist men of all races and conditions in
his cause. It needs no less the full scope of his intention for
a better world. With any smaller aim evangelism inclines
men to an unbalancing concern for individualistic salvation
—an impossibility against which Jesus warned his disciples.
If, therefore, evangelism would be true to him, it should set
as the goal for men nothing less than a society that will
foster the traits of character typified by him. History and
current events illustrate the necessity for this goal. They
show that the qualities of character exemplified by Jesus are
not developed without adherence to a corresponding social
vision and social goal. Where there is no such vision the
people perish.

They Have Support in Modern Thought about Society

The essential part which society plays in the development
of individuals is emphasized in various ways by the best
thought of our time. Rufus Jones explains the view of many

others: "It would be as impossible to develop a personality without human society as it would be to convey sound in a vacuum, or to maintain life without atmosphere." The child develops personality through his relation with persons. He reacts differently toward persons than toward any other part of his environment. "Much which was thought to be transmitted by heredity, we now know is *gained* by imitation both conscious and unconscious. The child is the most imitative being known to man." Almost from the first he imitates persons; and thus he learns to distinguish between his own self and others. Thus he gains also the first sense of power in his own act. By imitating sounds he hears made by other persons, he begins his slow mastery of language, through which his mental life is developed and his personality defined. The long dependence of the child upon his elders shows that individuality by itself is impossible, and that society could not begin as a "contract" between individuals. "Individuality does not come first and society next as a product. Society is fundamental; it is an essential condition for self-consciousness and personality. *Personality at every stage involves interrelation.*"[5]

Moreover, the ideal that deeply affects the development of persons is never an individual creation; it is born in a society. "Social customs, family traditions, established law, the ideals of art, literature, and religion—all these are indispensable to the formation of a personal ideal." Out of these elements our ideal emerges as an ever changing one, which grows more adequate the more we live for a community concerned for the best development of all its members.

Consequently, self-realization is never well under way until a person finds the task for which he is fitted and begins to take his part in the work of the world. Everyone needs well-directed work in order to find his place in the community and to discover what he, himself, may become. All such work for the common good helps to bring the true end and purpose of life into clearer view.

"Few moralists, of whatever school," Bishop McConnell shows, "would today insist that a person attains moral life by deliberately making his self-realization the end of his own effort. Selfishness has never at any time received less open support. All are at least approaching agreement on the position that a society of persons, in which each person aims at the good of the whole, is the field in which individuals come to highest selfhood."[6]

A similar trend in the philosophy of evolution, which shows the necessity to realize the solidarity of mankind, is corroborated by the effects of war. "We are now readier to stress mutual aid among all social groups as the condition of survival. All must rise or fall together; all must together struggle for existence, not against one another, but against disease and ignorance and selfishness on a world-wide scale, a struggle which can be successfully carried on only as the masses of mankind organize into humanity-wide unity."[6]

They Make Us Think about Class Consciousness

How can this ultimate goal of a warless and classless world be attained, many are asking, unless there is an intermediate stage of such solidarity among the workers as will issue in a united, class-conscious, labor movement? To this question, some reply: "Whatever else Christians should do they should not encourage class consciousness. The marks of Christianity are love and universality; the marks of class consciousness are hate and particularism. We are on the road to world brotherhood, and class consciousness would be retrogression." But another group replies: "Class consciousness is a necessary stage on the road to social justice, to a classless society."

Speaking for the latter group, John Bennett makes clarifying distinctions. He shows that there are many kinds of class consciousness, and that some are clearly incompatible not only with Christianity but also with any ethical view of life. The class consciousness that he defends would rally all workers, both the skilled and the unskilled, to the cause of their own emancipation and development. Because the workers are so close to the evils of the present system, and can feel those evils more keenly than can the privileged class, this kind of class consciousness may help the worker to achieve a wider loyalty than he now knows. Then, instead of trying to rise above his class and then forsake it, instead of playing safe for fear of losing his job, or seeking only the betterment of his own privileged group, he will be loyal to the cause of all the workers. Such class consciousness, therefore, is held to be good, as a means of attaining the emancipation of the underprivileged class—an emancipation that it is the duty of all to promote. But when members of a group put their own class interest above ethical considerations, class consciousness becomes an evil. And that evil surely will arise unless from the beginning class consciousness is ethical, relative, and provisional. "Ethical sensitivity must be developed in all stages of the struggle. It will not suddenly come into being when the workers are tempted by power."[7]

They Throw Light on Modern Church Problems

Coming thus to the opportunity of the Church, Bennett shows that there is a unity underlying class differences which must never be lost, and that the Church can do much to help us realize that unity. Moreover, the Church can show its constituency wherein the class struggle is a struggle for justice. The goal is a classless society. But long before that goal is achieved, churches, along with their other functions, can be outposts where such universal fellowship is being won and can be propagated. Whatever the particular theory or program of such churches may be, surely they, rather than any "churches" that are virtually well-to-do clubs, or places of racial discrimination, or competing institutions, will contribute to the kind of unity which Jesus and the early Christians found essential. And surely these churches, so far as they are true to him, will cultivate in their own life such community of interest as will make them zealous for social justice. Enough has now happened under the old competitive order to show that this unity of interest cannot be attained on the basis of acquisitive self-seeking, unrestricted nationalism, or communism. The needed unity of free men has come, however, and can come on a much wider scale, when there is a vast increase of such co-operation as the early Christians experienced and propagated through the fellowship of the Church.

On the basis of such experience, "the greatest church meeting since the Reformation" appeals to us: "Christians should seek to recapture for the Church the original Christian solidarity with the world's distressed people. . . . Christians who are beneficiaries of capitalism should try to see the world as it appears to many who know themselves excluded from its privileges and who see in communism a means of deliverance from poverty and insecurity. All should understand that the proclamation of racial equality by communists and their support of the cause of colonial peoples makes a strong appeal to the populations of Asia and Africa and to racial minorities elsewhere." On the other hand, "it is one of the most fateful facts in modern history that often the working classes, including tenant farmers, came to believe that the churches were against them or indifferent to their plight."[8]

In view of such conditions, Elton Trueblood seeks an answer to the question: "How is civilization changed? It is changed, early Christianity answers, by the creation of fellowships which eventually become infectious in the entire cultural order. . . . A society of loving souls, set free from the self-seeking struggle for personal prestige and from all unreality, would be something unutterably precious. A wise person would travel any distance to join it. . . . What we seek, then, is the emergence of the true Church, the company of loving souls, exhibiting the mind of Christ. . . . The major strategy is to turn the present church members, one by one, into participants in a truly redemptive society. . . . We must rid our minds of most current conceptions about what a church should be in order to try to see what the real needs of men are."[9]

If, then, the Church is to meet the real needs of men, if it is to be a pervasive and transforming influence for the survival of a worthy civilization, the essential changes in the Church must go much deeper than forms of ecclesiastical union. They must go much further than inspired preaching. Neither the organization nor the message of the Church will carry far toward a freely co-operating world unless there is a growing sense of economic and spiritual solidarity among the lay members. So long as they yield to speculative fever or scramble for profits, ignoring social consequences, we shall have mental and spiritual as well as economic depressions; and all attempts of the Church to point the way for civilization will be hindered by the practice of its members. They will lack the unity and power of the Spirit in themselves, and therefore will lack fitness and experience for helping the masses of mankind to organize into humanity-wide unity. So far, however, as laymen are led through their partnership with the Spirit into a common concern for men everywhere, they will encourage their ministers to deal frankly with the social implications of the gospel; and all together will seek to practice them in true community.

The world chaos which came because many flouted or never recognized the essential solidarity of mankind has raised questions for the Church, and for world organization, which must be faced by laymen, no less than by clergymen, on a wide front. To these questions we must return in the light of other conditions. Meanwhile we should remember an obligation toward youth which is relevant to all these issues. Adults must no longer distort the perspective of youth by separating into personal and social, or into economic, political, and religious compartments the life of man, which Jesus treated as indivisible. The needed unity will emerge when adults and youth, clergy and laity, learn in deed, through the effective fellowship of the Spirit, that "the whole drift of Christ's teaching is to demand public spirit on the largest and grandest scale in behalf of a great Divine-Human Commonwealth, toward whose consummation all God's ways with men converge."[10]

Questions for Further Thought and Discussion

To what extent has a group feeling of guilt and sin empowered Christians, ever since Pentecost, to make social changes?

How much should we be inspired to action by the social group to which we belong as Christians, rather than by individual relation to God's will?

In what way are the exclusively "personal" and exclusively "social" interpretations of Christianity each a refusal to face the other?

Is class consciousness humanly inevitable? Is it possible one necessary step in the building of the Kingdom of God?

Does the convinced Communist see life whole, better than most Christians?

I4

FELLOWSHIP IN SOCIAL DISCOVERY

The Fellowship Becomes the Organ of Insight

THE THINKING of the world on which the influence of Jesus dawned was confused by racial prejudice and internal division. These antipathies were the more inimical to clear thinking because they were not recognized as prejudices. They seemed, rather, to be well-justified attitudes. Both Jews and Greeks, proud of their older cultures, looked upon the lordly airs of the crude Romans, so lately come to power, as a refined aristocrat might look upon the pretensions of the *nouveaux riches*. Yet neither Jew nor Greek could see much to learn from the other; each was too confident that he belonged to a superior race. The Jews felt sure that they were the chosen people of God, and this conviction inclined many of them to exclusiveness and political ambition. The Greeks, on their side, nursed a feeling of superiority by dwelling on their leadership in philosophy and art, and on the contribution of their race to the science of government. The Romans, on the other hand, were confirmed in their attitudes of authority by thinking of themselves as the actual rulers of the world, the guardians of its peace and prosperity. What would be more natural than the assumption that they were the only people to put weaker races where they belonged and to keep them properly employed? Whatever the advantages of the Pax Romana, the arrogance of those who enforced peace

171

intensified the pride of subject peoples, and such contentious attitudes on all sides were not favorable to widespread fellowship of thought and purpose.

Yet, despite these hindrances, certain Jews and Gentiles, Greeks and barbarians, Roman citizens and slaves, came to know and love one another with an enlightening intimacy. As disciples of Jesus they gained a new outlook on life through the attitudes engendered by a friendly society in which various races began to understand and to enrich one another.

In the earliest days of acquaintance with Jesus, his followers seem to have had no idea of the interracial and revolutionary fellowship of which they soon became a part. Not until after the crucifixion of their leader, when they became aware that they were still in effective relation with him, and expected by him to carry on his work among all peoples, did their fellowship with him and with one another bring radical change in their thinking. The changes became more impressive after one hundred and twenty of the more resolute had spent days of waiting and thinking together in order to realize their Master's promise of enlightenment and power. As they came thus to a new unity of purpose and saw its transforming influence in the lives of rapidly enlarging circles, they became more eager to learn all that it might mean for themselves and for the new society. So we read: "They were steadfastly adhering to the teaching of the Apostles and to the fellowship." This translation suggests that it was "not the teaching and fellowship of the Apostles to which the community adhered, but the teaching of the Apostles and the Fellowship. It was a new name for a new thing, community of spirit issuing in community of life; that was the primary result of the coming of the Spirit."[1] This Fellowship was prior to the organized Church and prepared the way for it as a corporate expression of community of spirit. The Fellowship, in fact, helped to integrate differences that threatened the very existence of a universal church. It became a means of attaining a common Christian mind.

The very word which the early Christians chose to designate this unifying relationship helps us to understand how co-operative thinking became effective in a truly democratic community. They chose the word *koinonia,* originally meaning partnership, or common possession. In this sense Peter and sons of Zebedee were called koinonoi, or partners, in the ownership and use of fishing boats. So the related word, koinonia, seemed to the early Christians the most appropriate term to describe their relations with one another. They were partners in a great estate—the unique spiritual heritage of which they were joint heirs with Christ. "The ground of their corporate life was what they called partnership of the Spirit—a joint ownership in all that was most real and vital to them all. Our liturgical phrase, 'the communion of the Holy Ghost,' curiously obscured the vividness of the original words."[2] "The Greek word certainly means, not a general state of good will, but a partnership in some common treasure." As used by the early Christians, "it is a partnership in the Divine power and enthusiasm. And this is the chief Christian contribution to the understanding of fellowship."[3] By pooling their experience of this newly discovered power and enthusiasm, the early Christians were led to think together about a greater purpose of God for the world than they had ever imagined, and about what would help or hinder this purpose among men. They found such fellowship a means of enlightenment, a way of discovery in united thought and action.

So far as we can trace the origins of great forward movements in the early Church, we find them conceived in the increasing light that comes through fellowship. In an early crisis that threatened either to disrupt the Church or to confine it to a Jewish sect, we see differences of opinion harmonized at a meeting to consider the matter in Jerusalem. We feel a spirit of partnership bringing together opposing convictions so that they yield a larger synthesis without violence to any one's conscience.[a] It was, however, not in Jerusalem, where intense nationalism circumscribed thought, but

in Antioch, where interracial fellowship enlarged their outlook, that the disciples were inspired to send Paul and
Barnabas, two of their ablest members, on a daring mission
of fellowship to the Greek and Roman world.[b]

Through this international mission there came new evidence of the part that fellowship plays in discovering and
expressing the purpose of God for world-uniting community.
In his letter to the Philippians, for instance, Paul shows his
gratitude again and again for "your co-operation [koinonia]
in spreading the Good News," for "taking your share in my
troubles," for "fellowship with me in the matter of giving
and receiving."[c] He finds fellowship a way to distinguish between the vital and the nonessential, and to enter under-
standingly into the thoughts and needs of others. "It is my
prayer," he writes, "that your love may be more and more
rich in knowledge and all manner of insight, enabling you
to have a sense of what is vital." "If then I can appeal to
you as the followers of Christ, if there is any persuasive
power in love, if the Spirit has really created a Fellowship,
if affection and tenderness are really its atmosphere, make
my joy complete by being of one mind, united in mutual
love, with harmony of feeling giving your minds to one and
the same object, . . . each fixing his attention, not simply on
his own interests, but also on those of others."[d] So far as you
practice such fellowship, "treating one another with the
same spirit as you experience in Christ," you grow more
like him in moral insight and conduct.[e]

Another account of this early Christian fellowship shows
its intimate relation to Jesus: "It is what we have seen with
our own eyes . . . and touched with our hands; it is the very
message of life . . . that we announce to you also, so that you
may share our fellowship; for our fellowship is with the
Father and with his son Jesus Christ. . . . This is the message
that we heard from him and announce to you: God is light;
there is no darkness in him at all. . . . If we live in the light,
just as he is in the light, we have fellowship with one another. . . . Whoever loves his brother is always in the light

and puts no hindrance in anyone's way. But whoever hates his brother is in darkness, and is living in darkness, and he does not know where he is going, for the darkness has blinded his eyes."[f]

How Jesus Fosters Fellowship in Thought and Act

The way Jesus fostered fellowship as a condition for enlightenment and community among his first followers is told in the story, *An Unknown Disciple*. It is a vivid picture of how understanding grows whenever the same spirit pervades any group: "When Jesus walked with us, all went well, for he was gay of heart, and had a way of linking men together. He brought with him a feeling of kindliness and understanding which made all things seem possible, so that as we talked, no man spoke evil of another, and when we discussed, it was without floutings and carpings. We were his friends, and therefore friends one of another. His sympathy softened the hearts of men, so that they saw graces in their fellows to which they had been blind before. When he was there, all the diverse natures of his followers seemed to meet and blend, for he charmed and held even those most different from him."[4]

How he charmed and helped diverse natures to learn through fellowship is seen most clearly among the Twelve who enjoyed more intimate relations with him than were possible with a larger number. Again and again, as we have seen, Jesus took them into the quiet of the mountains or of some solitary place.[g] There, in moments of relaxation when their minds had freest play, he put himself unguardedly at their disposal. He courted their interruption and drew out their unpremeditated thought. By helping them to forget themselves, he helped them also to find themselves at unsuspected depths. His interest in all that concerned them was disarmingly spontaneous—never hampered by calculating motives. Then, too, he seemed to live in a brighter, freer world than their world of shortsighted expediency. Something about him reminded them of hopes lying in the buried past of their youth. The shy thought they had never dared to express, because it seemed to belong to some world of forgotten dreams, came out unafraid before him. Even difficulties and failures were freely confessed, and they seemed less formidable under the confidence, inspired by Jesus, that any one could get the better of evil.

Yet, when the disciples faced again the maladjustments of the world and desired to correct them as they had seen Jesus doing, they were hindered by old ways of thinking. They were obsessed by questions of personal precedence and national destiny. Nor had they yet learned that suffering is both inevitable and rewarding for disciples of Jesus. As they saw it, his whole mission was to triumph; and they were to share in his triumph.[5] When Jesus tried to tell them of the suffering that must follow where these secular ambitions prevail, Peter was so loath to face the consequences that Jesus had to warn him against conventional thinking. "You are a hindrance to me," he said, "because your thoughts are not God's thoughts, but men's."[h] Peter, like the others, was thinking in terms, not of the greatest final good, but of the usual standards of success, whereas Jesus saw the need of thinking in terms of enduring values and the good of all.

His way of preparing them to think in such terms was depicted years later, after they had learned more of his method of fellowship. Jesus was then portrayed (before his last supper with the Twelve) as washing his disciples' feet in order to end by his example the blinding folly concerning precedence, and to illustrate the attitude of humble service as a medium for truth. Then in friendly table-talk with the eleven, after Judas had gone out to betray him, Jesus shows another unchanging condition for the spread of truth: "Just as I have loved you, you must love one another. By this they will all know that you are my disciples—by your love for one another. . . . I have much more to tell you, but you cannot take it in now, but when the Spirit of Truth comes, he will guide you in to the full truth."[i] What is here meant by the full truth is more important than mental mastery of any collection of truths. It is rather the right attitude and approach to truth. This attitude and approach is always valid, and leads to further understanding. For "in the basal relation of the human spirit to the riddle of the universe, the same fundamental attitudes recur continually." The writer of the Fourth Gospel believed the most comprehensive of these attitudes to be "embodied in Jesus once for all time, to serve permanently as a type of what is best, truest, and most humanly fruitful."[6]

The Group Process: The Collective Idea

What, then, do these timeless essentials of social discovery require today for the survival and spread of truly democratic community? For a fresh approach to this question, we turn to Mary Parker Follett's book, *The New State*,[7] in which she considers the group process: "Perhaps the most familiar example of the evolving of a group idea is a committee meeting. . . . I go to a committee meeting in order that all together we may create a group idea, an idea which will be better than any one of our ideas alone, moreover which will be better than all of our ideas added together." When we meet the conditions of creative discussion, we find "that our problem can be solved, not indeed by mechanical aggregation, but by the subtle process of the intermingling of all the different ideas of the group."

What, then, is required of the individual in order that the group idea shall be produced? "First and foremost each is to do his part. But at the same time that we offer fully what we have to give, we must be eager for what all others have to give. If I ought not to go to my group feeling that I must give up my own ideas in order to accept the opinions of others, neither ought I to go to force my ideas upon others." To make the discussion creative each one should give his share in such a way that it fits in with what others are giving. Some people are so obsessed by what they are prepared to say that their attitude allows no give-and-take. Others want to be brilliant rather than to find agreement.

"Much of the evil of our political and social life comes from the fact that we crave personal recognition and personal satisfaction; as soon as our greatest satisfaction is group satisfaction, many of our present problems will disappear. . . . When one thinks of one's self as part of a group, it means keener moral perceptions, greater strength of will, more enthusiasms and zest in life. The things which we do and achieve together will give us much greater happiness than the things we do and achieve by ourselves."

If we are to find this keener perception and enjoyment in the group process, we must observe another condition in which the experience of the New State agrees with that of the New Testament: "Unity, not uniformity, must be our aim. We attain unity only through variety. Differences must be integrated, not annihilated. . . . The ignoring of differences is the most fatal mistake in politics or industry or international life: every difference that is swept up into a bigger conception feeds and enriches society." We should, therefore, always be on guard that diversity does not arouse hostility; for, without the unifying spirit seeking the larger idea, differences are not creative. They will defeat rather than further fellowship.

It follows that "the object of every associating with others, of every conversation with friends, should be to bring out a bigger thought than any one alone could contribute. How different our dinner parties would be if we could do this, without labored effort, merely by recognizing certain elementary rules of the game. Creation is always possible when people meet; this is the wonderful interest in life. But it depends upon us so to manage our meetings that there shall be some result, not just a frittering away of energy, unguided because not understood. This does not mean that we cannot sit with a friend by our fireside; it does mean that, private and gay as that hour may be, at the same time that very intimacy and lightness must in its way be serving the common cause, not in any fanciful sense, but because there is always the consciousness of my most private concerns as tributary to the larger life of men. But words are misleading: I do not mean that we are always to be thinking about it—it must be such an abiding sense that we never think of it."[7]

Yet we can never enjoy this abiding sense of my private concerns as tributary to the larger life of men unless in our personal relations we seek the truth through fellowship. My private concerns will impede group thinking, for instance, if I am either an autocratic parent or an antagonistic youth in my home, if I am either a domineering male in my relations with women or an antagonistic female in my relations with men, if I am either a dictator or a slacker in industry, or in civic life. These attitudes, if they exist, will carry their influence even where I least suspect it, far beyond the situations in which they first arose. They cannot be kept in thought-tight compartments, nor prevented from showing themselves in other ways than by words. They will continue to influence me, and to be felt by others, no matter what I say. If, then, I would do my part toward evoking co-operative thinking and real democracy in my community, or beyond, I must be seeking in all relations to experience the unifying truth in the depths of my own soul. This means, among other things, that I shall welcome the truth about myself, and about mistakes in which I have shared, even though the truth may humble me. For it may also help me to see my limitations and faults in such light as will enable me to work with others more effectively. Thus I forget myself, and yet unconsciously multiply myself, in the larger concerns which I share with those who supplement me.

Such attitudes and thinking of individuals become more important than ever because they affect so profoundly many a new and unsettled problem of group relationships. As Wallace Donham of the Harvard Graduate School of Business Administration points out, "Politics, business, and the labor movement in their present form are so deeply affected by the progress of science and by the industrial revolution that the whole problem of group relationships is new for each group. No one of the group has learned how to handle these changes well. None yet recognizes the magnitude of its responsibilities for the future of civilization, or that these responsibilities require restraint as well as action. . . . One necessity is a far greater development of group responsibility and group ethics to fit the new need. All the forces of the humanities and of Church and State are needed if we are to have time to work out these problems. For, without overlooking the outstanding men in each of these groups who have a sense of this overwhelming responsibility, politicians, businessmen, and labor leaders as groups fail to recognize the problem. The ethics of politics is wholly inadequate for the new functions assumed by government. Much of existing group consciousness in business is defensive in character. Men feel their common need for defense far more readily than they develop a sense of constructive group responsibility. Labor is as a group militant rather than constructive. Through religion a keener sense of group responsibility in all these groups might be aroused."[8]

How then can such attitudes and thinking as are essential to better group relationships and democratic procedure be cultivated and co-ordinated so that they will lead to effective action in every department of life? What is wrong with some procedures, and how can they be avoided or corrected? These are complex questions, only partly answered as yet in effectual practice. Nevertheless, there are good precedents to be followed in more thoroughgoing ways, and there are actual experiments that point the way for truly Christian and democratic community.

Questions for Further Thought and Discussion

How is rebirth (in the Christian sense) related to community attitudes? Does Christian insight always bring harmony, or sometimes division? Why?

Can community be achieved if one member or more is not committed to the same basic purposes and principles as the majority?

How does this apply in the world situation? In the interdenominational situation?

Why and how are all group loyalties safeguarded and transfigured, in a successful democracy, by Christianity?

Part IV

UNFINISHED TASKS FOR FELLOWSHIP

15

BETTER PROCEDURES FOR DEMOCRATIC
FELLOWSHIP

Debate Should Become Co-operative Thinking

EVEN WHEN INDIVIDUALS are eager to know the truth, and to practice democracy, they are often impeded in discussion by inadequate methods of procedure. Such hindrances are the more widespread because, until recently, "what happens when individuals discuss, or rather what happens in the relation between minds, is a problem which has been almost wholly neglected by psychologists and social scientists."[1] It has been neglected also, in spite of encouraging exceptions, by those responsible for procedure in political, educational, and religious discussions.

As a result of all this neglect, co-operative thinking, both in large assemblies and in groups, is often precluded because of a combative temper of debate. Although debate, which proceeds by settled rules of order, is an advance "on the road from squabbling to peace," giving both sides a chance to be heard, "debate is only a halfway house. For it is a clash between conclusions already held, rather than a seeking for deeper insight. Moreover, because it has the form, and uses the method of conflict, it is not favorable to friendly and candid examination of motives. It is not a method of self-criticism, nor of help to others in self-criticism."[2] How

183

the usual debate tends to stimulate pride of opinion, and to entrench rather than to liberate ideas, can be seen by anyone who will follow with detachment the debates in a legislative or ecclesiastical assembly, especially when partisan feeling runs high, or when members have ranged themselves on opposing sides of a question. We see then why debates so seldom encourage men to explore an actual situation and to consider together all its possibilities in a search for the best solution. The more debate can be transformed into truth-seeking discussion, the better for all concerned.

How neighborly dealing with a difficult situation, as contrasted with the more abstract discussion of a subject, may lead to better methods of discussion and co-operation is illustrated by the way an emergency was met in a farmers' co-operative marketing association. When many members had been selling their crops to outside distributors, in violation of their contracts with the co-operative, the very existence of the association was imperiled. Some of the executives wanted to start sweeping prosecutions. Instead, a representative meeting was planned to encourage the frank expression of different points of view. This showed that lawsuits would be interpreted by hostile middlemen as a sign of low morale in the association, and would intensify "the feeling of country folk against the airs of city professionals who seemed to dictate the very habits of farm life from the remote headquarters of the association at the capital. And it was sensed by several committeemen that what they had set out for, after all, was co-operation as a way of living—a thing which lawsuits, even successful lawsuits, would do nothing to bring nearer."[3] Therefore, all agreed that, instead of starting lawsuits in a distant court, the executives should arrange for hearings on local cases before committees of the association in each locality. These hearings were planned with the farmers to give different interests and feelings new opportunities of expression, and to show how each situation had been affected by particular circumstances and different points of view. Thus each officer and member was helped to consider with the others how to change the circumstances so that the essential needs of all could be satisfied. The whole project became education in what it really means to be a co-operator.

Experience like this helps to show why a forum, when led by a single speaker with the other participants confined to asking questions, is not the most effective way to develop group thinking. A forum so conducted is often handicapped because the speaker has too little in common with his hearers and is likely to treat the subject in a way that seems academic. Moreover, a speaker competent to present a subject may not be so well qualified to stimulate the thinking of a particular audience or to lead it in dealing with the actual situation it confronts. It is well, therefore, to have the entire meeting in charge of a competent chairman or leader of discussion, and to secure speakers and interrogators of different points of view who will co-operate with the leader in developing a good-natured discussion, free from personalities and irrelevancies. The teamwork of such helpers is likely to be more effective if they meet for friendly, open-minded discussion before the meeting, and plan not to take advantage of each other in combative debate but to prepare the audience for further discussion and action in smaller groups. To this end a chairman is needed whose disposition and training fit him to foster a truth-seeking attitude among all participants.

Meetings for discussion are sometimes opened by a panel of four or more persons holding various points of view who stage a discussion of some thirty or more minutes in which only this panel takes part, as preparation for a better informed discussion by the entire audience. Such a panel discussion at its best is also education, by example, in good procedure for group thinking.

It is significant that those who are skeptical about the practicality of group thinking are usually persons who have never taken part in this democratic experience. As Harrison Elliott remarks: "It seems absurd to those who take a strictly expert view of leadership to expect contributions of value toward the solution of life problems from any but highly trained individuals. Indeed, it is almost impossible to understand the creative power of a group unless one has participated in the process."[4]

All the more need, therefore, to realize that co-operative thinking is no untried innovation! George A. Coe lays stress on its long and suggestive history of achievement "in circles of friends who muse by the fireside without desire to win victories over one another; in some families and partnerships where the members pool their views and thereby attain harmony of action"; in assemblies to further scientific research where "each participant in discussion takes the attitude of inquiry"; in business meetings that follow the Quaker type of deliberation where no vote is taken but, after silence and listening (with freedom to speak), the progress or conclusion of the discussion is summarized by the clerk of the meeting with the words: "It seems to be the sense of the meeting that. . . ."[2] If it appears that sufficient agreement has not been reached, further time is given for silence and for comment, or the matter may be referred to a committee for further inquiry and later report to the meeting.[5]

How Improve and Record the People's Thinking

What needs to be done with these old and tried ways of thinking together is illustrated in a pithy book, *Practical Applications of Democracy,* through problem-centered groups and combinations of groups, dealing with specific problems in various areas of life.[6] Separate chapters depict this process in the community, in government, in education, art, and leisure, in journalism, in employment and vocational training, and in industry. In all these areas, "thinking in terms of specific problems is a prerequisite of action. We often attempt too much and get discouraged. . . . Often what we call problems are not problems at all. Instead, they are 'problem areas.' These have to be broken down into specific problems, so that they can be dealt with one at a time. Thus the problem-centered group opens the way to action—to taking part in democracy—by providing a method of meeting problems. Breeding such groups to meet everyday problems, and changing the nature of existing institutions by building problem-centered groups within, must be our task."

As we learn to deal in this way with public problems, we shall no longer be confused and frustrated by merely abstract ideas about democracy. "We shall use language which refers to something which can be experienced. Thus democracy will cease to be a mere word and will become an experience. We shall see how it is possible to do something about it, rather than just talk. In this way concrete thinking can lead, not only to action, but also to adjustment for the individual. The problem-centered group has a therapeutic effect on maladjusted individuals, inasmuch as it makes self-centered individuals outgoing, and focuses the energies of dispersed persons. . . . Democracy's success depends on the ability of individuals to think, and that can occur only in an atmosphere where they are not swayed by hysteria, as in a crowd, but are able to congregate in groups to deliberate on vital issues. . . . A truly democratic method of participation would involve individuals and groups in the activity of the whole of society. . . . Democracy today must answer the totalitarian challenge by a rediscovery of itself. The greatest offensive we can start against the dangers of dictatorship is to release the basic forces of our democratic society."

All this is considered with reference to world-wide communication in a dynamic little book by Charles W. Ferguson, which grew out of five years of inquiry at home and abroad into the citizen's role in world affairs.[7] He found that "with the proper democratic planning, small groups within organizations literally throughout the world might meet regularly over a period of three months, say, and grapple with the same problems that other groups are grappling with. By the time this happened it is not unlikely that a wider type of organization than we can now anticipate would be willing to accept fellowship in the effort. . . . It might

spread to embrace groups of every type and description—
many formed chiefly with the high purpose of world communication in mind." It was found also that we have not
yet given more than passing attention to the methods by
which well-matured opinions on public issues can be formed
and given effective expression in our society. "For the most
part, the efforts to date have been looked upon as incidental.
Canada, one of the most advanced nations in the field of
political education, has over a thousand listening groups
which take up issues raised in programs of the Canadian
Broadcasting Company. These groups are spread all over
Canada. They range in size from small groups in Saskatche-
wan to large groups in cities like Montreal. The genius of
the Canadian system is that each group has a recording secretary. The questions raised by the broadcast are thrashed
out by the people and then put to a vote. The declared
opinions of the group are sent to Ottawa. Experience with
these groups has been instructive in many ways."

All this is only a beginning. "The immediate extension
of the democratic experiment requires a fuller recognition
of the voice of the people through an intelligent use of the
referendum. Up to now it has been employed chiefly upon
issues of local or limited interest. . . . It is time that the
referendum be rescued and put to work in assembling public opinion on world issues." The encouraging experience
of Massachusetts and other states is explained, and also the
necessity to guard referendums against pressure groups and
mere salesmanship. Too often the tactics have been designed
to convince, rather than to give people a full chance to discuss and to decide. "New methods, with a fuller chance of
democratic back talk, might well make salesmanship less important. . . . We can now perceive dimly what form new
social inventions might take. The discussion group and the
extended use of the referendum may appear as crude as the
early trains and automobiles, but they adumbrate the kind
of apparatus which would put human energy directly to
work in the transformation of our world."

It is conceded that realists will protest the views just stated as far too sanguine. "But the only kind of realism that is worth the name will allow for the psychic factor in human affairs—the possible release of man's powers through the opportunity for democratic action. The inventions which made over our world in the nineteenth century were mechanical. The inventions which may change history in the future must be social and political. This is a truth too obvious to state if it were not consistently and learnedly ignored."

The inquiry we are reporting finds that there would be only scant chance for a democratic remaking of society if we could not count upon the aid of forces and agencies which, however inactive now in promoting democracy, are nevertheless geared to be allies of the cause. "Chief among these is religion. The democratic idea—with its emphasis upon the worth of the individual, the equal accountability of men before the moral law, and the dream of an ideal society to be reached by concerted effort—is a derivative of religion. The sources of democracy, the materials from which it is compounded in its present imperfect form and might be compounded in its finished form, lie particularly in the field of Christianity and its heritage from the Jewish religion. Whatever the failures of the Church, as Elton Trueblood has brilliantly pointed out in *The Predicament of Modern Man*,[8] it has been the one institution which kept faithfully before us the truths upon which democracy rests. Clearly the accumulated emphasis of religious teaching might very well be turned, under the stress of the present crisis, to an intense democratic awakening."[7]

Large Gatherings Plan for Better Thinking

How effective procedure for large assemblies may profit from the earlier work of individuals and groups is shown in the well-co-ordinated thinking which preceded, accompanied, and followed the Oxford Ecumenical Conference of 1937 on Church, Community, and State. The intimate account of the whole process by the organizing secretary, J. H.

Oldham,[9] shows how at least three or four hundred persons throughout the world, including some of the ablest minds in the Church, took part during two or three years in a continuous interchange of thought and drafting of papers, and how this preliminary work was used effectively in the genuine group thinking at the Conference itself. That this in turn continues to bear fruit in further discussion and co-operative writing encourages hope for the development of a common Christian mind throughout the world. It contributed in no small measure to the development of the World Council of Churches. Similar procedure has proved most fruitful in the sectional and plenary meetings of the first official sessions of the World Council at Amsterdam.

In a quite different setting, an attempt by democratic discussion to inject new life into the thinking of a whole community, not only made over the "small talk" of the residents in a city as large as Des Moines, Iowa, but led to similar, successful experiments in other cities, with the encouragement of the United States Commissioner of Education. Such projects, interrupted by World War II, are needed throughout the country as part of a great forward movement in adult education.[10]

The widespread interest that was aroused by these nonpartisan discussions of current issues, not only in the larger meetings at Des Moines and other cities, but in well-planned neighborhood groups as well, shows unrealized possibilities of a "participant electorate" as the hope of democracy. So do The Town Meeting of the Air and the listening groups throughout the country which carry further each week the public discussion; and the many listening and voting groups of the Canadian Broadcasting Company. These and other discussions over radio networks and in local communities show that the apathy of the average citizen is not what it has been supposed to be. "Every man has *his* interests; at those points his attention can be enlisted. At those points he can be got to take an experimental attitude toward experience."[11]

Begin with Groups; Enlist Communities

One's interest can be enlisted usually in one or more of the groups to which he belongs; for, as Miss Follett shows, "I am always in relation not to 'society' but to some concrete group. When do we ever as a matter of fact think of 'society'? Are we not always thinking of our part in our board of directors or college faculty, in the dinner party last night, in our football team, our club, our political party, our trade-union, our church? The vital relations of the individual to the world is through his groups; they are the potent factors in shaping our lives." Through them we can learn how to think and how to live with other men. "The whole labor movement is being kept back by people not knowing how to live together much more than by any deliberate refusal to grant justice." This, Miss Follett thinks, is partly because "for a good many years now we have been dominated by the school of crowd psychology, by the school which taught that people met together are governed by suggestion and imitation, and less notice has been taken of all the interplay which is the real social process that we have in a group but not in a crowd. . . . But already we can see that a political science which is not based on a knowledge of the laws of association gained by a study of the group will soon seem the crudest kind of quackery. . . . The group process contains the secret of collective life, it is the key to democracy, it is the master lesson for every individual to learn, it is our chief hope for the political, the social, the international life of the future."[12]

To learn this master lesson of the group process, one may begin in a group or help to form one that will deal in a practical way with his interests. For instance, the farmer, gardener, poultryman, or one who would like to develop an intelligent interest in such an avocation may take part in the discussions and demonstrations his county Farm Bureau arranges with men of wide and tested experience from the State College of Agriculture or Experiment Station.

Such a demonstration in the orchard or the field, the poultry plant or the dairy barn, or a discussion with such a background, is an excellent opportunity to learn not merely about a particular subject and situation, but about good procedure for bringing accurate information to bear upon actual problems. Here we may see how the general run of citizens may bring in an expert so that he can enter into the actual situation they must face, and thus help them to enlarge and test their own experience in dealing with it. And this procedure can be extended in annual or special meetings to deal with related questions of civic or international scope. Thus, occupational interests may feed the larger concerns of civilization, and these in turn may be dealt with in a way that will help the members of any occupational group to treat their more technical problems in the light of the public interest.

Any such group, a trade-union, an association of employers, merchants, lawyers, physicians, or clergymen, can aim to educate its members in the group process and can call in other participants from time to time, not so much to make speeches as to encourage the kind of questions and discussion essential in the democratic way of life. Fortunately there are an increasing number of groups that can experiment in this way to improve community relationships. A parent-teacher association can study at first hand ways in which its members can work with students in recreational and other projects for the enrichment of community life as a whole, and can bring to bear a wide range of experience from within and beyond its membership. An association that helps the district nurse or similar public servant has an approach to homes, to officials, and to others concerned for the general well-being that gives it an unusual opportunity to promote co-operative thought and action. The best work of the National League of Women Voters, both in "using small groups to discuss in advance the major items in the program of a general meeting," and in developing nonpartisan discussion of issues in a local field, points the way for further advance in a democratic procedure that should not be confined to women. Groups connected with churches, Christian and Hebrew Associations, schools, colleges, and other cultural centers have opportunities far beyond anything yet realized to bring together in fruitful thinking both the experts and the rank and file participants.[13]

To further such thought and action by all citizens, the community council, as explained by Arthur Morgan, "may well be one of the most important inventions of American democracy. . . . A community council *may* be made up of one representative of each live, active, public-interest organization in the community. That is, the Chamber of Commerce would appoint one member, as would the Parent-Teacher Association, the League of Women Voters, the Garden Club, the Rotary Club, the Trades and Labor Council, each church, the Farm Bureau or Grange, and so on through the list of community organizations." These representatives would study the needs and shortcomings of their community, and co-operate with governmental bodies and with the member organizations for the fuller development of the community. The council may itself select a few co-opted members, chosen because of their special ability to render service, either with or without voting power. For instance, a physician, greatly interested in public health, yet not chosen to represent any civic organization, might well be selected as a co-opted member of the community council.[14] There may be also a general membership that helps to support the work of the council.

Experts and People Learn to Think Together

The work of experts to secure and to appraise information on social problems is more than ever recognized as an acute need of democracy; but how to convey this information in a vital form to the people generally is still, Miss Follett finds, in large measure an unsolved problem. "For accurate information seems to bore people. How to give the people facts without an amount of dullness which leaves us with

empty halls is our problem. A good many experiments
should be tried in order to see if we could hit on one that
might be successful."[11] Miss Follett would like, for instance,
to try a new kind of experience meeting, which first of all
would so present the subject to be considered as to show
clearly its relation to all our daily lives. This, she observes,
"is very important and usually neglected. . . . The second
step would be for each one of us to try to find in our own
experience anything that would throw light on the question." Such meetings, becoming a part of our community
life, Miss Follett hopes, would encourage us to observe and
to analyze our experience much more carefully than we do
at present, so that it would no longer seem almost wholly
insignificant to us in social value. If we thus take an experimental attitude toward our experience, we should be prepared to unite our various experiences one with the other
and with the material provided by the expert.[11] Then more
effective teamwork would follow between farmers and the
agricultural expert, between workmen and the scientific manager in a factory, between mothers and trained workers in
school, church, or community projects. Far beyond the particular interests or individuals concerned would be the development of effective democratic procedure.

A chief difficulty in the use of an expert arises when he
is called in by a group to speak on some phase of a problem
without being familiar with its local conditions or the course
of the discussion. The danger then may be that his information and judgment may seem merely academic and be unduly discounted, or that his prestige may incline the group
to let him do their thinking for them. In either case the
supposed solution may fail to take into account all the local
factors or to win the convinced support of the group. The
best results usually follow, as Robert D. Leigh shows, "when
the expert is himself a member of the group or, when called
in, sits as a member and acquires the background necessary
to turn the results of his knowledge and experience directly
upon the problem at hand. He is given in advance as clear

a description of the problem and the status of its discussion as is possible. He makes his contribution to the discussion in the same informal manner as do other members, speaking either on his own initiative or in answer to questions. In such a position he is obliged to interpret his own experience, vocabulary, and outlook in terms of the background of the other members of the group."[15]

As the experts who fit themselves for such work are appreciated and widely used, we shall find more trained men available like Professor Ripley of Harvard. When he was called upon to sit as an expert in the major problems of railway management, "he found it useful to spend months in freight train cabooses, locomotive cabs, and switchyard sheds, in order to see the railway from the point of view of its employees; as well as to cultivate the more comfortable contacts with railway managers, owners, and accountants. This example furnishes a model to be followed by all who do responsible thinking in the principal fields of social conflict."[15]

Harmonizing Various Points of View

The experience of a group of experts from different fields, who worked together on a series of widely influential books, throws light on the best conditions for thinking together on any subject. Canon B. F. Streeter tells how the venture began. He had met for the first time Miss Lily Dougall in her home at Cumnor, near Oxford, England, where the subsequent meetings took place. "In the course of that same afternoon," he says, "we conceived the plan of attempting to thresh out the idea of prayer, and, in particular, the conception of God which Christian prayer implies, by the method of group discussion—the results to be embodied in a group book. This was the origin of *Concerning Prayer.*" Though Canon Streeter acted as editor throughout, he attributes to Miss Dougall the initial idea of this book and of the two that followed, *Immortality* and *The Spirit,* as well as the "atmosphere," giving special character to the co-operative

thought out of which each volume was produced. The
groups' members belonged to more than one religious denomination and included not only ministers of religion and
professional theologians but also men who had made their
mark in the fields of literature, art, history, philosophy, and
psychology.

The assumption with which they all set out was that there
can be no real opposition between true religion and true
science or true art. All truth, all beauty, all goodness, they
agreed, must ultimately be of God. "If there appears to be
opposition between science or art and religion, it is because
the human beings who are interested in these things partially misconceive or misunderstand their real nature."[16]
"Science is every day making new discoveries which bear on
the relation of the body and the soul. It is not the lack of
new knowledge but the difficulty of co-ordinating it which
holds us back; for no one person can have really first-hand
knowledge of all the various departments of thought concerned. Discovery comes whenever trains of thought or pieces
of information originally separate are seen to illuminate and
explain each other. But, when the things requiring to be
brought together exist in different minds, this fusion is made
harder or easier in exact proportion to the degree of sympathy and the range of contact between those minds. The
maximum possibility of such fusion is reached where there
is personal as well as intellectual understanding, and where
there is an overmastering passion for Truth which makes
each willing to put all he has into the common stock, to
hold back no half-formed thought as foolish or immature,
to secrete no bright idea as private property. Experience
shows that the intellectual activity and receptivity of each
person is raised to the highest pitch when fellowship is not
in work alone and in discussion, but in jest and prayer as
well—for humor and common devotion, when both are
quite spontaneous, are, though in very different ways, the
greatest solvents of egotism and a wellspring of fellowship
and mutual understanding. Such fellowship and co-operation

is not always an easy thing to compass, but when it exists, persons of quite modest gifts and moderate experience can do, relatively to their capacity, great things."[17]

Conditions that impede and others that foster such fellowship are elucidated by another member of the Cumnor circle. Arthur Clutton-Brock, art critic of the *London Times,* was one of the most regular attendants at the meetings in Miss Dougall's home. The attitudes and procedure impressed him by contrast with the lack in our common life of any adequate theory and practice of fellowship: "Men have felt rather than thought in terms of it; and their feeling has not led them to sustained and concerted action. There has been between the feeling and the action a lack of the connecting link of thought. We have not that theory of fellowship which we need, if we are to believe in fellowship enough to make it. Men are always in a right or wrong relation to each other; they are, in their nature, like notes, whose function it is to be in that relation which is music. . . . Out of it they are not themselves, but full of sound and fury signifying nothing. For, without that right relation which is fellowship, we cannot perform our human functions at all. . . . We neither feel, think, nor act rightly."[18]

Even Jesus during his life on earth could not make the men of his time understand these relationships, "because they were not capable of conceiving the universal fellowship which alone is the Kingdom of Heaven. To them a Jew was a Jew, and a Gentile a Gentile; and there could be no fellowship between them. This misunderstanding has persisted in one form or another to the present day. In the war, for instance, we have been aware of a new fellowship with each other." But so far as "fellowship is achieved through conflict there is only emotion, not the logic of the Kingdom of Heaven; and the emotion, lacking that logic, having in it no intellectual conviction, may turn easily from love of friends into hatred of enemies; indeed, the love and the hatred intensify and are confused with each other; the hatred seems a virtue like the love. But the vision and logic of the

Kingdom of Heaven give an intellectual conviction to love, make fellowship at least in aim, universal."[18]

When once we are moved by the vision and logic of universal fellowship, many "foreign" influences that may have repelled us begin to enrich our intellectual and emotional life. Diversity gives zest to international friendship. Commerce finds its best gains in the intercourse of souls. The sea, which once divided and estranged mankind, becomes both a parable and an actual medium of traffic between minds.

Questions for Further Thought and Discussion

Can democracy as we know it be historically traced to Christian sources?

What are positive and negative aspects of each of these means of arriving at group decisions: speech, debate, panel, open discussion?

To what degree does the Quaker-meeting way of deciding questions demand both balanced individuals, and a deep feeling of community?

How is democracy "harder," and how "easier," as a means for group action?

What experiments or projects can you add to the author's list illustrating his point here?

16

FELLOWSHIP IN EDUCATION

The Child a Touchstone for Education

"OF THE TWO PURPOSES of education—to make a person fit for the world as it is and to make him able to change it—the second is the more important. But an education for changing the world would be very different from any that we have inherited: for all education hitherto has been a method of moulding the new generation into the shapes admired by the old: and the old generally prefer things as they are."[1]

"It looks at times as if the young serve simply as a stimulus to an activity of the elders of which they, the children, become helpless objects, an activity which tends to increase without limit as leisure and the economic margin grow. Children create the necessity, but also the exciting opportunity for society's effort to make vocal the sense of its ideals, customs, laws, and (ominous word) to *inculcate* them."[2]

From this state of things two pertinent questions arise. How can we protect children and youth from the warping pressure of the particular class or generation of their parents, from their elders' more or less unconscious habit of thinking and acting in terms of their own ruling interests? How at the same time can we help children to learn for themselves from such contacts with real life as are needed

199

for their development, and also for conserving what is best in the past? In other words, while we expose them to the best type of life that we know, how can we "provide for growth beyond the type"?

Toward an answer to these questions Jesus gave decisive help by making the unspoiled, open-minded child the touchstone, not only for all our dealings with children and youth, but also for our own attitudes and character. He thus opened the way for more creative fellowship between young and old. When some of his disciples, craving the chief places in the expected Kingdom of God, disputed among themselves who should be the greatest, Jesus waited until they had come into the home at Capernaum. Then he asked them, "What were you arguing about on the road?" But they were silent. So he called the Twelve together and said to them: "If any one wants to be first, he must be last of all and the servant of all." Then he called a child, put his arms around him, and said: "I tell you truly, unless you turn and become like children, you will never get into the Realm of heaven at all. Whoever humbles himself like this child, he is the greatest in the Realm of heaven. . . . For it is the lowliest of you all who is great."[a] In so far as adults show this spirit and attitude toward the young, and cultivate in themselves such receptivity and response as Jesus found in a little child, they help to give children a determining part in the advance of education. They open the way for the spontaneous, trustful, childlike spirit at its best. They turn from their own conceits to learn with open minds the ways of a father-like God with his children. Thus education in the society envisaged by Jesus would become continuous adventure and growth for all in fellowship with children and youth.

Re-creation with Children

One value of such fellowship at its best is found in its re-creative power. It discloses sources and forms habits of recreation, which will never be outgrown but will be cherished for their life-giving values as the pace and pressure of life increase. All about us, men and women, many of them still young, are living with unrealized capacities because they have never been encouraged to develop the play tendencies of childhood, and so have never learned the wider play of mind. Both for our own future, therefore, and for that of our children, we need to share with their fresher minds in what art, music, literature, and drama may do toward recreating jaded humdrum lives. What Dr. Richard C. Cabot says of this influence is more likely to be realized by tired or preoccupied fathers and mothers when they share the experience with youth. Then, especially, "art carries us off into a far country, more beautiful, more poignant, more tragic, perhaps more humorous and sparkling, perhaps nobler and more heroic, than is shown us in the workshop or the home. We emerge refreshed by this intense experience, and for a few precious minutes we look upon the world as if our eyes had never been dulled and stupefied by repetition and inattention, never lost the child's divine power of surprise."[3]

Why do many adults and even children lose this power of surprise and forfeit the intellectual curiosity which is their priceless heritage? Why do many boys and girls come to high school or even college indifferent to their opportunities? They wake up too late, if at all, to the significance of their studies and fail to pursue them in their stimulating relation to real life. Yet these same boys and girls not long ago were living interrogation marks, frequently exposing the ignorance of their elders on matters that appealed to their inquiring minds. Their intellectual curiosity gave good promise of advance in science, religion, and government. What have we done to nip it in the bud?

If we face this question with an open mind and then work together to make amends, we shall find in our children's awakening interest in life re-creation and enlightenment for ourselves, as well as for them. The power of surprise, which we need to recover, the unspoiled child still finds in his contacts with the world about him. He needs wise encouragement and help. But on the other hand, as Jesus suggests, the child can help us to recover a freshness of outlook on the world, to develop habits of observation, and to grow in the awareness and response that add zest to life. These good things, therefore, must be sought by all of us together. For, like the best attitudes and purposes, they are caught from inspiring companions more surely than they can be taught by any formal instruction. It was by his joyful and contagious example, even more than by his teaching, that Jesus communicated to his disciples a deeper enjoyment of nature, a kindlier appreciation of men, and a keener delight in God.

Deeper, Wider Fellowship for Youth

Another reason for such fellowship in education and a way to further it are explained in a concise and still timely study entitled *What Ails Our Youth*. It shows "that the defects of youth pass down from us, their elders; but, of course, once fastened upon a generation of youth, they tend to give corresponding character to this generation's maturity. We face here something like a vicious circle. We, the elders who are in charge of the education and the other conditions that affect the health of youth, are ourselves infected; how, then, can we assume the part of physician? As our discussion goes forward we shall see that the answer to this question involves two considerations: *First,* we must attack our own ailments at the same time that we attack those of the young; *second,* the young must take part in the attack upon both their ailments and ours."[4]

For the diagnosis and cure of these ailments, we need wider, deeper fellowship. Adults, children, and youth need to think and work together more spontaneously in a wider range of common interests than is usual in modern life. Such relationships will avoid the deadening effect of lessons and discipline imposed by external authority, will enlarge the scope of self-government as compared with merely student government in schools, and will evoke the spirit that makes true democracy possible between those of different ages. When the right spirit prevails, the teachers will be welcomed as participants in the growing democracy of school life and their larger experience will be freely sought. For instance, when a group of children, who were engaged in the kind of play that involved constructive work, discovered that merely impulsive conduct interfered with their purposes they called a meeting, devised a government, and actually administered it effectively. But when their own information and experience were not sufficient, they voluntarily sought help from a teacher. Such co-operation in school life has often led to effective community service by the young. With the encouragement of teachers, for instance, young people have helped to solve playground problems, have co-operated with health, fire, and police departments, and have shown initiative in other directions.

Such enlarging of democratic living and community service is promoted also by a movement which began with the Battle Creek year-round public school camp—the first of its kind in the country. For two-week periods throughout the year a group of some sixty grammar-school children and teachers leave their classrooms to live and learn together in the school camp. Michigan school officials are founding similar camps as preparation for outdoor education on a state-wide basis. Teachers' colleges in New York and Michigan have set up camps to train teachers in the technique of outdoor education. "They are learning that citizenship, individual and community initiative and responsibility, tolerance, courtesy, appreciation of natural resources and natural beauties can be taught best out-of-doors, where the child can gather knowledge by sight, touch, smell, the pull of his own muscles—and group co-operation." Learning to co-operate and to apply science to business is gained in various practical ways: through supervised visits to near-by farms or industries, through managing the camp grocery store where food is sold to groups planning an all-day trip, through providing their own luncheons with guidance from the camp dietitian, through many projects in the camp workshop and in improving the buildings or grounds. "No wonder the regular school classes perk up after two weeks like this at camp."[5]

Almost any subject—arithmetic, science, history, for instance—can be made more interesting to the student when it is related to his life on the soil or in the home and community. More, however, than a merely personal interest of the student needs to be kept in view. Even progressive schools, John Dewey found, need to look beyond things that make schooling immediately enjoyable to pupils, and to put more emphasis upon things that will help them to deal with the issues of contemporary social life. While he recognized that much has been done to further creativeness in the arts and to teach science as an aid to intellectual enjoyment, he did not find as much being done to bring out "the relation of science to industrial society, and its potentialities for a planned control of future developments." He found that discussion based on current events is inadequate unless students are taken back of events and given insight into the basic forces of industrial and urban civilization. "Only schools which take the lead in bringing about this kind of education can claim to be progressive in any socially significant sense."

This socially significant kind of education is now carried beyond school and college walls by many competent agencies —by the American Friends Service Committee in opportunities for many kinds of voluntary service; by the Christian Student Movement in plans for enlightening contacts with life during vacation periods; by some colleges that arrange for intervals of employment in the industrial world; and by some professional schools that provide well-supervised opportunities for clinical experience, such as Dr. Richard Cabot urged for theological students.[6] Other projects which have brought volunteer workers to farms and gardens under wise supervision suggest that volunteer work in industry also should be directed toward better understanding of economic and social problems.

Experiences in manual or managerial work are especially valuable to youth when they are enjoyed under the best conditions of normal life in homes, on farms, in workshops, factories, or offices, and when mature workers are interested in the growing insight of their young helpers. With such help these ventures into the normal work of the world make for more flexibility of body and mind, greater initiative, and better understanding of persons and things as they should be, than does regimented, segregated, compulsory military training of teen-age youth. No wonder that so many educators, parents, and religious leaders object to the break-up of this important part of education, and to the perils of mass military living, at the very time when immature youth need the opportunities and helps for independent thinking and many-sided development that can be given to younger members of a normal co-operating community at its best. What is most needed in this formative period is wide co-ordination of homes, churches, schools, and other factors in community and national life to provide for the best development of body, mind, and spirit, and for clear insight into social problems through deep and varied fellowship.

This need led William Temple to emphasize the necessity for giving all future citizens ample time to take part in a democratic community of school life, because "the national community, or even his city or county, is too large a body for him to realize in it anything like living membership. He needs a society of people about his own age, in the activities of which he may take a share equal to that of any other member, so that it may reasonably claim his loyalty, and he may have the sense of being wanted in it. Nothing else will draw out from him the latent possibilities of his nature."[7]

If the full purpose of such democratic community in school life is to be realized, we must produce in schools a type of the society we should like to realize. We can attain democracy in our adult world, only as children and youth are reared in the practice of democracy.

A Better Environment for the Young

This primary need that school, college, and home should be a new world in embryo calls us further than changes in our educational system. We must go further because the necessary changes encounter difficulties beyond school walls. "Our industrial civilization itself is ailing, and it communicates its ailment to the young people. It is not organized in the interest of young life and its development, but of income, profits, and spending. . . . The system implies, for the vast majority, either routinized attendance upon a machine or else routinized obedience to superiors. This mechanization spreads into the clerical and managerial functions. This situation becomes unfavorable to the exercise of the powers that are most distinctively human—analysis, appreciation, choice, reflective co-operation. Thus the occupations of men impoverish the spirits of men, and then with ready money invite them to seek refreshment in things that can be bought rather than in things that can be had only by achieving them. This is true, on the whole, of academically privileged youth as well as of young people who are in occupations. For not only is this the system for which the student is consciously preparing; it is the system whence he draws his sustenance; and it is his dominant environment. To the question 'What ails our youth?' a part of the answer, then, must be, the occupation of adults, with the meanings for life that flow therefrom."[4]

Therefore, since "every child, more than he realizes, is infected with the parental malady," it is not enough to bring the young into more intimate relation with their elders and with the actual life of the world on the basis of things as they are. If education is to move toward things as they should be, we must provide, not only in schools and colleges, but also in the world outside, for growth beyond the type of life that now prevails. Education must pursue a larger social aim for both old and young. This larger aim, now more clearly seen, must be to develop persons as co-operative members of an ever improving human society. Such development should be lifelong. Then "it will progress from the simple habits of co-operative domestic life which little children should acquire to the wisest criticism of our social procedure and the most devoted efforts to improve it which are possible for adults."[8]

Adult Education and the Future

The more we see how this inclusive aim of education is curtailed by the occupations and attitudes of adults, the more evident becomes the need for a great enrichment and extension of fellowship in adult education. This need is emphasized by John W. Studebaker, former United States Commissioner of Education, in his comment on two significant facts: "First, there are approximately three times as many citizens in 'adult life' as in 'school life'; second, adult life is three times as long as school life. If these facts are coupled with our certain knowledge that school life is the period of immaturity, of childish and youthful interests, that it is in adult life that the responsibilities of government are assumed with serious purpose, and that swiftly changing conditions demand a constant reshaping of social insight and understanding, it becomes very clear that it is through a planned system of civic education designed for *adults* that the next great contribution to American democracy can be made."[9] Similarly, a committee appointed by the British government after the First World War found, as is now even more evident, that "adult education is a permanent national necessity, an inseparable aspect of citizenship, and therefore should be both *universal* and *lifelong*."

Possibilities of approaching this ideal are shown by results from the folk schools in Denmark. Various writers on adult education tell a thrilling story of how men and women from the farms of Denmark have flocked to their homelike folk schools in the countryside. "There they live for months at a time with the cultivated kindly men and women who are their teachers, live and work and play and talk with them

and with each other, most of their waking hours." The
Danes were a most backward, depressed people in 1864 when
a disastrous war with Germany took their richest provinces.
But later their residential kind of adult education helped
them to become "the most widely cultured nation of Europe,
the nation where the highest level of scientific agriculture
exists, the people who have developed to the highest degree
the difficult ability to act together harmoniously."[10] The
Danish folk school "is primarily a moral and spiritual force,
elevating the mind and strengthening the will by the vision
of great ideals. . . . It is not a church (though many of its
teachers were theological students at the university), but it
fulfills for its students something of the offices of a church
by steadily insisting on a spiritual philosophy of life suited
to the needs and capacities of the ordinary man. Its pupils
learn something more than history and literature and some
elementary mathematics, chemistry, and biology. They learn
a way and view of life. Spiritual inspiration has been the
heart of the schools since their origin."[11] The foremost leader
in the rapid development of these schools was a country
pastor, N. F. S. Grundtvig. "He believed that the hope of
the future lay in the education of adults, who were the key
to the opportunity for children and young people, and in
whose hands rested community and national life. He was
ably assisted by Kristen Kold, a working cobbler." These
men were contagious examples of the truth they declared—
that man is a spiritual being and that education, to be effective in the best sense, must help him to share the spiritual
heritage of the race.[12] They made even their country's meager
material resources an additional reason for all citizens to
work together in a nation-wide movement for adequate adult
education.

Equally encouraging, and even closer to the pressing needs
of a great majority of the world's people who suffer from
illiteracy, poverty, disease, and bad government, are the vast
campaigns for literacy and better living in many lands.

From personal knowledge of these campaigns in the Philippines, India, Africa, and Latin America, Frank Laubach, an expert in methods of teaching illiterates one by one and enlisting each one to teach another, reports: "The world is divided into an infinity of small groups, each expecting hostility from the other and therefore on the defensive. But self-restraint and tact can replace this defense mechanism with mutual good will. It has been thrilling to discover how quickly such ventures as literacy campaigns, disease control, and agricultural missions melt away these dislikes and suspicions. . . . On the other hand, the voices of hatred and prejudice are working to persuade Asia to gang up against the white race. There is terrible danger that a weakened white race may find itself in deadly conflict with the colored races. If Asia should unite against the whites, Africa would be with her—together they would have four hundred millions more than all the whites in the world. But it is amazingly easy to win the friendship of the peoples of Asia and Africa, if we will be Christlike enough to serve and love them unselfishly. The race problem is not a colored problem, it is a white problem. . . . While statesmen feel their way to political world union, we must found great enterprises like the common struggle against illiteracy to bring about confidence and the will to co-operate, without which political union will be impossible."[13]

Dr. Laubach stresses also the urgent need for an adequate literature and teaching of the way of love. "The literacy campaigns now under way are going to double the world's readers! A billion people now illiterate will be reaching out with hungry minds for something to read. Will they be fed with the message of Christ or with atheism? Will they read love or hate? Whatsoever is sown in their minds, the world will reap."[13]

Now, as never before, the plight of the whole world shows the urgency for "a world-wide program of adult education to provide intelligent popular support for political and economic reconstruction in the interest of justice and freedom. Education for children is not enough, because the fate of the world may be decided before they can grow up. Intellectual co-operation among scholars is not enough, for the movement must reach the people." For this reason the United Nations Educational, Scientific, and Cultural Organization (UNESCO) is working directly with agencies of mass education and opinion, instead of confining its efforts to intellectuals, as the cultural division of the League of Nations attempted to do. UNESCO seeks to maintain direct relations with civic, cultural, and scientific groups in all the member countries. In the United States its outreach will include about one hundred such organizations.[14]

Here are vast opportunities to extend education through the millions of families related to these organizations. For instance, churches, synagogues, schools, colleges, and other agencies could have direct contact with homes where some of the greatest educational possibilities remain to be realized by old and young working and thinking together.

Even in considering the immediate world-wide influence of adult education we dare not neglect the home; for we need to encourage and share without delay the unwarped thinking and fresh insight of youth. The generation now in our homes, and the decisions they will soon be making, are being profoundly influenced by the heritage of good and evil we now give them. Fortunately, examples multiply showing how this heritage may be improved by combining adult and juvenile education in the home and by enlarging its influence through interracial and interfaith co-operation in churches, schools, and other expressions of community spirit.[15]

The Home a Center of Creative Fellowship

The home is pre-eminently the place where creative fellowship in education should achieve early and far-reaching results. Many physicians and psychiatrists have discovered that the principal cause of maladjustment and nervous breakdown in adults is to be found in the wrong treatment of the patient by his parents in childhood. According to Dr. H.

Crichton Miller, the seeds of the present disorder have been sown long before, and often in love; through wrong ideals, or excessive affection through stupidity, or discouragement of real independence in the child—but seldom through the parent's neglect—the damage has been done. In his large clinical experience, he found so much good will with "so large an amount of damage done to the souls of these children, who are our whole asset as a nation. The need of the world is for new parenthood: the aim of the parent should be that the child should grow up a better parent for the next generation."[16]

To this end, it is imperative for the whole future of the child that he have as early as possible the companionship of those who embody an out-going purpose for a better world, and who will encourage him in its applications before the evil days come when he may say, "I have no pleasure in them." The child in his early years, Benjamin Kidd reminded us, is most responsive to the emotions associated with the larger social aim.[17] He is least affected by "the social lies which warp us from the living truth." But it is not enough to tell the child of this larger purpose; he must be given a chance to share it and to know the love and joy that come through its whole-hearted pursuit with others.

Only those who have known intimately some family where father and mother, brothers and sisters, have thus enjoyed one another in the interplay of adequate and kindred aims can appreciate what a safeguard and incentive such family life affords in all the other relationships of its members. In such a home, where the child is given the place Jesus intended him to have in the life of the group, where he is helped to show consideration for others as they show consideration for him, and where each member cultivates a friendly but not too inquisitive attitude toward the interests of the others, the family experience makes possible more intelligent deliberation about personal and public problems. It helps in the choice of vocation or life partner, and in making better adjustments throughout life. To the extent that its work and play, its attitudes and aspirations, approximate those of true children of God, such a family shows in epitome the kind of society we all should be seeking.

Home, Church, and School as Allies

To multiply and to reinforce such family outposts of a better society, school, church, and voluntary groups can bring students, parents, and other citizens together in various programs that help to realize what a true community can be and do for the good of all.[18] Families need some such fellowship in recreation and discussion with others in order to avoid clannishness and to foster a well-rounded life.

One way in which these groups can help home, school, and church to work together more effectively is by their support of the movement for more and better visiting teachers, and by co-operation with them. In many of our cities, and in some rural areas of most of the states, trained visiting teachers—far fewer than are needed—are restoring to school life youth whose chances for further education had seemed hopeless. In many cases the visiting teacher "has replaced the traditional truant officer, and has straightened out kinks of behavior beyond the skill of the classroom teacher. The visiting teacher is usually a first-rate teacher who has supplemented classroom experience by special study of child psychology, mental hygiene, and family case work." Much of the visitors most effective work is in the home, going to the root of the trouble in the pupil, his parents, or environment, and seeking a cure with the co-operation of all who can help in family, church, school, or neighborhood.[19]

A representative Committee on the Study of Christian Education calls for a great advance in the training of parents, teachers, and ministers with special reference to their more effective work in and for the home as the most potent influence in the development of personality. "Too much of our religious education is expected to take place within the church building. Not enough is expected of the home. The church school may have a rebirth of power if the church will go to the people where they live, if it will help them to establish and maintain a normal religious life within the home. Through this effort concentrated in the homes, Christian education may enlist the support of a large part of the laity of the churches because it will concern itself with what is clearly the business of everyone, instead of seeming to be a matter for the faithful few who maintain the traditional Sunday School. Thus many more may be convinced that what goes on in the church on Sunday is of supreme importance."[20]

Without a great increase of ministers, teachers, and parents exerting a transforming influence in both home and church, neither of these basic institutions can escape present destructive tendencies or fulfill their essential mission in a world adrift. The secularism and self-seeking to which we have more or less succumbed in the world at large have long been penetrating and perverting the life of both home and church. To these divisive tendencies others are now added by the policies of totalitarian, and sometimes even of so-called democratic states, which exalt a false nationalism and regimentation of life to the detriment of spiritual values. Thus family and church are both imperiled, and must stand together if they would expand their freedom and mutuality. From their co-operation there is coming a notable literature of tested experience. It shows in practice how the family can co-operate with the church school, and how the church can help the family through "the preparation of young people for marriage, through counseling those who are facing marital difficulties, through helping parents in the training of children, through building up an appreciation of the significance of the family, and through fostering those attitudes of trust and love in human relations on which the unity of society and the world depends."[21]

Questions for Further Thought and Discussion

Is the trend of education in America currently authoritarian, or toward the sharing principle advocated here?

How is "the mass mind" related to the loss of fresh and creative imagination?

What effect do war and military training have in this regard?

What progress, so far as we can note, is UNESCO making in promoting programs of adult education in various countries?

How could the Danish folk-school idea be put across in America's television-trained, baseball-loving populace?

How effective is adult education in (respectively ranked): Church, service clubs, lodges, school, movies, radio, television, newspapers, magazines?

How does the general method of Church education compare with that of the public school systems?

17

EDUCATING THE WHOLE MAN

The Home and Neighborhood in Well-rounded Growth

THE MOST ENLIGHTENING experiences of life, which we all need for well-rounded development, yet often miss under present conditions, are well illustrated in the life of Jesus. Some writers who pay high tribute to him as a "small-town religious genius" seem unaware of the wide experience he enjoyed from boyhood. To the inquiring mind of the boy of twelve, the days when he ventured to stay alone in Jerusalem must have been full of new discoveries. Not all his time could have been spent among the teachers in the temple, hearing them and asking them questions.[a] Perhaps he began to feel even then their remoteness from the common life and needs of men, which he later exposed. However this may be, he returned with his parents to make the most of the educational opportunities of Nazareth.

This community was not, as sometimes portrayed, a stagnant pool of rustic seclusion. In suggesting the advantages it offered to the growing boy, Edersheim shows that it was one of the great centres of Jewish Temple-life, and that the lower caravan route from Damascus to the sea passed through it. "Men of all nations, busy with another life than that of Israel, would appear in the streets of Nazareth; and through them, thoughts, associations, and hopes connected with the great outside world would be stirred."[1] When Jesus stood on the hill above Nazareth, he could see the world's life in epitome. Galilee, which lay at his feet, was not only cultivated to the utmost, and thickly covered with populous towns and villages, but the center of every known industry, and the busy road of the world's commerce. Also in full view, and within walking distance, was Sepphoris, "the ornament of all Galilee," and the capital of the province until Jesus was some twenty years old. As a carpenter, he may have worked at its rebuilding. In any event this commercial and political center, ranking in importance second only to Jerusalem, and much more cosmopolitan, would offer to an alert youth in a neighboring village many opportunities for observing the life of the early Imperial Age.[2] The pressure and problems of the world outside must have been felt by the youth of Nazareth as by few others.

How this varied experience of Jesus contributed to his later work is suggested by his quick understanding of the attitudes of men, and by the telling illustrations that came to him spontaneously from the various occupations of men and women. He talked with easy familiarity of a woman making bread, a sower planting in various soils, an employer or a landlord facing difficult problems, a merchant staking all on a single venture, or a builder calculating the total cost before he lays the foundation. The breadth and depth of his concern for men and women, wherever he found them, helps to explain the unique welcome that has been given to Jesus by people of all races and all stages of development.

This way of learning through dealing with people and events is precisely what John Dewey finds lacking in much modern education. He shows that learning through the ordinary course of living proceeds rapidly and securely before children go to school, because it is closely related to their needs and to the corresponding exercise of their powers. But in schools he finds a strong tendency that is opposed to this principle. "Teachers take accumulated learning of adults, material that is quite unrelated to the exigencies of growth, and try to force it upon children, instead of finding out what these children need as they go along. Probably the greatest and commonest mistake that we all make is to forget that learning is a necessary incident of dealing with real situations."[3]

Jesus used this dealing with real situations with great effect in the training of the Twelve and of the Seventy. He not only kept them observant of his own work; he encouraged them to do as he had done in meeting the needs of others. He brought them into closer relations with people and events by throwing them at times upon their own resources, sending them, "two by two, into every town and place where he himself was about to come."[b]

The disciples, whom Jesus thus trained to work for the new order of life, had been prepared for it in part by the same kind of discipline in early life which Jesus had found salutary. "Among the Jews, the contempt for manual labor, which was one of the painful characteristics of heathenism, did not exist. On the contrary, it was deemed a religious duty, frequently and most earnestly insisted upon, to learn some trade provided it did not minister to luxury, nor tend to lead away from the personal observance of the law."[1]

The Stunting Segregation of Youth

This invaluable part of education, which Jesus enjoyed through sharing in the various experiences of home and neighborhood, is precisely what many are missing in our day. Too often "the home dwindles toward a place for eating and sleeping; the neighborhood scarcely exists any longer. The people one meets are met under fewer human aspects, for briefer periods, in scattered places, on behalf of narrower interests. The youth is 'in' on few things with his elders. His human contacts are chiefly with other youth. Students have more contacts with mature persons, particularly teachers; yet these contacts are relatively narrow, and, as far as the colleges are concerned, there is general segregation of both work and play from domestic and neighborly experience."[4]

Moreover, parents who were thus segregated in their early life are later handicapped when dealing with their children. They may suppose that they enjoyed the best that school and college could offer, and the finest recreation out of doors, while in fact they never have cultivated a vital partnership with nature for the general well-being, or an appreciation of the needs and aspirations of those who differ from their own intimates. For all their advantages, they cannot or will not enter deeply into states of mind and feeling different from those of their own isolated class, or comprehend the baffling problems of the underpaid. This is true also of some who have come from the ranks of labor. Consequently many successful citizens fail to understand why their efforts, if any, to help the supposedly less fortunate are not more warmly received or more effective.

Many a man, however, who has enjoyed a supposedly superior education, and yet found himself more or less separated from the great majority of his fellow men, has come later to appreciate an education very different from his own. Matthew Arnold, for instance, quotes approvingly General Grant's story of his boyhood outside school hours. In his *Memoirs,* which became the best seller of its time, Grant tells how, when he was seven or eight years old, he began to help the choppers by driving the team that drew all the wood used in his father's house and tannery; how, from eleven, when he was strong enough to hold a plough, until seventeen, when he entered West Point, he "did all the work done with horses on the farm, besides tending two or three horses, a cow or two, and sawing wood for stoves, etc., while still attending school"; and how he was compensated for all this by freedom to go swimming, fishing, skating, or sleighing, and to use a horse to visit his grandparents in the adjoining county, or to take long trips with friends to Cincinnati or Louisville. Grant's father evidently believed that in order to grow in good judgment and decision of character a boy needs to take responsibility and to make decisions for himself. So the youngster was sent alone when eight years old to negotiate for the purchase of a colt he very much wanted, and later was allowed to trade the farm horses on his own initiative. Grant confessed that, due to his precipitate offer for the colt, this transaction caused him great heart-burning, but, like many another embarrassment, it carried a remembered kind of learning through mistakes. In commending the advantages of this young Ulysses, Matthew Arnold adds: "The bringing up of Abraham Lincoln was also, I suppose, much on this wise; and meager, too meager, as may have been the schooling, I confess I am inclined on the whole to exclaim: 'What a wholesome bringing up it was!' "[5]

Religion and Science Combined for Better Education

In order that our intimacy with nature and our fellow men may contribute most to the growth of the whole man and the whole society, there must be education of adults and youth that will harmonize religion and science for them in an effective partnership. Here also the teaching and practice of Jesus points the way. As one of our scientists, W. F. Luder, says, "Jesus was the first to apply science to life as a whole. He anticipated by fifteen hundred years our discovery of it" in relation to living abundantly. In fact we have not yet caught up with him. He can help us still further to apply both science and religion in the more generous, creative sharing of physical and spiritual resources.

Although Professor Luder sees that the teaching of Jesus was restricted by the backwardness of his audiences, he cites sufficient evidence to prove that Jesus had a remarkably scientific attitude, and can help us to apply both the religious and the scientific aspects of education. His attitude is shown by his rejection of the accepted teaching of his time that sickness and misfortune are invariably the result of sin, by his attitude toward the Law and the Sabbath, and by such sayings as, "You shall know the truth and the truth shall make you free," or "Whoever will do his will shall know of my teaching, whether it is of God, or whether I speak of myself." This latter statement can be tested by anyone who desires to know whether there is support in the universe for the teaching of Jesus. What is required is the open mind—demanded by the application of the scientific method to any problem. Whoever makes this experiment—whoever studies the records to learn what Jesus taught as the will of God, and then sincerely attempts to do it—will know whether the teaching does come from God. "In the process of studying the records different people may come to different conclusions about the exact meaning of the incarnation and the resurrection. But they will find something in themselves responding to the teaching in such manner that they will know that the way of Jesus is in harmony with the nature of the universe."[6]

The necessity for such an education is found repeatedly in du Noüy's scientific study of the methods and aim of evolution. After showing the disastrous influence of some scientists, and of some teachers of religion, all misled by their fragmentary knowledge of the universe, he says: "Today, things have changed. We can conceive a harmonious cosmos the laws of which reinforce our intuitive, religious aspirations without ever contradicting them." Therefore "it now becomes imperative for the rational and the intuitive efforts to blend. This imposes a broadening of science, but also a unification and clarification of religions. This clarification, which simply means a return to the elemental teachings of the gospel, must be progressive."

A beginning must be made, du Noüy concludes, first with children, then with students. This requires the preparation of teachers who will be responsible for the orientation of the coming generation. "The teacher must be honestly and sincerely convinced that the so-called conflict between science and religion does not exist in the light of modern science. To obtain this result his scientific culture must be free of all social or political influence, be in accord with the *present* state of our knowledge, and not be inspired by a science fifty years old.

"We know now that intelligence can turn against itself and destroy man, unless it is controlled by a moral force. . . . Today we are faced with the question of whether intelligence or morality will win. If intelligence alone should rule, all the human traits of which we are proudest, the sense of duty, of liberty, of dignity, of the beauty of disinterested effort, would disappear little by little until civilization would vanish without even an afterglow. On the other hand, if the moral law dominates, it will not oppose itself in any way to the free development of the mind. It will progressively gain ground and will allow all the human, intuitive, and intellectual characters to develop in perfect freedom."[7]

Morals and Religion Needed for Sound Education

The necessity that the intellect must be supplemented in education by moral and spiritual forces appears from various points of view. Phillips Brooks shows why the greatest men who ever lived, the best-beloved and most influential for good, "are those in whom you can not separate the mental and moral lives. You cannot say just what part of their power and success is due to a good heart and what to a sound understanding." This harmony appears in the intellectual life of Jesus. "The great fact concerning it is this, that in him the intellect never works alone. He never simply knows, but always loves and resolves at the same time. Truth which the mind discovers becomes immediately the possession of the affections and the will. It can not remain in the condition of mere knowledge." On the other hand, "merely to see that things are right or wrong and not to feel a pleasure in their rightness, and a pain in their wrongness, does not indicate a finely molded character. The moral perceptions, even the moral obediences, do not make a full moral life. The moral emotions must be there too. For the man who lacks emotion lacks expression. That which is in him remains within him, and he can not utter it or make it influential. And on the other hand the man who lacks emotion lacks receptiveness. That which other men are, if it does not make him glad or sorry, if it gives him neither joy or pain, does not become his."[8]

When we find ourselves turning away from many a learned man whose knowledge has not been pressed into character, and when we discover in well-rounded characters a power more than intellectual, calling out the best in others, we see more clearly the need for a vast increase of competent parents and teachers whose moral and emotional natures are well developed. Unless enough teachers and parents of future citizens can communicate unselfish, co-operant emotions and purposes, education will fail in the most important phase of social evolution. This failure, of which Benjamin Kidd warned us, now imperils the world. "The intellect," he said, "continually comes into conflict with those larger evolutionary forces which, through the instrumentality of religious systems, are securing the progressive subordination of the present interests of the self-assertive individual to the future interest of society. . . . But, like all movements of the kind, the evolution is proceeding very slowly. One after another, races and civilizations appear to be used up in the process. When the intellectual development of any section of the race has, for the time being, outrun its ethical development, natural selection has apparently weeded that section out like any other unsuitable product."[9]

This process has reached a stage which shows anew the danger of neglecting ethical and spiritual development. Yet we may easily become so preoccupied with the results of secular dictatorships abroad that we ignore the danger of moral and emotional starvation at home. The danger is intensified in the public education of a democracy, because education in a democracy feels obliged to avoid the conflicting opinions of various religious groups. As a result, *the best places will be left blank,* because it is on the most vital matters that men most differ. The prewar experience of France in secularized education has furnished a striking instance of the principle that in education a vacuum is equivalent to a negation. In one case as in the other, instinct is robbed of its possibility of response. Children have rights which education is bound to respect. The first of these rights is not that they be left free to choose their way of life, i.e., to make bricks without either straw or clay. Their first right is that they be offered something positive, the best the group has so far found. Against errors and interested propaganda the growing will has natural protection: it has *no protection against starvation,* nor against the substitution of inferior food for good food."[10]

The present danger of politically guided education is not confined to a negation. There have ben increasing attempts to inculcate in the young, and to impose also upon adults, the theory of a deified state as supreme over the conscience of the individual. This theory, whose ramifications are laid bare in a penetrating book, *Educating for Citizenship,* is essentially "the same educational philosophy that controlled the schools of the German Empire before 1914. Here the pupil was habituated to the assumption that the will of the sovereign is ethically right, an ultimate determinant of duty for the citizen, and in fact, an obligation of religion." This theory of state supremacy, which has brought chaos in Germany and Japan, is not confined to dictatorships. It can be found openly or insidiously at work in our own country, to the detriment of free mind and conscience, and of democratic institutions. For particulars we must refer to books like that just cited and others, such as *The New Leviathan.*[11] This much, however, should be said here. It is no longer safe to dismiss these dangers at home on the ground that the authority to teach is not committed by the Constitution to the Federal Government, but is reserved to the several states and to the people. This little understood safeguard of our democracy is too easily overridden by zealous officials, whether federal, state, or local, or swept away by mass hysteria. Before that comes on a wide front every friend of freedom is needed to guard against the regimentation of minds by either governmental agencies, class interests, mob violence, or local prejudice.

Moreover, the danger that the majority of our youth will be impoverished in their moral and emotional development is intensified because, as a careful investigation shows, "little attention has been paid to religious education by those who are the leaders in America's great system of public schools. The dearth of writings on religious education from the pens of public educators shows a corresponding failure to grapple with the problems of a complete education which includes education in religion as an integral part. Both general education and religious education await for their future growth the development of a philosophy of education which shall take adequate account of their interrelatedness."[12]

Such dearth of moral and religious education is not confined to our public schools. It threatens education everywhere because "moral education is impossible without the habitual vision of greatness"; and for lack of such vision much current education fails.[13] Wide experience supports Professor Hocking's verdict: "If I were to name the chief defect of contemporary education it would not be that it turns out persons who believe and behave as their fathers did—it does not: but that it produces so many stunted wills, wills prematurely grey and incapable of greatness, not because of lack of endowment, but because they have never been searchingly exposed to what is noble, generous, and faith provoking."[12]

The lack of vision in contemporary education is traced by William Temple to the tendency of modern culture to "regard faith in God as a dispensable indulgence. . . . We have supposed that it is possible to provide education which is religiously neutral, to which religion can then be added in greater or less measure. But, in fact, an education which is not religious is atheistic; there is no middle way. If you give to children an account of the world from which God is left out, you are teaching them to understand the world without reference to God. If he is then introduced he is an excrescence. He becomes an appendix to his own creation. Now if God exists at all, it is obvious that he is the most important of all existing things; we can understand nothing properly until we see it in its relation to God and his purpose."[14]

It is because of this omission from the philosophy of John Dewey that many who appreciate his great service to education think that he unwittingly opens the door for a religion of nationalism. For instance, Francis P. Miller says, "Professor Dewey himself would be horrified at the suggestion that he is playing into the hands of nationalistic forces. He supposes that by appealing to the imagination as the source of ideal ends he has suggested a religious attitude capable of supplying mankind with a common faith. His suggestion will have exactly the opposite effect. It will have this effect because an appeal to the imagination of the natural man in the actual world of our day means an appeal to national culture as the ultimate frame of reference. The human imagination, which was supposed to possess universal qualities capable of inspiring flesh and blood men of all lands and races to enter into a common faith, turns out to be a specific American imagination. This is the very stuff out of which religions like the Nazi religion are eventually compounded. And that is the reason why the movement of thought which is associated with Professor Dewey's name is preparing the way for an American religion which will parallel the national religions of other countries."[15]

The omission of God from much modern education, as explained by Harry Emerson Fosdick, comes to this: "It isn't simply that positive religious teaching is shut out. What often happens is that irreligious teaching is permitted. To know what materialistic science teaches—that is education. To learn all about Freud, not simply as a genius in psychiatry but as an atheist who thought all religion an illusion —that is education. But to acquaint our youth with the great prophets of the Old Testament, or with the personality and principles of Christ—that is religion, and must often be bootlegged in if it gets in at all. We cannot go on that way. Some day a book must be prepared by Catholics, Jews, and Protestants, presenting to American youth in the schools the spiritual heritage of our Western World, not as propaganda but as basic knowledge, if they are to understand even where our democracy came from and what it means."[16]

A similar obligation is stressed by a representative committee appointed by The International Council of Religious Education. They declare: "As leaders of thought in the community, the churches have a responsibility to public education in general, but in particular also to the religious content of the curriculum. . . . The time has come for a drastic review of this whole situation on the part of both churchmen and schoolmen. It is our contention that to lay foundations in religious education is a part of the responsibility of the general schools. Unless they take this responsibility, it is questionable whether the task of Christian education which has been undertaken by the churches can ever be satisfactorily accomplished."[17]

The responsibility of the public schools is emphasized by another representative committee speaking for leaders in both public and religious education. They conclude: "It is a grave mistake to suppose that the public school, holding as it does in so large part the power to determine the scope of intelligent interest and concern on the part of youth, can be neutral in this matter. The failure to play a part in acquainting the young with the role of religion in the culture while at the same time accepting such responsibility with reference to other phases of the culture, is to be unneutral— to weight the scales against any concern with religion." On the other hand, "it is not the business of public education to secure adherence to any particular religious system or philosophic outlook." But the committee agrees that the school has a responsibility for removing religious illiteracy, for laying the groundwork of intelligent approach to religion as an aspect of the culture and to "impel the young toward a vigorous, decisive personal reaction to the challenge of religion. . . . There is much evidence that the study of the Bible as a unique piece of religious literature, conducted with at least as much respect as is given to the great secular

classics, and devoid of arbitrary interpretations to the same
extent that we expect in connection with the latter, could be
carried on without offense to any section of the community."[18]

On the relation of religious faith to the democratic way of
life, the committee says, "For us, the democratic faith means
that the worth of persons and the increasing perfectibility of
human institutions rests on a religious conception of human
destiny. We believe that the Judaeo-Christian affirmation
that man is a child of God expresses an authentic insight
which underlies all particular theological formulas. We think
the effort to sustain a social ethic that has been severed from
its cultural roots will not succeed generation after generation." Hence the committee holds that a failure to preserve
and capitalize the Judaeo-Christian tradition as an asset of
democracy "is sheer cultural madness."[18]

The impressive agreements just summarized show why both
adults and youth need the best mankind has so far found as
an aid to growth beyond the inadequate types of life which
have prevailed. And there is wide agreement that the best
came to life in One whom young and old, the learned and
the unlettered, through many generations and of many races,
have found to be the wellspring of whatever is best and
purest in the Christian life. Nor should we forget that even
Christian lives do not adequately express or explain him.
Those who have gone farthest with him would be the first
to appreciate the view of H. G. Wells "that to this day this
Galilean is too much for our small hearts." More than ever,
as we have seen, leading Jews recognize this successor of their
great prophets as one through whom both Jew and Christian
may find new light and hope in dark days, and the greatest
unifying influence between them. He it was who, for the
first time in history, absolutely trusted the Unseen, who had
utter confidence that love was at the heart of all things,
utter confidence also . . . in the liberty of that love to help
him. How then can those who differ in age, race, and culture
be given not only religious freedom, but also ample oppor-

tunities to gain intimacy with the mind and heart of this
"pioneer of life"? With him, education is nothing less than
teachable fellowship in the search, the discipline, and the
enjoyment of that Realm of God which he foresaw as both
a growing community on earth, and the consummation of
history.

Questions for Further Thought and Discussion

*How is it possible for children in this urbanized day to have such simple,
elemental experiences as Grant and others are here shown to have had?*

*Are most of those who speak in Jesus' name today concerned with "total
evangelism," which deals with the whole life of the individual and
society?*

*Can you account for the retreat of faith back to the mere "spiritual" or emo-
tional or Sunday life of people, leaving the rest of their lives to the
state and business and amusement?*

*Why is it hard for American students in big universities to achieve education
of the whole personality there?*

*How does current interpretation of the separation of Church and State (in
schools) affect this purpose? What should the Church be doing in this
area?*

18

RECURRING HINDRANCES TO FELLOWSHIP
AND COMMUNITY

Racial and Class Rivalries

THE HINDRANCES to such community as we are seeking can
be better understood and overcome if we study them as they
have prevailed under varying disguises. More than ever the
light of candid inquiry is being turned upon them. So we
have a better opportunity than had earlier generations to see
how primary hindrances, like selfishness, lack of confidence,
and rivalries, are often concealed by plausible expedients.

The work of Jesus was hindered from the start by the
exclusiveness and racial ambitions inculcated for generations
among the Jews. In the time of Jesus, the Jewish rulers were
so absorbed in personal or racial interests that few of them
would even try to understand the universal aspirations of
their great prophets. They thought of God as especially concerned with their own race, and with certain ordinances that
seemed to them essential to prevent contamination from foreigners. They tended, therefore, to exalt legal restrictions at
the expense of fellowship, and to think of God as preoccupied with punishment and repression.

This conception of God as the repressing guardian of a
legal code rather than as the creative Spirit of an expanding
community has persisted in Christianity, despite the larger
aspirations of Hebrew and Christian prophets. It still grows

upon men, as it grew upon the Jewish rulers in the time of
Jesus, when they try, more or less unwittingly, to use God as
a bulwark for special rights or privileges. Then those who
hold political, ecclesiastical, or other positions in the established order become unduly concerned about the institution
to which they owe their power or livelihood; and those who
enjoy the hereditary rights of a ruling or exploiting class
cling to their perquisites. Some groups then accept or promote the concentration of wealth with shortsighted disregard for the general welfare. Others seek monastic or academic seclusion that isolates them from the needs of their
fellows. Thus the fear of change is engendered; and legal or
ritualistic minutiae take precedence over human values.
Then a remote or complacent deity, who will not unsettle
the status quo, is preferred to the intimate and disturbing
God of Jesus. Speculative disputes about God take the place
of enlightening co-operation with him.

Compromise before and after Constantine

Other hindrances to wider social influence by the early
Church, which have their modern counterpart, are typified
by the idolatry on which the Roman government insisted in
public functions. The early Christian found no way to accept office in minor local magistracies, which might have
given wider application to his religion of love; he felt compelled to absent himself even from public ceremonies, because public life was steeped in idolatrous usage.[1] The earliest Christians were less compromising than some of their
successors. They would not burn incense to Caesar.

Yet a clearer understanding between emperors like Marcus
Aurelius and Christians like Origen might have moderated
the idolatrous demands by the Empire, and made possible
more co-operation by Christians. The results of wider outlook on both sides at an early stage might conceivably have
been less disastrous than was the later compromise under
Constantine.

One has not far to look for modern equivalents of the

emperor worship by which the supremacy of the Roman State was symbolized and enforced. The equivalents are found in the restrictions which governments, corporations, and even families, try to place upon the freedom and initiative of the individual. The idolatrous tendency to put the immediate aims of one's own group or nation above the enduring interests of a divine-human community is no small impediment even now; for this idolatry is not confined to an Oriental empire or a European dictatorship. It is present wherever the interests of a government or a class are considered sacred.

A related difficulty in the early Church was the influx of pagan thought and life. This influence became more demoralizing after the alliance between the Church and the Roman Empire had made Christianity fashionable. But even before this alliance was consummated, pagan influence intensified other difficulties. After the second century there was an increase of moral laxity, personal and sectional jealousy, and dependence upon forces very different from those on which Jesus had relied. There was a definite movement in the Church toward centralization of authority, and a hardening of spirit which made the compact with Constantine a less difficult affair than it might have been at an earlier stage. This growing institutionalism made the Church seem more like an end in itself, and obscured the compassion and purpose of Jesus for the world.

Consequently, the Church was more easily persuaded that great advantage would be gained from uniting with the State. Instead of persecution there would be support from the government; instead of poverty, resources of empire; instead of obloquy, the favor of the emperor. The reasons seemed urgent for the union of Church and State.

On the other hand, before the Church began to compromise with the Empire, its members, even under persecution, had become a transforming influence out of all proportion to their numbers. They were little more than a twentieth part of the population of the Empire, but what they lacked in numbers they more than made up by their organization, unity, wealth, and driving power. The Empire was decadent, the Church still full of youthful vigor. The impression made by the vitality, power, and unity of the Church upon Constantine first led the Emperor to consider whether it was not indispensable to the preservation of the Empire.

But after the union of Church and State, the emperor brought his own ways of doing things into the Church, and found not a few who were ready to adopt them. Political methods that had nothing in common with those of Jesus were used on both sides of Church controversies. Coercive measures were relied upon to enforce decisions of Church Councils. Power and position became dangerous incentives. In seeking such things, leaders in the Church, as well as the Church itself, lost vision and independence. Those in authority, no less than their supporters and their opponents, were led further and further from the way in which Jesus sought to give his cause a universal currency.

Instead, therefore, of becoming a distinctively Christian factor in world affairs, the Church won a kind of empire under Constantine and his successors at the cost of its real power. What it gained in external authority, it lost in the more persuasive power of love. It lost in large measure the power to transform the motives of men and to unify their purpose. Wealth, prestige, political methods, and persecution, even to the point of torture and death, were used to enforce outward conformity. But such enforcing bred suspicion, bitterness, antagonism, and other evils born of authority and of subservience. As a result there was inevitable loss of good will and spiritual unity, with a corresponding dissipation of energy in secondary issues.

Long Continued Influence of the Roman Empire

The habit of enforcing conformity and other evils of institutionalism have been intensified ever since by a pervasive though often obscure hindrance—the long continued influence of the Roman Empire, its kind of morality, and its way of governing. "To this day," as John Macmurray explains, "our culture has remained in the Roman mold. It is essentially imperialist, that is to say, its governing ideal is the maintenance and perfecting of an efficient organization of social life, depending on law, industrial management, and the maintenance of power for the defence of law and property. . . . We are Romans at heart, even in our extremes of Fascism and Communism, though like the Romans we are willing to use art and religion so long as they agree to play the part of menials to our ideal of social efficiency. . . . The Romans were deficient on the artistic and on the religious side. They adopted the Greek culture, and then the Christian religion, when they found that mere organization and administrative efficiency could not serve to maintain the unity of the Empire. But they accepted them as tributaries and servants of imperialism, while despising profoundly both Greeks and Christians."[2]

To understand how the liberating religion and ethics of the Hebrew prophets and of Jesus have been hampered by the Roman influence, we must take account of the decisive part that Stoicism has long played in European civilization. Macmurray shows how the Stoic philosophy provided the moral basis for the ruling classes of Rome, and the intellectual framework for Roman law. He traces Stoicism as a determining influence in much Semitic and ostensibly Christian thought and organization, even beyond the Roman pale. We need not accept all his findings to profit from his view that, in large part, European religion became Stoic and Roman rather than Christian or Greek. He shows that Stoicism was most congenial to the instinct for organizing efficiency and to the worship of it as a social ideal, traits common to the Semitic peoples and the Romans. Among the Semitic races this instinct for organization, applied to business, made the Phoenicians the great traders of the ancient world. Applied to religion, it enabled the Hebrews to produce the efficient social system of the Jewish law. Among the Romans the instinct was applied to the organization and legal administration of a vast, expanding government. In the modern world their example has been followed by the English and American peoples.

Side by side with this worship of law and efficiency, however, Macmurray depicts the spirituality of the Hebrews expressing itself in their long line of individual prophets, "who stand out against the background of legal organization and in opposition to it. The prophetic tradition was one of inner vision and emotional response, not of the fixed plan of law and formal obedience. This prophetic tradition culminated and completed itself in Jesus, who insisted that the Sabbath was made for man, not man for the Sabbath, that legal rationalism must be the servant of personal freedom, and that life should be based upon an emotional principle, not an intellectual one."[2] But this principle of love for God and one's neighbor, in which Jesus summed up the Law and the prophets, was limited throughout later history by the dominance of Roman and Stoic legalistic influences. Here we find a real clue to the history of Europe—to the development which has resulted in us and our world.

Lack of Historical Perspective

When we follow such clues through critical periods before and since the fall of the Roman Empire, we see more clearly that another hindrance which brings mental and moral confusion is lack of historical perspective. Many people fail as citizens because they act as though a knowledge of history in relation to human well-being were unimportant. Consequently, they are ignorant of the economic and psychological forces that so largely determine an age and its people. They fail to see how the future depends upon the past, and what of the past should be built upon and what should be discarded or reformed. Without some knowledge of the past, modern men cannot explain failures of earlier years, nor can they have a clear view of the course which leads forward. Lacking knowledge for correcting their own distorted assumptions, they have tried to build a modern culture by mass production in amusements, labor-saving mechanisms, and the ravage of natural resources. "But one cannot build a culture *de novo;* one cannot *build* a culture at all. It must grow. In American life there were seed plots from which a sound and significant culture might have flowered. But the whole impact of modern life has tended to cut connection with that tradition, and to advertise the 'new culture' of a machine age."[3] Fortunately, the barrenness of this imitation of culture is now more evident. There is an awakening also to the importance of those creative spiritual elements in the past of our own country, as well as in the longer experience of the race, which are needed now for a growing democratic culture. If such awareness grows sufficiently, citizens will demand corresponding changes in both juvenile and adult education, in government, and in economic life.

The Fallacy of Abstraction

Another prevalent hindrance to real community is the fallacy of abstraction. Henry Van Dusen throws light on this neglected hindrance: "By abstraction, we mean the mistaking of the part for the whole, or the reading of the whole in terms of some fragmentary part."[3] For example, "Religious folk fasten upon the distinctive experience and creed which have brought liberation to their spirits, and forthwith pronounce heretical, religion which has come to others in radically different fashion. Educators are intrigued by some single theory or branch of knowledge or period of history, exaggerate its significance out of all true proportion, and deny their pupils exposure to other vast areas and periods of knowledge."[3] In research, each science tends to abstract its own selected material from the data of other sciences, often with serious distortion to conclusions. From such abstraction contemporary science is in vigorous reaction. Alfred North Whitehead protests, for instance, that "the increasing departmentalization of universities during the last hundred years, however necessary for administrative purposes, tends to trivialize the mentality of the teaching profession."[4]

Moreover, the *laissez faire* abstractions about freedom, which were used to justify unregulated self-seeking in business, left out of account the resultant suffering of underpaid workers during the industrial revolution. These abstractions convinced many people that the incentive of private profit under *laissez faire* was the cause of the increased prosperity. The prosperity, however, was really due to the release, by scientific discovery and consequent control over Nature, of man's capacity for production. This part of the truth is still omitted from much abstract talk about free enterprise, which often is not free enough, but works for monopoly. Another part of the omitted truth is that a living wage and good working conditions are needed for the well-being of workers, as also for their training in democracy, and therefore should be a first charge upon industry.

At present industry itself suffers from abstractions. The supposed exigencies of mass production too often confine each workman to his particular act or machine. They abstract him from the broader educational experience of the process as a whole, and shut him out of the creative craftsmanship which is the essence and redemptive principle of all true labor. Fortunately, there are increasing attempts, educational and industrial, to correct this tendency. But when an industry is absorbed in making the greatest private profit, it tends to abstract its participant, not only from history, Nature, and culture, but also from the deepest fellowship with his comrades and with God. Obviously, any one thus isolated is in no position to appreciate a commonwealth of universal values such as Jesus envisaged; for then the worker tends to think of his work in terms of the money it will bring to him, rather than in terms of its own worth. His standard of values is debased, and life itself becomes shoddy.

Self-centered Aims of the Church

Thus, racial and class rivalries, the continuing influence of the Roman Empire, the lack of historical perspective, and the lopsided views caused by abstractions, together with economic and vocational factors, considered later, all helped to perpetuate another agelong hindrance to the purpose of Jesus—the adherence by the Church itself to a smaller purpose than his. Long ago the Church began to act as though it were an end in itself. Studies by representative churchmen attribute the collapse of medieval civilization chiefly to this narrowing of aim. "Medieval civilization identified the Church with the Kingdom of God. The Church, instead of promoting the Kingdom, replaced it. This usurpation by the Church, and its disparagement of other modes through which the Kingdom is built, brought with it the inevitable consequences. Catholicism degenerated into the slavish worship of its own organization, and that organization became a tyranny from which men at length revolted."[5]

Nor was the tyranny of organization overcome in the revolt of Protestantism. When that revolt issued in other ecclesiastical organizations with large vested interests, the tendencies toward self-seeking were multiplied. Each growing division of the Church was subjected in turn to "the temptation of all large vested interests—the temptation to make the protection of its own material well-being the dominating influence in its policy."[5] Then the Church suffered, more or less unconsciously, from the related temptation to accommodate itself to the prevailing standards of the business and political world.

With this centering of the Church upon itself, and the emergence of different standards of conduct for clergy and laity, other difficulties were accentuated. Not only the aim of the Church, but the kind of character it engendered, was narrowed. As the churchmen just quoted affirm: "The Church suffered its conception of sanctity to become stereotyped. Its enforced asceticism encouraged a kind of detachment from so-called secular things, which has often been used as an excuse for avoiding the obligations of the common life." When these obligations and many forms of creative work were avoided or disparaged by a rigid asceticism, the religion of the Church appeared emasculated; it lost its appeal for many types of mind. Indeed, "Christian faith becomes insipid and ineffective unless it confronts the world and is proved in the actualities and conflicts of life."[6]

As the Church centered upon itself it narrowed the range of what had been a more communal life. "Religion tended not unnaturally to become a special rather than a pervasive interest. And like other special pursuits, it came to be regarded as primarily the concern of distinct vocational groups, clerical and monastic; whereas for most people it was expected to come in mainly on special occasions, from outside the daily round." Consequently, "for most people busy with everyday living, religion has become increasingly unreal or at least unfamiliar and irrelevant."[7]

Excessive Specialization

The dangers inherent in specialization have not been confined to religion. Groups specializing in science, art, law, finance, or industry became so absorbed in their own abstractions, half-truths, and occupational interests that they neglected the inclusive and teachable kind of fellowship which a more creative society requires. Some benefits of this wider fellowship are suggested by what the Church accomplished in sheltering devotees of learning during the Dark Ages, and by what has been done since then under religious influences or agencies to encourage both the physical and the social sciences and the arts. Nevertheless, the dogmatisms and limited outlook of many spokesmen for religion, interacting with other dogmatisms and limitations among scientists, economists, and other groups, have long tended to separate many who were trying to be, and others who might have become, disciples of Jesus—all of whom should have been working together on the problems of an increasingly interdependent civilization.

Only brief illustrations can be given here of ways in which the professions have been limited in their larger public service. In commending a volume by Jerome Frank on legal procedure, Judge Julian Mack writes: "The last two decades have made it abundantly clear that the just decision of causes requires a careful weighing of social and economic considerations not to be found in the strict body of the law itself. . . . Now Mr. Frank serves timely notice that it does not suffice to consider merely the social and economic facts upon which legal decisions should properly be predicated, but that the very thought processes of the judge and jurist himself must be tested and freed from persistently resurgent childish notions that have no place in an adult civilization. We must become increasingly aware of the difficulties inherent in our necessary use of words to convey thought, of the limitations implicit in the use of formal logic, of the delusive manner in which an oft-repeated legal fiction becomes an axiomatic rule of law. . . . Not the least value of Mr. Frank's study is that it serves to bring home to lawyer and judge alike a better understanding of these deficiencies in his own thought processes. . . . Only when thus awakened can bench and bar achieve their common desire to make the law 'the trewe embodyement of Justice.' "[8]

The profession of teaching is beset by no less serious hindrances to democracy. Forces in the modern world, as H. A. Overstreet points out, "have invaded the teaching profession in a way insidiously destructive of the services which the teaching profession ought to render. . . . In subjects having to do with social, political, and economic relationships, the teacher has been subtly bound by the conventions and opinions of dominant minorities within his society. . . . He has had either to ignore injustices and maladjustments or to suffer the consequences of teaching what powerful interests have found it to their advantage not to have taught. Thus, as economic forces have increasingly controlled our modern life, the teacher has more and more become their instrument, or their victim, or both. . . . It is therefore not surprising at the present time that there are stirrings that indicate an unwillingness to be the mere yes-men of a system that looks suspiciously like one that ought to be renovated. But the grip of the dominating powers can be incredibly great, and the teacher in the end may be defeated. Whether genuine democracy in education will prevail would seem to depend upon whether we shall be willing to take seriously the admonition to seek the truth that it may set us free."[9]

Consolidation of Economic and Political Power

The predicaments of these and other professions, including public servants in many capacities, are complicated by another major hindrance—the consolidation of economic and political power in the hands of comparatively few individuals and groups. This concentration of power has malign influences that reach far beyond the intention or even the knowledge of its manipulators. The danger is exposed in a parallel drawn by Louis Brandeis (later Justice Brandeis) between what has been done in present-day America by the manipulation of other people's money, and what was done in the days when the Roman Republic was undermined. He came to the disquieting conclusion that by similar processes, even in part under republican forms, Caesar Augustus was made master of Rome.[10] This analysis of Brandeis may be too lightly dismissed on the ground that since he wrote, conditions have been changed by recent legislation. Not a few, however, who know the situation from the inside are solicitous about the concentration of power that still exists in comparatively few hands, and about the temptations, subtly disguised, that will press more insistently, even upon patriotic men, when that power is threatened seriously by either democratic or violent measures. The kind of dictatorship sometimes resorted to when property interests are endangered, Bishop McConnell found "more openly advocated today by what are called the favored classes than is a workers' dictatorship by labor leaders. . . . Almost any form of dictatorship might be put upon the American people as long as that control worked secretly, but it could not continue with high effectiveness if it once had to act in the light of full publicity. There is, however, much more danger in an hour like the present of the dictatorship of moneyed groups than of socialist groups."[11]

Some moneyed groups may, even yet, hide behind a streamlined variation of Huey Long, and use the terms and some of the methods of democracy or even of Christianity. They may partially deceive themselves, salving their conscience with benevolent promises. Yet, under this plausible front, they may quietly plan to consolidate their own economic power, only to find themselves at last the supporters and victims of a specious dictator.

On this danger, the history of Germany under Hitler throws much light. It shows how completely freedom may be lost before the people, or even most of the financial, industrial, or political leaders, are fully aware of what is going on. In Germany it was the consolidation of political and economic power that made possible the suppression of democracy. "Whatever part the great barons of the Ruhr and the Rhine played in the early days of the National Socialist movement, there is no doubt that as they saw approaching the crisis of their regime they threw their millions behind Hitler and saved their system. Always a dangerous policy— for a dictator is not fond of acknowledging his debts to his financial benefactors—fascism is entered upon only as a last recourse. Usually the dominant economic group will prefer to manipulate democracy, leaving intact the camouflage of civil freedom. But it is essential to note that the final test for modern democracy does not appear as a clear issue, and the demoralization of public thinking tends to become so chronic that faith in democracy has vanished before the death blow to democracy is struck."[12]

Need for a New Birth of Religion and Democracy

The plight of the church in Germany before Hitler and the related loss of liberty there suggest how essential it is that complete religion and genuine democracy work together, if a civilization of free men is to be achieved. "The Evangelical churches in Germany maintained a rigidly other-worldly emphasis, to the exclusion of a concern for those mundane social and economic matters which play so large a part in the everyday life of the common people." As a result of this attitude and policy of the churches, "the whole field of social reform and critical radical movements was left to the state or to radical secular organizations. The latter, with considerable justification, regarded the church as an institution which had not the least concern in matters of social reform, regarded it even as hostile to movements directed to the social amelioration of the lot of the people." These attitudes have had two very serious consequences. One was so blind a devotion to the state in all its activities "that the church was slow to perceive the true character of the Nazi state, and made no effort to oppose it until the church's very life was menaced. In the time of its greatest need the church found little sympathy from the masses. The other and even more serious consequence of the German church's general social attitude was that it made no contribution whatsoever to those forces and movements which, had they been stronger and more firmly grounded upon ethical conviction, as well as upon political realism, might have prevented the rise of Hitler and carried through the social revolution to a successful conclusion."[12]

In other lands, as well as in Germany, the Reformation started Protestantism in the direction of a more complete democratization of life, but it soon encountered unexpected hindrances. In theory the Reformation set men free from the divine right of kings, ecclesiastics, and all authoritarian usurpers. It began to recover the priesthood and prophetic function of each believer. It stressed the primacy of a transforming faith rather than a legalistic attitude in religion. Before long, however, these vital principles were obscured in a controversy with Catholicism about the Bible as a substitute for an infallible church. "Gradually the absolute book replaced the absolute church." Authoritarian tendencies and the letter of the law once more quenched the prophetic spirit and hindered wide applications of the gospel of love. This result was inevitable where churches tried to interpret the entire Old Testament, including vindictive passages and wars, on the same ethical level as that of Jesus, and judged heretical those who differed from their particular theory of revelation.

There was another reason for the failure of many to make prophetic applications of the gospel to current social issues. "The distinctive doctrine of justification by faith was so misinterpreted as to give men assurance of salvation while ignoring their complicity in those sins of the corporate life which according to the prophets and Jesus inexorably alienate men from God."[13]

For the completion of the Reformation and its democratizing of life we obviously need a new birth of fellowship and prophetic insight, seeking universal practice of "justice and mercy and faithfulness," as Jesus and prophetic statesmen sought them.[a] Fellowship in these "weightier matters," disclosing unrealized possibilities of human and divine love, would make for a democracy not merely political, but also economic, ethical, and spiritual. Such democracy is more than a form of government; it is a way of seeking complete community. It needs the wholehearted co-operation of many more citizens, inside and outside the church, seeking ways to overcome in themselves hindrances to adequate community.

Questions for Further Thought and Discussion

Must Christians always be a dynamic minority to be effective: is this a faith which withers when it is adopted by the great majority?

What are the greatest obstacles to fellowship and democracy in your local community today?

Why are temptations for the Church to become over-institutionalized today just as great as they were under Constantine or the medieval popes or nineteenth-century denominationalism?

What evidences can be given that the Church today has sold its prophetic birthright in return for acceptance by the everyday world?

Can you point out tendencies in religion today to over-emphasize doctrine or liturgy, while under-emphasizing Christian social claims?

What do Christians pledge when they unite with the Church?

19

HALF RELIGION VERSUS COMPLETE COMMUNITY

A Divided Mind in the Church about Aims

FOR MORE LIGHT on how the growth of community is constantly hindered in the modern world, we turn now to what D. S. Cairns called the root of the trouble today in Christendom. It is the absence of a common Christian mind in the Church about the great questions and aims of civilization. In explaining this trouble, he begins with the weakness of faith, hope, and love in the European and American world. In what these qualities involve for personal and family life he finds Christians more or less agreed; but when he asks what kind of world-society corresponds to these qualities in the individual, he finds confusion. "There is no common mind or standard as to what constitutes a Christian civilization. . . . The Church has never thought out in its fullness the kind of nation, of international life, of industry and society that are alone in harmony with faith, hope and love, and the Christian idea of God. Having no such adequate ideal itself, or clear objective at which to aim, it has, of course, failed to capture the world for it. . . . It has left great places in its moral demands, and into these empty houses there have entered the seven devils of national self-interest and the greed of personal gain."[1]

244

This moral confusion, in which the modern Church partook of the spirit of the age, was intensified by its increasing withdrawal from the sphere of public and corporate morality. In spite of limitations, the Church at the high point of the Middle Ages had a conception of religion which included all of life. "It dominated the state, regulated public and private conduct, and gave laws to govern economic and political behavior." As Professor Winfred Ernest Garrison says, "Early Protestantism carried over the idea of giving religion control of all conduct. The Genevan state, for example, virtually destroyed the distinction between sacred and secular authority; and the basic idea of Puritanism was that of a 'holy state' in which all laws should be expressions of the will of God."[2] Whatever we may think of the way this theory was applied, we must admit at least that it did not undermine the independence of the Church or its obligation to educate its members in public morality. In Germany, however, as a result of unhappy circumstances in which both church and state were involved, the moral authority of the Church was confined to the sphere of personal conduct. In Protestant lands generally the rising spirit of nationalism and the increasing demands of business came gradually to exert such influence that the Church was relegated to a secondary place. "The state became the inclusive category, and the Church merely one of the institutions which existed within its shelter—a unique one, to be sure, but only one among many. By the middle of the seventeenth century, especially in England, political action no longer sought religious sanctions; and economic policies were judged as profitable or unprofitable rather than as right or wrong. The new science of political economy took the place of the Church's moral authority as the guide for Christians in their economic transactions. John Wesley could simplify the rules of Christian economics to this: 'Get all you can; save all you can; give all you can.' But how should a Christian get? The Church had little to say about that, so long as the more obvious forms of theft and fraud were avoided. And so it continued with only slight exception through the eighteenth century and the early part of the nineteenth."[2]

Half-truths Obscuring the Aims Shown by Jesus

This confusion about the relation between private and public morality has long been worse confounded by certain half-truths of wide currency, which still control policy even when they would be rejected in principle. A summary discussion of these half-truths, for which we are deeply indebted to John Bennett, may help to clear up the confusion.[3]

First half-truth: "That individuals can rise above any conceivable combination of social circumstances, and that therefore it is misplaced zeal to become deeply concerned about changing those circumstances." There is one simple answer to this half-truth: "Only the spiritually developed person can rise above all external circumstances; and the world is inhabited chiefly by persons in the early stages of spiritual development. It is not enough for the world to be a gymnasium for saints." It should be a good school for the rest of us. Most of us are influenced adversely, directly or indirectly, by certain factors in the modern world: poverty, wealth, concentration of power, war, a profit-seeking society, and as an inevitable consequence of these, a depersonalizing of the common life. This depersonalizing of relationships makes it difficult for youth or adult to feel that he "belongs" to any real community or cause, and to be sensitive to divine and human realities. The insidious consequences of all these factors in modern life are so ramified that even a strong man by himself is unable to escape the entangling web.

Second half-truth: "That since individuals control institutions and systems it is enough to change individuals." This half-truth is one of the most common assumptions of Christian people. It gains plausibility because, when we change laws or systems, we often find that without changed men we have gained nothing.

But changed men may not be changed enough. Even devoted Christians may suffer unwittingly from distorting blind spots. A general conversion does not necessarily remove these blind spots, especially when they result from the interests, habits, and prejudices of a privileged group. All this may be seen for our warning in the ominous conduct of certain English evangelicals of the last century who ignored the plight of suffering workers in the industrial revolution, though at the same time they were most zealous for the abolition of slavery. One of their leaders, William Wilberforce, saw clearly the evils of slavery. He fought against these evils all his life, in spite of opposition and reproaches from his own class. Yet he regarded trade-unions among the poor workers of England as economically unsound and politically dangerous. His biographer admits: "Genuinely anxious as he was that the state should relieve the poor he would not allow the poor to use the one weapon by which they could relieve themselves."[4] His indifference to removable causes of their poverty was characteristic of a group of Christians who were exceptional in their devotion to the antislavery crusade. Yet even they were so limited by the perspective of their own class that they were "as callous as the employers and landlords, themselves, to the sufferings of the English poor under the changes wrought by the industrial revolution."[5]

Moreover, "in the present economic system the best individual employers may be quite helpless in living up to their own insight unless there is general political and economic change. They are caught by the system at two points. They cannot remain solvent unless they can compete successfully with other employers, and unless the masses of people can buy their goods. If they alone pay higher wages, abolish child labor, establish social insurance, etc., they are in constant danger of being undercut by less enlightened competitors unless they have monopolistic control, which is in itself a menace."[3] Also the individual employer and employee are both at the mercy of the market. If the economic system is not adapted to distribute wealth more equitably, and to create generally adequate purchasing power, there will be constant danger that the enlightened employer will lose a sufficient market, even though he does pay high wages, and that eventually his own workers will lose their jobs.

Other dangers grow with this exclusive emphasis upon converting the individual employer. Even if exceptional circumstances permit him in an individualistic capacity to give higher wages or other advantages to his workers, he runs into the dangers of paternalism—the danger of developing servility and dependence in the workers, the danger of feeding his own will to power and of enlarging his own blind spots, and the danger of making all improvement depend upon the whim or the conscience of the employer, who is subject to change. No paternalistic experiment is a substitute for a real sharing of economic power.

Third half-truth: "That you can change society without changing individuals." This half-truth is not as prevalent among Christians as are the other two. Many Christians see clearly that good systems, unless operated by good men, will inevitably be perverted by selfish men, who can use any system for their own ends. The evils in any system are rooted partly in human nature, in its love of power and prestige, of comfort and pleasure. What is needed in any new or changed system is that the system itself shall give greater opportunity and incentive to the best in every man, and discourage the worst, and that it shall be progressively adapted to serve the general well-being. There will always be need for those who can do their best work in changing systems, and for those who can do their best work in changing persons. To do their best work, however, each must appreciate and foster what the other contributes in a common cause.

The Wider Outlook of the Christian Community

To attain this wider outlook, to outgrow the blinding effects of half-truths and one-sided religion, we need to think and live as members of a growing community like that which Jesus proposed to his first disciples. "What he stood for was a real community of equals whose standards of prosperity were personal and not impersonal, whose bond was service, whose foundation was good will, whose scope was international, and whose method was love. Christianity, therefore, is by its nature committed to the cause of the democratic movement; if it is true to its own genius and loyal to its own Founder, it stands squarely with the vast mass of the toilers of the world."[6]

When we share a real community of interest with the toilers of the world, as thus interpreted by B. C. Plowright, we find certain sayings and acts of Jesus that may have seemed vague or remote, suddenly becoming pertinent for present conditions. When, for instance, Jesus saw that his nation, which expected to rule in the Kingdom of God on earth, would not provide the conditions for its coming, he told its leaders the parable of the wicked husbandmen who played false with the resources entrusted to them. Then he added: "That, I tell you, is the reason why the Kingdom of God will be taken away from you and given to a nation producing the fruits of it."[a] To understand this pronouncement we must remember that the Aramaic word translated "nation" is easily susceptible of being translated "community" or "people," and does not necessarily imply the politically created and circumscribed nation as we know it. Accordingly, the translation, "the Kingdom of God will be given *to a people* producing the fruits of it," helps us to understand the thought of Jesus. He meant that the new order of society must come through a new kind of people— a people profoundly different in attitude, purpose, and method from the leaders to whom he spoke. This necessity for a changed people gives point to his assurance to the disciples, "Fear not, little flock, for it is your Father's good pleasure to give you the Kingdom."[b]

These statements throw light also upon the purpose of Jesus as it emerged in the training of those who were to carry on his work. His purpose became more evident during a closing period of his ministry, when he gave them unhurried time in regions remote from interruption by the popu-

lace or by his opponents. Other careful students share Plowright's view that the purpose of this training was to prepare
disciples to be the fellowship and community that could
represent and further the Kingdom of God in this world.
"In his despair of his own particular nation, Jesus turned, as
an alternative and as embodying the true, actual and yet
ideal community, to the Christian fellowship. *The Christian
fellowship is Christ's alternative to political community. He
had ceased to trust to a political community based on race,
blood, and self-interest for the inauguration of the Kingdom,
and now looked to a community based on faith in himself
and loyalty to himself, organized on the basis of good will,
as the harbinger and bearer of the principles and conditions
which God could answer with the Kingdom of God.* He
trusted for the redemption of society to a Christian community—if we choose to state it so, to the Church."[6]

If we use the word "church" in this connection, we should
remember what the word so translated meant to those who
first used it to designate the kind of community inaugurated
by Jesus. They chose, we have seen, a word used in the old
free commonwealth of Greece for the general assembly of
all free citizens by which their common life was governed—
a word that survived in the restricted municipal self-government permitted by the Roman state and was taken over by
brotherhoods and guilds. "Among the Jews who spoke Greek,
this word, *ecclesia,* seemed the appropriate one to describe
the commonwealth of Israel as ruled by God."[7] The history
of the word, which the New Testament writers used to designate the early Church, supports the view before us of what
Jesus meant the Church to be and to do. "He could not and
did not think of it as an occasional fellowship, but as a true
community, a real society. All the conditions which were
characteristic of true community were to be true of the new
community."[6]

This explanation does not imply that the New Community or Church is identical with the Kingdom of God, or
that it is the only mode through which the Kingdom comes.

It does make clear that a society which is true in practice to Christian principles helps immeasurably to foster moral personality and a Christian social order, whereas a society that practices unchristian principles does much to distort both the personal and the collective life of men. Consequently, we must beware of all presentations of the gospel that do not have as their background God's concern for the creation of true community. "We must suspect all forms of evangelism—especially if they be financed by wealthy laymen or women—which try to insulate God and Man from the concerns of community, and dub matters of social righteousness, secular. That is a form of religion which puts God in an almost complete moral vacuum, asserts that God is related to the world only through individuals and not through the society which, humanly speaking, is God's instrument in shaping their life and controlling their thought."[6]

From this separation of sacred from so-called secular, of spirit from body, of the individual from a transformed and transforming community, we should have been saved, as Plowright explains, if the Church and its members had continued to live as Jesus lived and called his disciples to live. He spent himself to bring health, wholeness, to the bodies as well as to the spirits of men, and he united his disciples in a fellowship of faith and love, designed to give the Spirit of God free course to transform the entire life of men. To live thus in true community as sons of God "makes religion a real adventure of the whole man instead of an adventure of the emotions and the intellect. It bids men do and dare in the world of affairs, and not simply make tentative experiments in the world of private and semiprivate relationships. And Jesus offers only one warrant for such bold decision. God is a God who cares, cares as the early Church rightly saw, to the point of giving himself to the uttermost."[6]

Communist Challenge to the Christian Community

Through this insight of Jesus and the early Church, we are brought to a fundamental component of faith in God not confined to church, synagogue, or any organized religion. Many in the modern world, repudiating what they suppose religion to be, yet devoting themselves to what they hope will be a classless society, are sustained by an underlying confidence in some power or process in history which furthers, they believe, the growth of a world-wide community. In explaining this fact, John Macmurray presents both a contrast and a possible point of contact between Christianity and communism in their better forms. He presents communism also as a challenge that Christianity be put to the test of its initial beliefs. All this goes to show that it is not safe to dismiss the appeal of communism and its propagating power on the ground that some of its self-constituted leaders have been discredited, or that others have turned from its earlier aims. Communism at its best, as Macmurray shows, "seems to have recaptured the capacity to live as part of the whole of things. The communist lives by a faith in a power, which he calls in his own jargon 'the process of history,' which guides and determines the destiny of mankind. As a result he feels himself to be an instrument through which this power is here and now achieving its purpose of creating a true and universal society in the world. The Christian would call it the 'Kingdom of Heaven on Earth'; the communist, of course, would not. But what he means is a real, universal brotherhood of mankind based upon equality and freedom."[8] He sees his own life as merely a single incident in the process by which this purpose for humanity is being achieved. Therefore he can endure hardship, suffer persecution, and even give his life willingly for this great purpose; for he believes that he must resist at all cost whatever opposes the "process of history." He is convinced that in spite of, and even through, all human opposition it must eventually triumph, because it corresponds to the reality of the world. His belief is more than the recognition of this truth; it is the capacity to live in the confidence this truth inspires. This capacity is not all of the Christian belief in God, but it is an essential part of it.

Although this much of the communist confidence in the possibilities of complete community resembles that of the early Christians, most communists do not find corresponding attitudes or practices in organized Christianity as they know it; and, for that reason in part, they have repudiated all religion, at least in name. They do this in accordance with the dictum of Marx: "Let us turn from ideas to reality, let us look not at people's theories but at their actions. It is by seeing how societies and their institutions work in practice and not by accepting their own ideal accounts of what they are after, that we shall understand their real faith." Accordingly, the communist thinks that the significance of believing in God can be discovered by finding what attitudes to life and what forms of social behaviour are fostered by the Christian churches. He concludes from what he has seen of them that, however they may talk about it, they are not urgently concerned with establishing throughout the world a society of free and equal brotherhood. He thinks that the adherents of the churches shrink from the demands that such a brotherhood makes upon them, retreat into passive or active opposition in defense of their own private or national interests, and conceal their retreat by a smoke screen of idealistic verbiage. He counts these church members, therefore, as in some ways the most dangerous, because the most disingenuous, of the enemies of real human brotherhood. "These are the people," he says, "who believe in God, and therefore this is the true practical significance of religion." So he thinks that "nothing is left for him but a total repudiation of religion. Only by a profession of atheism can he maintain his own faith."[8]

The fact that communism provides a faith for living for millions of people, especially young people, who have never encountered any faith which put so much meaning into life, gives urgency to John Bennett's statement of a well-tested alternative: "There is no other faith which can compare with communism except Christianity. Christianity, when its full meaning is not hidden by one-sided teaching or distorted by

alliances between the Church and privileged groups, is a
faith that can meet the need of those who struggle for more
equal justice in the social order. It will help them to understand how quickly new collocations of power may become
the source of new forms of injustice. It will enable them to
relate all that they do for the transforming of society to the
depths of their personal lives and to the ultimate purpose of
God. The first responsibility of the Christian community is
not to save any institutions from communism, but to present
its own faith by word and life to the people of all conditions
and of all lands that they may find for themselves the essential truth about life."[9]

Why Communism and Some Rivals Fail Community

The evidence multiplies that something essential to community is lacking in the faith and practice of Marxist communism, as surely as in half-religion and its half-truths. What
this Marxist faith and philosophy lead to, in spite of their
plausible ideals, is well summarized by one who shared with
deep devotion in the struggle of labor, and who can speak
from intimate knowledge of both general labor and communist movements: "The startling thing about the labor
movement, especially in its more thoroughly Marxist phases,"
says A. J. Muste, "is not its anti-capitalism, but precisely that,
in spite of surface differences, its underlying assumptions are
similar to those of our industrialist, capitalist civilization at
its worst, and that unless the labor movement is purified,
deepened, and spiritualized, it too will contribute to the
dissolution rather than the redemption of our civilization.
Among devotees of Marx and Lenin, as among those to
whom our industrial capitalist economy is God, one encounters the same preoccupation with material abundance as the
master key to all human problems, with consequent subordination of cultural and spiritual life to economics; the same
faith in the sufficiency of external changes, with corresponding indifference to the inner life of the soul; the same degra-
dation of morality into expediency, with easy resort to the

doctrine that the end justifies the means; the same reliance upon power, domination, violence, with the same lapse into ruthlessness at critical times; the same contempt for humility and fellowship; the same inability to break with war; the same confining of man's life exclusively to this world—the secularizing of all life."[10] These tendencies, obviously, are not confined to totalitarian states. They have long been gathering head everywhere; and they still threaten both democracy and religion throughout the world.

An Awakening to "Christ's Christianity"

All this corruption of good ends by pernicious means and the failures of half-religion give poignant urgency to what the church and other organizations and individuals could have done and should now do. It is now recognized more widely than ever, as affirmed by that harbinger of a more united Church, the Oxford Ecumenical Conference on Church, Community, and State, "that the irreligion of modern radicalism was in large measure due to the failure of the Church to understand the problem of social justice in the modern age and to bear clear testimony in favor of justice in the various crises of our era."[11]

Yet this responsibility and failure of both Church and synagogue in the past does not excuse any individual, least of all at this time when the most promising movements for effective, united thought and action are under way in and through the Church. Whether one has been blinded or repelled by the half-truths and half-religion, which we have examined, he now has a unique opportunity to further the awakening that already has begun. Not only is there now increasing dissatisfaction with the conventional compromises of religion; there is also greater eagerness to discover just what the faith and purpose of Jesus really mean for the increase of community, both on a world-wide scale and at our own door. Herbert Gray voices widespread misgiving and aspiration when he says: "What if our common Christianity is in some essential respects different from Christ's Christianity? What if in his name we have been proclaiming something less and even something different from the gospel of the Kingdom of God? That would at least explain the disconcerting facts of today. It may be that from very early times we have taken from him so much less than he meant to give that the religion we have professed and practiced is actually a religion without power."[12] This much, at least, is more than ever admitted: partial acceptance of the teaching of Jesus and makeshift procedure at variance with his aim and method have disastrously failed to meet the needs of free and equal brotherhood. To admit that the policy of compromise and expediency has failed may be a turning point in the affairs of men, if only enough of them will make a fair trial, personally and corporately, of the whole truth and practice of the gospel of the Kingdom of God. "This is the opportunity of today," as Kenneth Latourette and many others see the Christian outlook. "The Kingdom of God can be entered. The world waits for those who will even now live as in the Kingdom."[13]

All this and much more about the relation of Christ and the Kingdom of God to history, and about our consequent opportunity, is brought together in an essay, written in consultation with many British and American leaders, by Archbishop Temple. He was deeply concerned to find with others a basis of common understanding and action for the postwar years.[13] In contrast to the still current and confusing Greek view that "history makes no fundamental difference to our understanding of reality," he explains the Christian view: "It is in history that the ultimate meaning of human existence is both revealed and actualized. If history is to have a meaning, there must be some central point at which that meaning is decisively disclosed. . . . For Christians the decisive meaning of history is given in Christ."

This view of history "confronts us with two urgent practical tasks. The first is to disabuse the minds of people of the notion, which is widespread and infects much current preaching, that Christianity is in essence a system of morals. Thus many people have lost all understanding of the truth, so prominent in the New Testament, that to be a Christian is to share in a new movement of life, and to co-operate with new regenerating forces that have entered into history.

"The second task is to restore hope to the world through a true understanding of the relation of the Kingdom of God to history, as a transcendent reality that is continually, though partially, being embodied in the activities and conflicts of the temporal order." (This means, as the Archbishop said elsewhere: "We may not hope for the Kingdom of God in its completeness here, but we are to pray for its coming and to live even now as its citizens. And here we find ourselves actually belonging to a fellowship which is an earthly counterpart of the City of God, though many of us are hardly aware of it and all of us are frequently forgetful of it. The City of God, which has sometimes appeared as a beleaguered fortress, again stands before us with gates wide open so that citizens of all nations may enter. Yes; here is one great ground of hope for the coming days—this world-wide Christian fellowship, this ecumenical movement, as it is often called.")

All this is part of the background for the conclusion: "In the tasks of society Christians can and must co-operate with all those, Christians or non-Christians, who are pursuing aims that are in accord with the divinely intended purpose of man's temporal life. But Christians are constrained to believe that in the power of the gospel of redemption and in the fellowship of the Church lies the chief hope of the restoration of the temporal order to health and sanity.

"What none but utopians can hope for the secular world should be a matter of actual experience in the Church. For the Church is the sphere where the redemptive act of God lifts men into the most intimate relation with himself and through that with one another. When this is actually experienced the stream of redemptive power flows out from the Church through the lives of its members into the society which they influence. But only a Church firm in the faith outlined earlier can give to its members the inspiration which they need for meeting the gigantic responsibilities of this age. Spiritual resources far beyond anything now in evidence will be needed. It may be that the greatness of the challenge will bring home to Christians how impotent they are in themselves, and so lead to that renewal which will consist in rediscovery of the sufficiency of God and manifestation of his power."[14]

Questions for Further Thought and Discussion

Is Communism's challenge to the Church nowadays waning or growing?

Which seem uppermost in Christianity today: "individual" or "social" concerns?

So far as we can judge by our Lord's definition of The Kingdom, are there many people today who are outside the Church and yet members of The Kingdom?

Has Communism a more realistic sense of "living in history" today than Christianity?

What dangers lurk in sharing efforts with those who work today the same ends, but from presuppositions different from ours?

20

THE USE OF POSSESSIONS TO FOSTER FELLOWSHIP

Early Christian Possessions Fostered Fellowship

WHAT HAVE THINGS to do with fellowship or with those inner conflicts that disrupt fellowship and hinder the growth of community? Much more than at first appears, the early Christians discovered, and this discovery revolutionized the use of their possessions. They found many ways in which things could either enlarge and enrich their relations with one another, or else limit and distort them. And they became so keenly aware that everything of enduring value for them was dependent on that right relation which is fellowship, that they made it the determining factor in the use of all possessions. Of the original company in Jerusalem "no one said that any of the things which he possessed was his own," because "those who believed were of one heart and soul,"ᵃ and they desired to use all that they had to foster the growth of a community of love, which was for them the supreme temporal good.

The spontaneous way in which they made the development of fellowship decisive in all questions about their possessions has been obscured by different interpretations. Sometimes their conduct has been belittled as fanaticism. Sometimes it has been either extolled or denounced as a systematic application of communism. Yet the freedom from any enforced system is seen in the treatment of the notorious two who tried to gain credit on false pretenses for what they had done with their property. The offence with which Ananias and Sapphira were charged was deception, not refusal to obey a communistic rule. It is evident from what Peter said to them that their land and the proceeds from its sale were both at their own disposal.[b] What was expected of them, however, was a voluntary sharing for the good of the entire brotherhood, and this illustrates the early Christian conception of property as a means to foster fellowship.

The freedom shown by these early groups in using their possessions for mutual advantage may be hard for us to understand. We are so enmeshed in a system which subordinates human values to property rights that we are often unconscious victims of a standard of values very different from theirs. All the more, therefore, may we profit from the insight that came with their sense of detachment from their possessions.

Their attitude was one of freedom from the dominance of things. The inalienable rights of property did not loom forebodingly on their horizon, nor obscure for them the greater human values. They were not afraid that they might be committed to some dangerous economic theory. They did not even approach the question from the side of economics. They had few, if any, vested interests, no institutions to be supported, no large contributors who might be offended. Despite notable exceptions, they were carried beyond the inhibitions of fear and excessive caution that so often follow in the wake of wealth. The further they went in the discoveries and projects of fellowship, the greater was their zest in using things for the good of the entire brotherhood.

They helped the destitute not only in their own communities but also in distant lands. At the same time they discouraged idleness: "If any man will not work, neither let him eat."[c] And they found work for those who were in need of it. The right to employment was recognized. "What bound the members together," said Harnack, "was not merely the duty of supporting one another; it was the fact that they formed a guild of workers in the sense that the churches had to provide work for a brother whenever he required it. . . . The churches were also labor unions."[1]

The fearlessness of these early disciples in making all possessions tributary to the growth of brotherhood doubtless came more easily to them because they expected an early end of the age. This expectation has often been emphasized to belittle their experience with property. Their hope of an early return of their Master would make them less concerned about accumulating earthly goods; but it by no means invalidates their insight into the results of piling up wealth and hankering after it. This insight has been confirmed so often in history that it cannot be lightly dismissed or safely ignored. Its relevance for us is clarified by what Jesus said and did about property.

Jesus Shows Peril and Possibility of Possessions

When a man out of the crowd appealed to Jesus in a dispute about an inheritance, Jesus refused to take part in dividing it because he could see from the man's attitude that no mere division of property would establish right relations between the brothers who were at variance. Instead of attempting any external solutions, therefore, he went to the root of the difficulty by saying: "Take heed, and beware of all covetousness: for a man's life does not consist in the abundance of his possessions." He warned them by the plight of a rich man who made a failure of himself when he planned to enlarge his barns. "So it is," Jesus said, "with him who amasses treasure for himself but has no riches in God."[d] Such a man fails also to enrich fellowship among men. The self-seeker loses his capacity for neighborliness. He has already failed in his relation with God.

Jesus saw the double danger that, frequently, while "the rich man's heart is lost in his treasure, the poor man's heart is lost in his worries." So he sought to relieve the anxiety of his disciples by instilling deeper confidence in God and in one another. He asked them to consider the birds and the wild flowers for which God cares, saying: "How much more are you worth than birds . . . and how much more will he care for you! O men how little you trust him! So do not seek food and drink and be worried; pagans make food and drink their aim in life, but your Father knows quite well that you need that. Only seek his Kingdom and these things shall be given you in addition. Dismiss your fears, little flock; your Father finds pleasure in giving you the Kingdom."[e]

In other words, Jesus held that no insurmountable difficulties in providing the necessaries of life for all exist in the nature of things. On the contrary, he believed that right relations of men with one another, and with the creative power and natural resources in the universe, would meet the needs of everyone. He saw that these relationships and resources had never been adjusted and cultivated for the good of all. If they were cultivated with confidence and good will, he was sure that they would overcome paralyzing fears and wasteful rivalries; they would reveal the things most worth living for; they would provide a simple sufficiency for the ordinary needs of men. Jesus was not deluding men with a dream of an easygoing or miraculous supply of food and clothing; he was proposing a widespread community of love as the one far-seeing, realistic way to meet all the needs of a developing society. Many of the ablest men who are familiar with present conditions are in substantial agreement with this conviction of Jesus. A commission of such men, investigating the actual difficulties of modern industrial life, found that "the supreme claims of the Kingdom of God and the world's need of deliverance coincide."[2]

Jesus saw, however, that men will never discover the relation between their own deliverance and the supreme claims of the Kingdom of God unless they make this new order of faith and mutuality the determining factor in the use of everything they possess. If they seek first private profit or personal ambition they will disrupt the process. They must make all things tributary to this better state of mind and of affairs in which each will seek his neighbor's good as he would seek his own.

It follows, therefore, as Jesus taught, that this art of loving one's neighbor as one's self requires an attitude of detachment from the things which might hinder it. There are those who cannot attain this attitude without actually parting from their possessions. Under such conditions there is no alternative. "Sell all you have—then come and follow me," Jesus told the young ruler who came to him eagerly, but went away sorrowful because he was rich.[f] With the insight of love, Jesus discerned the young man's master passion and could not acquiesce in the frustration of a divided heart and mind. He knew that "where your treasure is, there will your heart be also." "You cannot serve God and money."[g] And, "What does it benefit a man to gain the whole world and forfeit his life? For what could a man give to buy back his life?"[h] Jesus saw that the young man must turn his distracted attention from the possessions by which he was obsessed; he must fix his mind upon something larger and better than his conflicting interests. What Jesus asked him to do, therefore, was to throw off his chief handicap, the better to serve his fellow men in a new society—and to find his own fulfillment in so doing.

Even where wealth is not a chief temptation, Jesus saw that it tends to disqualify its possessor for the best service in a neighborly society. The false feeling of security engendered by wealth tends to divert men from a wholesome dependence upon their neighbors, and upon God. Not only does large wealth make men unduly independent of others, it "gives them a power over their fellows which is good for neither."[3] It tends also to confine its possessor to the intimacies and interests of the privileged few, and to permit only a superficial acquaintance with the life and thought of the vast majority of mankind. Even when he has the best intentions, the rich man is likely to be treated as one apart from the great body of his fellow men. Then, on both sides, fel-

lowship is limited; unbiased judgment and disinterested co-
operation become more difficult; the brotherly life is handicapped. This often happened in the later history of the
Church. "Fellow Christians, despite their occasional emotional unity, never really got together in their religion, because the common business of life was excluded from their
hours of religious fellowship. Economic well-being never became a common end. They pursued it separately."[4] The rich
man, moreover, is peculiarly tempted to accept these conditions as inevitable. It is easy for him to be lulled to contentment with things as they are. And such contentment blinds
him to the changes that are needed to realize the unity of
the Family of God. Hence the warning of Jesus: "How difficult it is for those who have money to get into the Realm
of God."[i] The more a man's aim and way of living separate
him from the common needs of his fellows and from comradeship with them, the more likely he is to miss many
fruitful experiences of fellowship.

These tendencies, however, lie deeper than any external
manner of life and are by no means confined to the rich.
Riches, as both Jesus and his early disciples realized, imperil
not only those who possess them, but all who trust in them,
who hanker after them, who are unduly absorbed by them.
The difficulty, the early Christians saw, is not in property
itself, which has vast possibilities for the good of all, but in
selfish desire and struggle for it. They traced this struggle
even in the lives of some who did not acquire wealth: "What
causes wars and contentions among you? Is it not the passions which are ever at war in your natures? . . . You are
envious and cannot gain your end; you fight and make war.
You have not because you ask not. You ask and receive not,
because you ask amiss that you may spend it in your pleas-
ures."[j] From another part of the early Christian world the
same difficulty is emphasized: "From love of money, all sorts
of evil arise." "People who want to be rich fall into temptation and a snare, and into many unwise and pernicious
cravings which sink mankind in destruction and ruin."[k]

An Acquisitive Society Intensifies the Peril

Careful investigations show that these pernicious cravings are encouraged by the present industrial system: "What is fundamentally wrong is the present emphasis on self-interest."[5] This conclusion of a representative committee in the United States is reinforced by the findings of a similar commission in Great Britain. Both groups voice the collective judgment of able men, familiar with modern industrial and economic life, who approached their investigations from various points of view. The British commission finds that "if anything stands out clearly today, it is that the policy of self-interest has brought and is bringing ruin in its train."[6]

What, then, do these investigators find to be the first essential? The committee in the United States came to this conclusion:[5] "The one thing now most essential is to have done with the idea that the chief purpose of an industry is the private profit of those by whom it is carried on. Industry must be regarded as a social function, carried on to serve the community. Instead of an 'acquisitive society' organized around the promoting of individual wealth-getting, we must have what an English economist has called a 'functional society,' aiming to make the acquisition of wealth contingent upon the discharge of social obligations, to proportion remuneration to service and deny it to those by whom no service is performed, to inquire always 'not what men possess, but what they can make, or create, or achieve.'[7] In the language of recent psychological studies, we must subordinate the acquisitive impulses to the creative. With these conclusions may be compared the words of a distinguished American industrial engineer: 'A nation whose business system is based on service will in a short time show such advancement over one whose business system is operated primarily [for] profits for the investing class, that the latter nation will not be long in the running.' "[8]

Acquisitive impulses are found to be strong under the present system largely "because we organize our industrial

life around an appeal to this motive. . . . We do not know
what resources of human nature are latent and unused, because we constantly assume that competitive seeking of private profits is the only foundation for our economic life. . . .
We have an elusive circle in which men are selfish largely
because our social order appeals to selfishness, and in which
our present social order has so many evils because men are
selfish. We shall effectively break the circle only as we definitely undertake to center our industrial life around another
motive than the pursuit of private profit."[5]

As a matter of fact, when the motive of service is given a
fair chance it often becomes a transforming power. This is
seen in the lives of many Christian ministers, teachers, physicians, and also industrial managers when personal contacts
are maintained. Experts and salaried managers frequently
respond to the motive of service without regard to personal
profit. "They give themselves to their work because they
find in it the satisfaction of the instinct of workmanship and
of the desire to do things worth while. . . . The stupendous
achievement of the Panama Canal is carried through by an
army officer on an army officer's modest salary."[5]

To foster this better motive, however, "outer changes are
necessary, because either for good or ill the surroundings
affect the inner spirit. The individual and the social environment constantly act and react on each other. . . . The new
motive and the better organization must therefore develop
together. The transformation of character should lead to
transformation of environment and the bettered environment in turn minister to further transformation of character."[5]

Social Motive Seen at the Heart of Industry

Although there is much in modern business to obstruct
these larger social motives, the necessity for them is demonstrated at the very center of our industrial life. Here we find
progress dependent upon men whose entire work compels

them to cultivate disinterestedness. "Whatever the motives which cause men to endow laboratories, to work patiently in laboratories, or to buy the products, the fact remains," says Walter Lippmann, "that inside the laboratory, at the heart of this whole business, the habit of disinterested realism in dealing with the data is the indispensable habit of mind. Unless this habit of mind exists in the actual research, all the endowments and honorary degrees and prize awards will not produce the results desired. This is an original and tremendous fact in human experience: that a whole civilization should be dependent upon technology, that this technology should be dependent upon pure science, and that this pure science should be dependent upon a race of men who consciously refuse, as Mr. Bertrand Russell has said, to regard their 'own desires, tastes, and interests as affording a key to the understanding of the world.'" This does "not mean merely that scientists tell themselves that they must ignore their prejudices. They have developed an elaborate method for detecting and discounting their prejudices. It consists of instruments of precision, an accurate vocabulary, controlled experiment, and the submission not only of their results but their processes to the judgment of their peers. This method provides a body in which the spirit of disinterestedness can live." Scientific discipline has become, as Graham Wallas would say, an essential part of our social heritage. For the machine technology requires a population that in some measure partakes of the spirit which created it.[9]

And yet, Lippmann admits, "the influence of the scientific spirit becomes more and more diluted the further one goes from the work of the men who actually conceive, discover, invent, and perfect the modern machines."[9] That is to say, with notable exceptions in management, scientific disinterestedness has been too much confined to laboratories of physical discovery and invention or to the narrower training of men as instruments of a process. It has not yet been applied with anything like the same thoroughness to the appreciation and use of art and craftsmanship in industry, or to the

268 CHRIST AND COMMUNITY

progress of industry and business toward its true goal—the development of persons, whether producers or consumers.

Consequently, industrial civilization, Delisle Burns shows, "is without the vital current which invigorates when it flows from one aspect of community life into another, when art affects manufacture and manufacture, art," and when science makes its maximum contribution to both. Despite the claim that industry is scientific, "science has not really affected the outlook of manufacturers, workers, or consumers: for it is not a real influx of reason into industry when a fool has a better machine given to him." Although the machine age has led to larger use of natural resources, "there is no real saturation of social life or of its economic aspects by scientific knowledge and the scientific attitude."[10] To investigate this relation of science to all aspects of modern life, Julian Huxley, the English scientist, made a tour of British science. His report says, "I became more than ever impressed with the lack of appreciation and understanding of science among business men, financiers, educational authorities, politicians, and administrators. Almost equally serious, however, is the absence of a broad scientific outlook on life, too often to be noted in the scientific specialist as well as in the layman."[11] In another connection, looking into the future, he said: "The coming years will present one of two pictures—either science in chains to the profit motive, or science set free to do its possible service to human welfare."[12]

Religion with Science Can Bring Better Industry

How, then, can science and religion at their best co-operate in industry for the greatest good of all? The way in which the C.O.P.E.C. Commission on Industry and Property, already quoted, dealt with this question is itself an illustration of how to find an answer. This commission was probably as adequately representative of statesmen, economists, businessmen, technicians, labor leaders, artisans, distributors, and consumers as any group that ever tried to face these problems with scientific detachment in the light of Christian principles. In presenting their report for discussion in plenary sessions of the conference, the chairman of the commission told how their work had brought them to a common mind: "Most of us were already familiar with the leading features of modern industry and the problems which they present. As employers or workers, as economists or social students, as members of different political parties, we saw these problems from different angles. If our varying views meet and are harmonized in this Report, it is mainly because as we worked together, wide differences of outlook converged gradually to a single strong conviction—the conviction of *responsibility*. The unrest, the suspicion, the class wars which are the menace and reproach of our civilization and Christianity alike are not growing without a root. They are growths from roots of man's planting."

"Acquiescence by one-half of the nation in degrading conditions of life and work for the other half over a long stretch of years, a false theory of economics dominating the marketplace and buttressed by the eloquence of great statesmen throughout the period of *laissez faire,* the Church silent and apparently indifferent—by these things was the seed sown long ago. The plant reared from that sowing finds abundant nurture in our own time. . . . Here comes in the consideration of responsibility, individual and collective. We know now that these conditions are not the result of inevitable laws; they are not God-imposed but man-created. Man who made may also unmake, though truly he will find unmaking the harder process of the two. . . . No responsibility is so wide as that of the consumer. Yet of all responsibilities it is the least generally recognized and the most imperfectly understood. . . . We have powers, civic and political, which enable us to work both individually and corporately for change in our social system and for higher standards of social life by common action."[7]

Out of the work of this commission and of the conference as a whole came impressive agreement on definite objectives, which subsequent events confirm:

1. The aim of Christians with regard to industry, commerce, and finance should be to procure the predominance of the motive of service over the motive of gain.

2. Industry should be a co-operative effort adequately to supply the needs of all. This does not involve one particular type of organization universally applied. It does involve a perpetual effort to find the organization best suited to each industry.

3. Industry should be so organized that all those engaged in it shall have an increasingly effective voice in determining the conditions of their work and lives.

4. The first charge on industry should be a remuneration sufficient to maintain the worker and his family in health and dignity.

5. The evils of unemployment are intolerable to the moral sense. The causes must be sought and removed.

6. Extremes of wealth and poverty are likewise intolerable. A Christian order involves a juster distribution.

7. The moral justification of the various rights which constitute property depends on the degree to which they contribute to the development of personality and to the good of the whole community. If such rights subserve those purposes they deserve the approval of Christians: if not, they should be modified or abolished.

8. The duty of service is equally obligatory upon all. No inherited wealth or position can dispense any member of the Christian society from establishing by service his claim to maintenance.[13]

To attain these objectives, as the commission shows, personal conviction is essential in order to make collective action effective: "No organization can be of use unless first shaped and then energized by the living conviction and purpose of men. History shows that legislation or administration too much in advance of public opinion is at least ineffective and sometimes harmful. This means that those who believe in the Kingdom of God and pray for its coming must both be in earnest about it themselves and make others enthusiastic in the true sense. This is an essential part of the mission work of the Church at large. . . . Those who would remake our industrial world to the pattern of the Kingdom of God must endure the sense of loss and face the complex risks that all great changes bring with them; not otherwise will the work be done."[14]

Another important agreement on economic justice was formulated in a series of conferences by a representative group of 122 Protestant, Catholic, and Jewish leaders in the United States, and published jointly in October, 1946.[15] The progressive tenor of the eight principles on which they agree is well illustrated by three which are closely related to each other and to the present economic needs of the world:

> II. *The material resources of life are entrusted to man by God for the benefit of all.* . . . It follows, therefore, that the right to private property is limited by moral obligations and is subject to social restrictions for the common good. Certain types of property, because of their importance to the community, ought properly to be under state or other forms of public ownership. But in general the aim of economic life should be the widest possible diffusion of productive and consumptive property among the great masses of the people. Co-operatives, both of producers and consumers, can effectively assist in promoting this end.

> VII. *It is the duty of the state to intervene in economic life whenever necessary to protect the rights of individuals and groups and to aid in the advancement of the general economic welfare.* . . . The amount of government action on federal, state, and local levels will be determined by the extent to which the common good is not being achieved by the efforts of the functional economic groups. As far as possible, however,

these functional groups should be encouraged to participate responsibly in the formulation of governmental programs and in their administration.

VIII. *International economic life is likewise subject to the moral law.* Organized international economic collaboration of groups and national governments to assist all states to provide an adequate standard of living for their citizens must replace the present economic monopoly and exploitation of natural resources by privileged groups and states.

The joint declaration from which we have just quoted, as well as the agreement in C.O.P.E.C. and in the sectional and plenary meetings of the World Council of Churches at Amsterdam in 1947,[16] shows possibilities of such experimental procedure between free enterprise and democratic socialism as Arnold Toynbee finds most needed now in our international and economic problems. He finds this need so urgent now because "the different peoples of the world, who have suddenly been brought into close quarters with one another physically through the many inventions of the West, are still divided from one another politically, economically, socially, and psychologically by differences that it will take time to overcome. In a world in this stage of social evolution, a particular local and temporary solution of a world-wide problem cannot be applicable, as it stands, outside the country where it has been worked out by trial and error to fit the local conditions of the moment. But perhaps here we have put our finger on the service which the western European countries can perform for the world today. An awkward feature of the American ideology of free enterprise— as well as of the Russian ideology of communism—is precisely that it presents a social 'blueprint' as a panacea for every conceivable social ill in every known set of social circumstances. But this does not fit the facts of real life. In real life, every social system that can be observed at first hand or reconstructed from records is a mixed system, lying at some point between the two theoretical poles of undiluted socialism and undiluted free enterprise. . . . What the world needs above all now is to get the issue of free enterprise versus socialism off its ideological pedestal and to treat it, not as a matter of semireligious faith and fanaticism, but as a common-sense practical question of trial and error, of, more or less, circumstance and adaptation."[17]

The world's need, thus stressed by Toynbee, becomes more significant when coupled with two others which he finds also essential to survival: the need to "establish a constitutional co-operative system of world government; and to put the secular superstructure back on religious foundations."[17]

These urgent needs evidently require further scrutiny and testing of such interracial and world-uniting fellowship as can surmount divisive rivalries and make possible a working accord between various economic, political, and religious interests.

Questions for Further Thought and Discussion

How far should the Christian renounce "abundance of things," and how far enjoy them (as hallowed by the Incarnation) and seek to secure them for all people?

What examples come to mind of contemporary Americans who work not to profit but to serve?

Can we ever hope to have a whole economy based upon that attitude?

How do you explain the fact that the three fields most vital for a democracy (Church, State, School) are by-and-large the most poorly paid today?

What evidence do we have that acquisitiveness is immaturity, and an index of personal insecurity?

Is the scientist "disinterested" in a sense all Christians might share?

How can you bring about the result that one human being feels responsible for any or all others?

INTERRACIAL AND WORLD-UNITING
FELLOWSHIP

Interracial Fellowship Brings Better Understanding

MANY GREEKS AND ROMANS once failed to understand the purpose of Jesus for an inclusive brotherhood because some of his Jewish disciples were exclusive and clung to racial or nationalistic hopes, refusing to welcome into the church Gentile converts who had not conformed to Jewish ritual. So now, in all parts of the world, many have no chance to understand true Christian brotherhood because of the rampant nationalism of so-called Christians, their cultural and racial pride, and their coercive methods. These unchristlike attitudes are associated in many minds with the religion that Western civilization is supposed to represent. Christianity is under suspicion as the cat's-paw of an exploiting commercialism. It is thought to have succumbed to machinery and physical force, to have surrendered the supremacy of spiritual values, and to be inimical to the best that the older civilizations have to contribute. Therefore many people in the East suspect that the West is trying to impose upon them a type of Christianity and culture which they cannot admire. Its apparent materialism and hauteur obscure what would most appeal to them in the character and purpose of Jesus. Consequently, many remain ignorant of the influence for good which he might have in the social and international life of the world.

How this misunderstanding can be corrected, and interracial fellowship be furthered, has been summarized by Mahatma Gandhi. When asked by Stanley Jones how Christianity could be naturalized in India so that it would contribute more to India's redemption, Gandhi replied: "I would suggest, first, that all of you Christians must begin to live like Jesus Christ. Second, I would suggest that you must practice your religion without adulterating or toning it down. Third, I would suggest that you must put your emphasis upon love, for love is the center and soul of Christianity. Fourth, I would suggest that you study the non-Christian religions and culture more sympathetically in order to find the good that is in them, so that you might have a more sympathetic approach to the people." By love, as Stanley Jones explains, Gandhi "did not mean love as a sentiment, but love as a working force, the one real power in a moral universe, and he wanted it applied between individuals and groups and races and nations, the one cement and salvation of the world."[1]

That these suggestions are supported by facts is seen in the changing attitude of the East toward Jesus. When "India, a non-Christian nation, wanted to pay her highest compliment to her highest son, she searched for the highest term she knew and called Gandhi a Christlike man."[1] Thus India is more or less clearly apprehending that Jesus typifies the ideal for the race, and that in harmony with this ideal its development must proceed. This is the conclusion of many of the finest minds in the East. A leading philosopher of India, deeply read in the philosophy of East and West, replied to a question about Jesus: "We had high ideas of God before Jesus came. But Jesus is the highest expression of God that we have seen. He is conquering us by the sheer force of his own person even against our wills." Similarly, a Hindu lawyer of fine ability, giving an address on "The Inescapable Christ," said: "We have not been able to escape

him. There was a time when our hearts were bitter and sore
against him, but he is melting them by his own winsome-
ness. Jesus is slowly but surely entering all men in India—
yea, all men."[1]

To interpret all statements like these, however, as imply-
ing an acceptance of Western Christianity would be to con-
fuse and obstruct the influence of Jesus in the East. The
fear of being counted as converts to a foreign and false kind
of Christianity, P. O. Philips of India believes, would "drive
many sincere seekers after truth, who now feel impelled to
follow Christ in their spiritual quest, to barricade their souls
against influences that may proceed from professed followers
of Christ." For many are drawing sharp distinctions between
Jesus and what they understand as the religion of the West.

These oriental attitudes to Jesus deepen the obligation of
Westerners: "Orientals see that western material civilization
is beginning to dominate their lands; they would like to see
Christianity able to dominate western material civilization.
From this standpoint the conversion of ourselves to Chris-
tianity would be the greatest service we could render to the
East."[2]

The deeper appreciation of Jesus is not limited to the
East. We find it in another race which has long suffered from
the un-Christlike conduct of professing Christians. A modern
Jew recognized in Jesus a further reaching purpose of love
than many professing Christians have yet taken to heart. In
commenting on the conduct and teaching of Jesus when the
scribes and Pharisees complained because he welcomed pub-
licans and sinners, C. C. Montefiore said, "Surely this is a
new note, something which we have not yet heard in the Old
Testament or of *its* heroes, something which we do not hear
in the Talmud or of *its* heroes. 'The sinners drew near to
hear him': his teaching did not repel them. It did not palter
with, or make light of sin, but yet it gave comfort to the
sinner. The virtues of repentance are gloriously praised in
the Rabbinic literature, but this direct search for, and appeal to, the sinner, are new and moving notes of high import

and significance. The good shepherd who searches for the lost sheep, and reclaims it and rejoices over it, is a new figure, which has never ceased to play its great part in the moral and religious development of the world."[3]

This response to Jesus of many races in the modern world reveals a condition not unlike that which we have noted in the early Church. Now, as then, the prime difficulty is not in the response of other races when they have a fair chance to understand Jesus; it is in the attitude and conduct of the race that professes to know him, and that is supposed to represent the religion called by his name. Customs and actions of exclusiveness on the part of this dominating race, which assumes its own superiority, have become so habitual that the embittering effect upon those of different race and culture is seldom realized by the offenders.

Repudiating the Fallacy and Practice of Racism

In spite of such hindrances throughout the world today, great advances are still possible if those who profess the Jewish or the Christian faith, and who desire peace, take the attitude of their great scientists and prophets and repudiate the fallacies and practices of racism. Racism is the dogma that one ethnic group is condemned by Nature to hereditary inferiority and another group is destined to hereditary superiority. But scientific findings, as well as the best Jewish and Christian insights, now run counter to this dogma. In 1938, the American Anthropological Association stated: "Anthropology provides no scientific basis for discrimination against any people on the grounds of racial inferiority, religious affiliation, or linguistic heritage." The American Psychological Association, in the same year, declared: "In the experiments which psychologists have made upon different peoples, no characteristic inherent psychological differences which fundamentally distinguish so-called 'races' have been discovered. . . . Certainly no individual should be treated as an inferior merely because of his membership in one human group rather than the other." Leading biologists stated a similar conclusion at the Seventh International Genetics Congress, held in Edinburgh in 1939. These independent conclusions were based upon prolonged investigation of two kinds— "field study by anthropologists of peoples widely scattered over the face of the earth, and laboratory study by psychologists and biologists dealing with the functioning of the human mind and the working of the laws of heredity. . . . As the years have passed new studies have made ever clearer the correctness of the findings."[4]

Similar findings come from research into the rise and fall of civilization. Arnold Toynbee, for instance, examines and rejects the theory that a superior race, in one part of the world after another, has been responsible for the creation of civilizations. He advances the view that man achieves civilization, not as a result of superior biological endowment or geographical environment, but as a response to a challenge which rouses him, in a specially difficult situation, to make unprecedented effort.[5]

Such findings of science and history lead to this significant fact: In the troubled affairs of men, race is of consequence because of what men think and feel about it and not because of anything that race is of itself. That is the cardinal fact. The more we ponder all the implications of this fact, changing our attitudes and conduct accordingly, the better we shall be prepared to practice interracial democracy at home and abroad.

Co-operation of Races in Africa and Asia

Hindrances and possibilities in these pressing interracial problems are well illustrated in the white man's treatment of colonies and of the African and Asiatic races in general.

Wilfred Wellock, who was a member of the British Select Commission of East Africa before the Second World War, explains a condition that is even more ominous now. He found Europe seemingly unable to get away from the idea that Africa exists in order to be exploited. He recognized the official British policy in Africa as that of the "sacred trust," by which Britain declares that the interests of the natives are "paramount" over all other interests, and accepts the duty of educating them and of advancing self-government among them. "But in practice," he adds, "the principle of the 'sacred trust' is often lost sight of, and in many cases openly repudiated. . . . The white populations of East and Central Africa have for many years been pursuing a policy which has for its aim the creation of a vast self-governing dominion stretching from the Nile to the Limpopo. Were that dream realized it would involve the domination over considerable millions of natives by some two per cent of the population. We do not say that the white minorities are more wicked than the rest of us, but that so great a temptation to profit by human exploitation ought not to be presented to any- one."[6]

To prevent such exploitage and to forestall the spread of communism in vast areas of Africa, the possibilities and need of large scale, many-sided projects that would help to build true communities, and be eventually self-supporting, are il- lustrated in a great East African project of the British Gov- ernment. The difficulties encountered by the British show also the need for some form of international co-operation.

This project was planned to distribute object-lessons of good farming and community life over vast, disease-breeding areas of Tanganyika, Kenya, and Northern Rhodesia in one hundred and seven mechanized farm units of thirty thousand acres each. Every unit would provide a community with ade- quate housing, medical, sanitary, and educational facilities, and a welfare program. The main crop, the groundnut (called by us the peanut), a leguminous, soil-enriching plant, is also an important source of supply for the world shortage of edible fats and oils. The income from large sales of these nuts could raise the native standard of living, and the tops of the plant could increase milk production and cattle rais- ing.

Hitherto, Africans have used fire to clear the bush. This destroys all organic matter, leads to soil erosion, and often to abandoned, disease-breeding land. Mechanized bush clearing on a large scale and contour ridges, crop rotation, and other measures are necessary to save the soil and to raise the water level. To carry out such long-range plans, including better water-supply, transportation, and education, capital beyond the present reach of East Africans and protection by government are desperately needed.

The initial capital for this interracial project was to be secured by the British Government; but the plan called for its transfer eventually to the local governments, and for some kind of co-operative arrangement with the African people themselves. "Co-operative farming is well suited to the African culture, in which communal agricultural activities have long been carried out; and the project would not be economically practicable if individual subsistence farming should replace large-scale mechanized farming when the enterprise is turned over to native management."[7] Beyond the benefits to those working on such projects, the research, experiments, and object-lessons, which they would provide, if adapted to various crops and conditions and carried through with wholehearted support from all concerned, may well become a major contribution to the recovery of the plundered planet, and to a great increase in the world's food supply from tropic and subtropic lands.

In its initial stages, however, this vast peanut-raising scheme, as seen by a London director of the Union for Democratic Action, "has turned out to be a bitter and heartbreaking struggle against brush, drought, and stone-hard ground. . . . The task is so great that, in the present-day world, only the United States has the means to tackle it. In any circumstances, the co-operation of the Africans themselves is essential to progress. The Labor Government is determined to achieve this. Alone among the European powers who dominate Africa, Britain has declared ultimate independence as her policy. . . . If British rule in East Africa ended tomorrow, the settlers would take over. The East African people have a long way to go before they can be certain of taking power for themselves in an independent state. Some sort of trusteeship is essential, although many Americans would undoubtedly prefer international rule to the present British monopoly of power."[8]

In any event, an essential "prescription against both communism and nationalist dictatorships is economic development so designed as to accomplish two important purposes— to give the educated minority of Africans opportunity to develop and apply their talents, and to effect some perceptible improvement in the grinding poverty which is the daily lot of millions of African peasants. Much depends on the manner in which Americans approach the responsibilities which will inevitably fall upon them. Economic development of the wrong sort will give the communists—for the first time —a real opportunity. They have indeed done some effective missionary work among the three thousand Africans studying in London, largely at the expense of the Colonial office. But the masses of the African people are conservative. . . . Economic development on sound democratic lines will give British Africa the essential basis for responsible self-government."[6] Nigeria, almost as large as Texas and California together, is another example of various ways in which the British Government is seeking such development. But where white settlers seize control sound development is jeopardized.

The need for international co-operation in these urgent affairs, in order to allay the fears of the African people and to secure their wholehearted support, is recognized increasingly by competent observers. Dean Liston Pope of Yale Divinity School, in reporting his extensive investigations in Africa, said: "As a whole, the African leaders are as embittered, confused, and without hope as any group of men on earth. Grievances vary, but there is almost universal bitterness against white men—a small minority in every country who have arrogated to themselves all the most important political prerogatives, economic resources, and cultural opportunities." Dean Pope found also that settlers and governments of European origin are especially distrusted, and that many Africans do not expect much help even from Christian missions of these countries in the struggle for equality. "In fact, they often look upon the mission as in the camp of the opposition, due to the white control of the mission program and arrangements whereby governments support mission schools. . . . Perhaps missionaries need to get back to the day-to-day life of the African again. . . . The new kind of missionary that Africa needs is a moral and spiritual technician who will not preach the gospel vaguely, but relate Christian philosophy to the needs and aspirations of the people where they are. . . . Missionaries must view with personal sympathy the legitimate aspirations of their native followers; every trace of racism must be obliterated from mission programs, like the unchristian plague it is. Those of us who stay at home have the same imperatives; the news of what we are travels faster than the missionaries we send out."[9]

These conditions, and those explained by Mr. Wellock of the British Commission, show that a suggestion made by him should now be adapted as widely as possible to present exigencies: "As an interim measure, the natives of Africa should be placed under the supervision of an international commission, in co-operation with a council composed of representatives of the various territories."[6] We can see now why mandates under the League of Nations lacked adequate guarantees and supervision in the interest of the great majority of impoverished and undernourished people. It remains for trusteeships under the United Nations to be extended and administered for the general well-being, and for the preparation of the people concerned to govern themselves as soon as possible. This involves an obligation upon the United States to be scrupulous about adequate supervision of all trusteeships, including those in which we share direct responsibility.

At the outbreak of World War II, colonial administrators in some parts of the world were better prepared than formerly to co-operate in a self-governing policy. Here, as Gerald Heard explains, the colonial service was reserved increasingly to those who had an anthropological training.

"Anthropology, however, is itself a rapidly developing science. The first stage taught the colonial administrator a great deal about new and efficient methods, that nonviolent technique of which Pennell on the Northwest Frontier of India and Livingstone in Africa were pioneer experimentalists. The second stage teaches an even more surprising lesson about aims." If the administrator must give up the impossible task of making natives commercialized Europeans or European serfs, "he must either leave them alone and throw up his job, or he must have a goal far beyond nationalism to which to lead them. Such a discovery means a great chance not merely for the native but for the administrator. He too must see through and rise above nationalism; he becomes part of the emerging Civil Service of the world. It is here that he meets another pioneer—the new missionary—the man who gives his life not to impose his ritual on the native but with the native to find out humanity's way to God."[10] Here, too, the United Nations and its affiliated agencies, together with the World Council of Churches and related bodies, if well supported, can help to train for more effective service "a new trans-national force of men" who might lead both the native people and the "civilized" out of the impasse to which exploitation and violence have brought them.

These considerations are not confined to colonial problems. They have a bearing on possibilities already examined for the development and co-ordination throughout the world of agricultural, industrial, medical, and democratic resources and techniques.[11] The urgency for this creative reconstruction is shown by a widely representative group of leaders, who emphasized the vast importance of an address of Nehru, given at Columbia University: "Nehru proposes a drastic reconsideration of the methods by which we can attain that world community of freedom, understanding, and co-operation longed for by the masses of mankind. He reminds us that the emergence of his own country into independence was accomplished by determined effort but with no reliance upon force as its major method of implementation.

"Competition in the use of force has come to a dead end. For no matter who wins, all lose. There is still a possibility that the world may not be destroyed. But there is no longer a possibility that force alone can be the means of the world's escape.

"If we put our billions into a positive program of world aid with no hope or expectation of monetary return, if we share with the world our industrial skill and our technical superiorities in scientific food production, we shall go far to strengthen the faith of the world in our disinterestedness and in our leadership for freedom. Lord Boyd-Orr in his concept and work for a world food organization, President Truman's Point Four program, and countless scientific and technical international organizations outside of government—these are the seedbeds of the future.

"In fact, our present trends need immediate rethinking. And Nehru's visit to this country may result in deeper discussions, in less timidity of expression, and in finding for ourselves, and in the light of our own traditions, new openings."[12]

These new openings should lead also to more comprehensive economic co-operation. For instance, "Sir Arthur Salter, for many years director of the Economic Section of the League of Nations, says that, if the countries of Western Europe would establish among themselves a market liberated from nationalistic governmental interference, they could manufacture enough articles for export to pay for *all* their imports of raw materials and food." This economic balance would mean that "Western Europe's trade deficit would disappear, and with it would disappear Western Europe's chief reason for needing dollars from the U. S. taxpayer." to hasten this generally desired result, which the Council of Europe is designed to advance, many Europeans "would doubtless wish to suggest to us that possibly some of our import duties and quotas, our export controls, our immigration provisions, are not entirely conducive to the general welfare of the whole North Atlantic Economic Community. In discussing such suggestions, we may find mutually advantageous solutions."[13]

Related Interracial Problems at Home

In this critical time of interracial tension, as a thorough and impartial inquiry shows, the citizens of our democracy have now an unprecedented opportunity:[14] "America will have the major responsibility for the manner in which humanity approaches the long era during which the white peoples will have to adjust to shrinkage while the colored are bound to expand in numbers, in level of industrial civilization, and in political power. . . . In this crucial time, as the international leadership passes to America, the greatest reason for hope is that this country has a national experience of uniting racial and cultural diversities, and a national theory, if not a consistent practice, of freedom and equality for all. . . . In this sense the Negro problem is not only America's greatest failure but also America's incomparably great opportunity for the future. . . . America can demonstrate that justice, equality, and co-operation are possible between white and colored people. In the present phase of history this is what the world needs to believe. Mankind is sick of fear and disbelief, of pessimism and cynicism. It needs the youthful moralistic optimism of America. But empty declarations only deepen cynicism. Deeds are called for. If America in actual practice could show the world a progressive trend by which the Negro became finally integrated into modern democracy, all mankind would be given faith again—it would have reason to believe that peace, progress, and order are feasible. And America would have a spiritual power many times stronger than all her financial and military resources—the power of the trust and support of all good people on earth. *America is free to choose whether the Negro shall remain her liability or become her opportunity.*"[14]

In this choice, all citizens need help in learning to cooperate. If anyone is indifferent or hostile, he not only throws his influence against the cause of brotherhood and peace throughout the world; he does irreparable injury to his fellow citizens. For instance, in the United States the feeling of many Negroes, both in the North and South, that "they do not belong," and that "no one cares," has been found to be a prolific cause of delinquency and crime.

The story of "Hill City" in Pittsburgh is a vivid object lesson of what can be done when Negro youth are helped by their white and Negro neighbors in dealing with their own problems. Before white people were roused to their responsibility, "the Hill bred twice as much crime per capita among Negroes as among whites. Causes were easy to detect. On the Hill there was a richly endowed settlement house for white children but nothing for Negroes, though they formed the largest racial element. No meeting places, no recreation, only their miserable tenements, cold and dark, and the bleak and ugly streets. And behind that, the grim, inescapable fact of poverty and unemployment."

Fortunately, the director of public safety in Pittsburgh, Colonel George Fairley, had led a Negro regiment and had learned to appreciate the fine qualities of Negroes. He gave Howard McKinney, who had been a leader of his fellow Negroes in the Y.M.C.A., an official standing as city detective, and a free hand in dealing with youth. Beginning without cash, but with the help of other Negroes, McKinney had soon turned abandoned stores into a dozen meeting places and recreation centers, with a thousand boys and girls enrolled in groups. Juvenile delinquency dropped, but McKinney felt that something more was needed to satisfy the craving of Negro youth for drama and action. He asked them whether they would like to set up a self-governing city. The response was enthusiastic. At the meeting for the election of mayor, city council, district attorney, and other Hill City officers, the acting mayor of Pittsburgh gave importance to the occasion by attending and swearing the newly elected officials into office. Many citizens helped to equip headquarters for the new government. Applications for citizenship poured in. Boy or girl investigators looked into each application, interviewed parents, examined school records, and reported whether the applicant would make a worthy citizen. Within a year Hill City had 2,600 citizens nine to twenty-one years old—2,100 Negroes (half the Negro population of those ages on the Hill) and 500 white boys and girls of a dozen nationalities.

The officers of Hill City were not given actual police power. But they have the almost irresistible power of the youngster in his own world. The largest five and ten cent store in Pittsburgh used to catch four or five Negro boys every day for stealing; now, said the manager, "there isn't one a month. If we do catch a colored boy, we report to Hill City's district attorney, not to the police." Colonel Fairley said, "When a kid is put on probation at Hill City, he's really on probation. A kid may fool an adult parole officer, but he can't fool a bunch of kids his own age."[15]

From this experiment in self-government, the youth of Hill City branched out in new relationships between their community and the city as a whole. They focused the attention of public and private agencies upon the problems and the aspirations of young people, and paved the way for the improvement of general social and economic conditions. Merely to combat racial tensions is not enough. Citizens young and old must co-operate to remove causes of racial conflicts, such as poor housing and health, lack of jobs, and denial of basic human rights. Without an active and intelligent public opinion on these problems, public officials are often disinclined to tackle them.[15]

Hence the general need for some such agency as the "Unity Commission," an effective part of the Pittsburgh city government, which consists of leading representatives of fifteen races, has a full-time director, and the bishop of the Episcopal diocese as its first chairman. There are already at least three dozen cities with interracial and intercultural committees, sponsored and paid for by their governments, and many times this number where voluntary interracial committees have helped to focus public opinion upon remedial measures. In several instances, state-wide affiliation of these various agencies helps to promote personal initiative and official action. Every state in the Union, Carey McWilliams urges, should be thus organized and the state organizations united in a single national organization, including "seven hundred-odd other organizations which have an interest in various phases of the problem. In other words, an army has enlisted or is willing to enlist in the fight against discrimination; but we still lack a general staff and a well-defined strategy."[16]

What can be done is explained in the widely approved Report of the President's Committee on Civil Rights. It shows the need of federal, state, and local agencies for inquiry and education, as well as for legal action, and stresses the part that the individual and the community must play.[17]

An important part many can play in the cause of civil rights is to help open doors to good jobs for Negroes. For instance, the co-operation of white residents in New York City's "Harlem" was needed to convince the management of stores serving many Negro as well as white customers that they should employ a fair proportion of Negroes. This instance of persuasion suggests possibilities for church and school, labor union, the press, and other molders of opinion to help educate citizens for specific action, so that citizens in turn can provide and support wise leaders for all civil rights and for the constructive resolving of differences through fellowship. The more such molders of opinion become creative of the larger, enlightening fellowship that we are seeking, the less will citizens follow the delusive hopes and methods that menace their freedom.

Questions for Further Thought and Discussion

What cultural forces besides religion tackle the ideal of interracial community, and how effectively?

How does the Christian answer to race problems differ in Asia and Africa as over against America and Europe?

Does wise, socially aware statesmanship in any instance maintain colonialism today rather than granting immediate independence?

How can Christian strategy in Asia and Africa go about to combine Christian missions and anti-imperialist movements for independence?

In what ways does Christianity justify complete, nonsegregated racial equality?

22

THE CHURCH AS A WORLD-UNITING FELLOWSHIP[1]

A Possible Church as Seen by duNoüy and Toynbee
BECAUSE OF THE RACIAL and political tensions threatening
the world, and because of the strategic position of the
Church, it behooves a good citizen, even if he is not a member of any church or synagogue, to keep abreast of what the
co-operating agencies of the Church are doing, and what
more they could do with adequate support, to further world-
uniting fellowship and equal rights. Many citizens disparage
the Church as a whole because of what they see, or what they
fail to find, in some local congregation. They would do better to consider the need and opportunity for a universal
Church as shown in du Noüy's scientific study, *Human Destiny*.[1] He concludes that the only salvation for mankind will
be found in religion, and that the religion which the Church
is called to implement "must be a sound Christian religion,
vitalized by its own primitive ideals, aware of the progress
of science, rid of prejudice against fair speculative intelligence, and soaring high above frontiers. Never in her two
thousand years has the Church had a more urgent call and
a nobler opportunity to fulfill her obligation as the com-
forter and guide of humanity."

The necessity and also the possibility for the Church to rise above frontiers, and even above an existing civilization, in order to fulfill its mission as a world-uniting fellowship is noted also in Arnold Toynbee's comprehensive work, *A Study of History*. Writing of the disintegration of the Graeco-Roman society, he says: "The Empire fell and the Church survived just because the Church gave leadership and enlisted loyalty, whereas the Empire had long failed to do either the one or the other." In other cases also Toynbee found that "the social link between two societies has been a universal Church, which has been created by the internal proletariat of the old society and has afterward served as a chrysalis within which the new society has taken shape. . . . When we examine the universal churches we shall find ourselves compelled to raise the question whether churches can really be comprehended in their entirety in the framework of the histories of the civilizations in which they make their historical appearances, or whether we have not to regard them as representatives of another species of society. This may prove to be one of the most momentous questions that a study of history can suggest to us. . . . What is the destiny of the universal Church, in which every higher religion seeks to embody itself?" These questions are especially pertinent now because, as Toynbee shows, there has often been a close "relationship between disintegrations of civilizations and new initiatives in religion," and because Western civilization, the only existing one, if any, that is not disintegrating, is even now in a precarious plight and needs for its salvation a revived and reuniting Church.[2]

These findings of Toynbee are supplemented by his later statements: "Future historians will say, I think, that the great event of the twentieth century was the impact of the Western civilization upon all the other living societies of the world of that day. They will say of this impact that it was so powerful and so pervasive that it touched chords in human souls that are not touched by mere external material forces—however ponderous and terrifying." And even later historians, he thinks, "will say that the impact of the Western civilization on its contemporaries was the epoch-making event of that age because it was the first step towards the unification of mankind into one single society. By their time, the unity of mankind will perhaps have come to seem one of the fundamental conditions of human life." And those living later, who perceive how this came about, "will say, I fancy, that the importance of this social unification of mankind was not to be found in the field of technics and economics, and not in the field of war and politics, but in the field of religion."[3]

In our own time, however, Toynbee sees the possibility of catastrophe. This is partly because Western civilization, while it has been antagonizing other peoples by exclusiveness and exploitation, has also been destroying itself by fratricidal strife among its nationalistic states. This is a process that Toynbee perceives in the suicide of earlier civilizations. Failing to solve their differences creatively, they have been forced to accept the solution of a military conqueror. And the resultant universal state has merely prolonged the life of a dying civilization. "There is nothing to prevent our western civilization from following historical precedent, if it chooses, by committing social suicide. But we are not doomed to make history repeat itself."

Facing these alternatives, Toynbee answers his question: "What shall we do to be saved? In politics, establish a constitutional co-operative system of world government. In economics, find working compromises (varying according to the practical requirements of different places and times) between free enterprise and socialism. In the life of the spirit, put the secular superstructure back onto religious foundations. Efforts are being made in our western world today to find our way towards each of these goals. If we had arrived at all three of them, we might fairly feel that we had won our present battle for our civilization's survival. But these are, all of them, ambitious undertakings, and it will call for the hardest work and the highest courage to make any progress at all towards carrying any one of them through to achievement. Of the three tasks, the religious one is, of course, in the long run by far the most important."[3]

Such historical and scientific findings about religion and the Church in times of transition show their increasing importance in helping to solve what Toynbee considers our most urgent political and economic problems. One way in which religious work may have vastly greater scope and effect is in the co-operation of the churches and their members with the United Nations and its specialized agencies. For instance its Food and Agriculture Organization (FAO) and World Health Organization (WHO) have to deal with problems in which the Church has long been a pioneer in countries like India and China. Not only have various agencies of the Church much to contribute out of this experience, but the Church as a whole is needed to support, through its members and its influences on public opinion, other agencies also of the United Nations, such as the Security Council, the Trusteeship Council, the Economic and Social Council and its important Commissions.[4] UNESCO, for instance (United Nations Educational, Scientific, and Cultural Organization, which has autonomous powers of initiative beyond the veto of any nation) not only offers opportunities for wider collaboration to churches throughout the world; it desperately needs the motivation and approach to people which churches at their best can give. Without such help UNESCO will be fatally limited, as we have seen much current education limited, by lack of adequate purpose and spiritual influence.

Recent Growth of International Fellowship

All such opportunities and perils call citizens to take a more active part in the world-uniting work of the Church. The Christian world mission has become more than ever a co-operant enterprise of various races, encouraging self-government by indigenous churches, and promoting interracial fellowship, mutual aid, and general well-being. The increase of co-operation across national lines was shown when the German hordes overran Norway, Denmark, Holland, Belgium, and France, and thus cut off from these supporting countries about one-eighth of all Protestant missionary work in the world. Then Christian churches in other lands rallied to the support of these orphaned missions. From tens of thousands of parishes in twenty free countries all over the world contributions were sent to destitute Christian communities in forty countries on five continents. As Henry Van Dusen concludes: "Aid was given without regard to race or creed or denomination, but only on the basis of need. Not one missionary was withdrawn or one mission closed, so far as is known, for lack of funds. It is the most impressive concrete demonstration of the underlying unity of Christ's Church Protestant which has been given in the whole of Christian history."[5]

Equally promising is the efficiency shown by the young mission churches when their homelands were invaded. In 1942, when the Japanese swept over Siam, Burma, and Malaya to Singapore, through the Philippines, the Dutch East Indies, and most of the islands of the Western and Central Pacific, this vast area included more than one-fourth of those who had been brought into the Church by its missionary work. Then these native Christian peoples, in country after country, took over responsibility not only for churches but also for schools, hospitals, orphanages, and publications, which had been directed and financed almost wholly by foreigners. They maintained not only their own Christian life and work but also those missionary friends who remained with them, cut off from the rest of the world. Thus was shown the maturity and loyalty of these youngest and least experienced Christian churches.[6]

Moreover, in many places invaded by the Japanese, both native Christians and missionaries were aided so far as possible by fellow Christians among the Japanese. Let one incident illustrate the situation. Some months after the con-

quest of the Dutch East Indies by the Japanese, the first message came through in cryptic words to report that the Dutch
missionaries there were well, free, and able to continue their
work—"thanks to the friends of K. A. Gawa."[5]

Many of the most discerning tributes to this Christian
world fellowship have come to us through the unsolicited
testimony of men in uniform, telling of what they have seen
in widely scattered outposts of so-called foreign missions.
"No enterprise in history aimed at the amelioration of hu-
mankind and the building of a fairer common life has ever
received more decisive approbation."[6]

Christian co-operation in virtually every aspect has advanced farthest and fastest among the younger churches of
the mission field. Every major land or region of the younger
churches has the equivalent of a National Christian Council,
including most if not all Protestant bodies.

All these achievements and the expanding co-operation in
recent years of leading Protestant world organizations is
prophetic of still better things to come. Just before World
War II almost all these organizations—the World's Y.M.C.A.,
the World's Y.W.C.A., the World Student Christian Federation, the World Alliance for International Friendship
through the Churches, the European Central Bureau for
Interchurch Aid, and the World Council of Churches, then
forming—had their world headquarters in Geneva. On the
outbreak of war, these bodies united in an Emergency Committee of Christian Organizations. "From 1943 onward their
headquarters at Geneva was practically cut off from all of
the world except the European Continent. Nevertheless, the
staffs and committees there continued to act as an enlightened general staff for the churches throughout the world,
and to direct the most extensive program of practical Christian activity which Christ's churches united for action have
ever undertaken."[5]

In addition to co-ordinating much of this work through
its own expanding departments, the World Council of

Churches, acting with the International Missionary Council, has sponsored jointly the Commission of the Churches on International Affairs. This commission aims in part: "To encourage the formation, in each country and in each church represented in the parent bodies, of commissions through which the conscience of Christians may be stirred and educated as to their responsibilities in the world of nations; to formulate the bearing of Christian principles upon immediate issues; to suggest ways in which Christians may act effectively upon these problems in their respective countries and internationally; and to represent the sponsoring Councils in relations with international bodies such as the United Nations and related agencies." The New York office of this Commission (297 Fourth Avenue) has special responsibility for following the work of the United Nations, and is equipped to supply authoritative documentation on virtually all aspects of its work.

At times it has seemed, says a *Primer for Protestants,* that "the so-called ecumenical movement was an enthusiasm of the clergy alone, but the Second World War proved it to be sustained by a deep and fresh awareness among the laity of the essential oneness of Christ's body everywhere, across all military and cultural frontiers. Just as the leaders of this movement were able to bring together representatives from the recently warring peoples after the First World War, and just as representatives of the Younger Churches actually at war were able to worship together at Madras, so today the fellowship and trust of Christians is almost the sole channel of healing among the shattered peoples of Europe. And in all the great assemblies of the church universal in recent years, at Stockholm, Jerusalem, Lausanne, Oxford, Edinburgh, Madras [and Amsterdam], the basis and reality of union was found, not in theological or ethical discussion, but in common adoration, in the memorable services of worship when the 'communion of saints' became actuality."[7]

This linking together of evangelical Christian forces throughout the world gathers strength so rapidly that no account written today could do justice to its promise of more fruitful world fellowship tomorrow.

Church Union and Federation within Nations

The achievements of united or federated churches within national areas have been notable also. In the organic union of such churches, the decade preceding World War II (1927-36) was most encouraging. It witnessed ten unions. The six years of war (1939-46) witnessed seven unions. At the same time the national federating of churches has made great progress. Before the war there were five important national church councils; at its close there were thirteen, including the British Council of Churches and the Canadian Council of Churches—probably the most important since the formation of the American Federal Council in 1908.

This Federal Council is merging with seven other national interdenominational agencies into the National Council of the Churches of Christ in the United States of America. Even before this merger, its example was at work in almost every state and many countries and cities of the United States, and throughout the world. There are over eight hundred and fifty state and local interchurch councils in this country; and there are national federations or councils of churches in almost every country of Europe, Asia, Africa, Australia, and Latin America where there are different Protestant churches of sufficient strength. The American Federal Council has had great influence also in the movement that has resulted in the World Council of Churches.

Of all the types of interchurch co-operation, this type of federation is the most recent, and many regard it as the most influential. "Indeed the question is widely mooted whether such federation rather than organic union is not the ideal method of expressing the union of Christians in Christ. As a matter of historical fact, the rapid spread of church federations throughout the world is probably the greatest achievement of the many-sided impulse toward Christian unity."[5]

Forecast of the Ecumenical Movement

These many achievements since the World Conference at Edinburgh in 1910 open the way to far greater advance, if a reborn Church grapples with the disorders that threaten civilization. As Walter Horton shows, our leading social prophets, including "still active thinkers such as Toynbee and Trueblood, agree essentially upon the role that a deeply dedicated minority may play in the transfiguration and redemption of an apparently moribund civilization. . . . The Christian Church in its first great centuries, and in several critical times since then, has been a disciplined revolutionary minority—an *ekklesia*, 'called out' of the existing order to live by faith the life of a new order. It is a matter of history that Western civilization has been transfigured and renewed more than once by what Toynbee calls the 'withdrawal and return' of revolutionary Christian minorities."[6]

This revolutionary function of the Church has been recognized increasingly in recent decisions and plans of the ecumenical movement. All four of the volumes drafted by representative leaders of the Church in preparation for the Amsterdam Assembly Sections of 1948 called for great changes in the relation of the Church to the world. "Of larger scope than the Amsterdam program is another project of the World Council's Study Department, the *Ecclesia Militans* series. . . . The most important study in this series, so far, reveals a world-wide 'Back to the Bible' movement, affecting the Eastern Orthodox and Roman Catholic as well as Protestant churches. 'Back to the Bible' movements have created reformations many times before in the history of the Church; this time there is hope that the Bible may help to *reunite* the Church as well as to *reform* it. . . . A century of historical criticism has taught us to use the Bible less mechanically and more inspirationally. When Christians put their heads together over the Bible, not to find proof texts with which to fortify themselves and to judge one another, but to find common inspiration for facing and navigating a sea of troubles, they are drawn into very close communion with one another. This proved true at two Bible conferences called by the World Council in 1946 and 1947."[8]

The most promising step so far taken by the World Council to meet the new world situation, Walter Horton thinks, is the founding of the Ecumenical Institute at the Chateau de Bossey, near Geneva, on the Swiss shore of the lake. "The Institute undertakes to raise up new leaders (especially *lay* leaders) to rethink the tasks of the Church in the light of the searching demands of the Bible, and the unprecedented conditions of the modern world." The full significance of this institute is seen in its relation to the whole series of conference centers which have recently sprung into being in various parts of Europe, and which have asked to be kept in touch with one another through the Ecumenical Institute. For this purpose there is an annual Round Table at Bossey, and a new member of the staff stationed there, who corresponds with all the European movements and investigates similar movements outside of Europe, with a view to a world-wide lay movement for a reborn Church and a reordered society.

In the light of his careful study of these centers of new life in Europe,[9] Walter Horton says: "I shall continue to advocate the founding of centers in America—at least one interdenominational center to each principal group of states, plus as many local and denominational centers as possible. . . . The laymen attending conferences at these centers would become evangelists and missionaries as well as builders of a new society. Their activity in social reconstruction would by itself exert a powerful evangelistic influence in a world where destructive forces are driving men to despair. The goal of the new missionary evangelism should be nothing less than the conversion and redemption of *whole classes and whole nations*—not just a few more church members—and ultimately, the salvation of our lost and dying world order. It is wonderful to note how rapidly this larger idea of missionary evangelism is spreading today. The alienated laboring class in France is beginning to be won for Christ by Catholics and Protestants who have identified themselves deeply with French labor, and bridged the cultural gap. A commission appointed by Archbishop Temple before his death has lately reported on the conditions under which the 'Conversion of England'—England, not just a few Englishmen—might become possible. Nothing less than the 'Conversion of America' would be a proper aim for our new regional centers in their evangelistic capacity."[8]

Obviously such evangelism, combined with social reconstruction, on the scale of the whole gospel and of the whole world's need requires a rebirth of the Church and its members. For "only a reborn Church, which is literally a piece of God's New Order, a 'colony of heaven' on earth, 'in the world but not of the world,' will have power to restore order, soon or late, to a world so deeply disordered as ours. Neither a worldly Church nor a wholly other-worldly Church has any such power."[8]

The Ecumenical Spirit in Home and Community

The goal of a reborn Church in a reordered world, we must remember, cannot be approached without devoted co-operation of many local churches, their members, and the homes which nurture them. For instance, resolutions of federal or world councils, denouncing segregation in the churches, cannot produce interracial fellowship unless it is practiced in local congregations, homes, and communities. Without effective co-operation in many a parish, "ecumenical headquarters will find itself in the unhappy predicament of being generals without an army. The local parish on the other hand needs headquarters to dramatize in vivid ways the fact of the campaign and its stirring goals."[10] What laymen can do for a world Church is told with many instructive examples by John Oliver Nelson in *Young Laymen—Young Church*.[11] This book shows how any layman can find and develop tested ways to serve the ecumenical movement in his own home, church, and community, and how he can make them an influence for good in local and world affairs. It shows also the necessity for a vast number of laymen who will seek and improve various ways "to help build Christian principles into the everyday life of the world." This is the avowed purpose of The Laymen's Movement for a Christian World.[12] The more laymen demonstrate this purpose in the day's work, the more effectively they will enlist many others within and beyond the Church.[13]

A primary need for the solution of local and interracial problems of Christian unity and world order is friendly personal relations in home, church, school, and wherever members of different groups or races should meet. Leading oriental statesmen and educators have expressed their deep indebtedness for the hospitality shown their students in this country by our colleges, churches, and Christian homes. Such hospitality and other Christian influences account in large measure for the loyalty shown to this country on the outbreak of war with Japan by the Japanese then living under our flag. Accordingly, educational, social, and religious institutions in all countries should become more and more congenial centers for those creative interracial friendships on which so much depends. Such friendships can overcome deepseated prejudice. When racial and national antagonisms are provoked either at home or abroad, these friendships will be more than ever needed in dealing with the misunderstandings and unfair practices which inflame the world.[14]

Especially among the young, informal and friendly relations between members of different races are of the utmost importance in order to forestall the antipathies and misunderstandings which so often arise later in life. The earliest attitudes and conduct of children when left to their own initiative help to substantiate the conclusion of leading anthropologists that racial antipathies are not instinctive, and that we must make the most of their absence in the uncontaminated child. For these antipathies are usually fomented by economic, political, and social rivalries from which the child is free—until he catches them from others.

The adults who can help most to foster the finest interracial fellowship among the young are those who themselves are freest from such rivalries and the other causes of racial prejudice. Even in churches and so-called Christian homes, one often finds the dislikes and the feeling of superiority that are quite enough to distort the freer attitude of the child. The difficulty is not so much in what parents or teachers do, as in what they fail to be. There is often an absence of that positive good will, of that absorption in the larger, Christlike purposes which would encourage the child's own inclination to ignore divisive tendencies in the world about him.

Hence the importance that churches and schools co-operate with homes in such educational programs for all ages and races as are increasingly productive of better community spirit and performance. Thus the conviction spreads that racial antipathy can be forestalled or overcome when young and old of different races are given adequate opportunities to meet one another with mutual respect and friendliness, and to share interests and purposes great enough in the long run to transcend the world's rivalries. Toward such fellowship everything that is found applicable in the foregoing and following chapters should be applied in order to realize the conditions for a co-operating and Christian society.

Questions for Further Thought and Discussion

What evidence is there that Church leaders see the role of Christianity today in history as urgently as does Toynbee?

Granting that religion often shows new life as the culture around it disintegrates, what signs do we discern of both these phenomena today?

How can the message of the World Council of Churches be most realistically brought into the consciousness of the grass-roots layman?

In what ways must the new ecumenical breadth of the Church affect its sanction of war among the nations?

Why is federation rather than organic merger the characteristic ecumenical movement in this age? What likelihood is there that one leads to the other?

What intercultural Christian projects can you list? Have you taken part in any of them?

23

PRAYER, A WAY TO BETTER FELLOWSHIP

Man's Need for Fellowship Is God's Opportunity

Toward the close of his amazing life of scientific research and invention at Schenectady, Charles Steinmetz said: "Some day people will learn that material things do not bring happiness, and are of little use in making men and women creative and powerful. Then the scientists of the world will turn their laboratories over to the study of God and prayer and the spiritual forces which as yet have hardly been scratched. When this day comes the world will see more advancement in one generation than it has in the past four hundred years."[1]

At this time when scientific method, as we have seen it used by Jesus, is needed on all sides, a friendly caution from another leader of ripe experience may help those who hesitate to pray. He says: "It would be both psychologically absurd and contrary to Christian principles to expect everyone to pray in exactly the same way. I suspect that many who are disheartened about their prayers have never had this fact made clear to them. They have too narrow a notion of prayer. A man might really live very close to God, and yet rarely offer long and formal intercession. He might have the habit of referring everything to God. . . . I knew a small boy who was not very bright at school until it was discovered

303

that he had a gift for music. When that was allowed to develop it was found that his mind became alert and alive all
round. The mind is a unity, and when one part of it takes
fire the rest will glow. So it is with our spiritual capacities.
We must begin where we can; if we are faithful there, the
other aspects of prayer will be ours."[2]

The disciples whom Jesus led to new ventures in prayer
had been seriously limited, as our generation is still limited,
by current misconceptions of the character of God. In their
time the prevalent idea of God fell far below the more spiritual conceptions of Old Testament prophets and poets.
Broadly speaking, we may picture the God worshiped by most
of the disciples before they knew Jesus, as an austere Being,
difficult of access, save by way of ritual sacrifice, a patron of
their own nation, "though distantly interested, it may be, in
other races, sternly righteous, and manifesting his righteousness through the punishment of the guilty."[3] Many of our
own generation suffer like limitations in their thought of
God. They think of him as an absentee ruler or an impersonal power—in either case as inaccessible in any intimately
co-operating way. Such ideas, more than we know, affect the
thought and conduct of all of us. In the uncertainties of our
time, however, many are coming to realize their need for
a dependable God who is "a very present help in trouble."[a]

It was nothing short of a revolutionary experience for the
first disciples to turn from the worship of a God who seemed
like a glorified Eastern Potentate, jealously guarding his prerogatives, and to be drawn into fellowship by a father-like
Spirit, inspiring his children to behave like brothers. Such
a transition required more than a change of opinion about
God, more even than the teaching and example of Jesus. It
required, as we have seen, the pressure of that extremity of
human need which is God's opportunity of making himself
known.

So, when the disciples faced the responsibilities and dangers of carrying on the work of Jesus, and when they became
convinced that his unusual influence grew out of his com-

munion with God, they tried to learn more than they had yet gathered from the practice of Jesus in prayer. The apostles doubtless remembered that, just before he chose them for their special work, he had spent the night on a mountain alone with God.[b] They remembered also that it was after, as well as before important events, that Jesus sought solitude with his Father. It was after the Sabbath filled with teaching and healing that he went out before dawn to a solitary place where Peter found him praying in the quiet of the early morning. It was after the multitude had tried to make him king that the apostles found him withdrawn to a secluded place for prayer.[c] By the time the Epistles, the Gospels, and the Acts of the Apostles were written, the writers were convinced from their own experience in trying the way of Jesus that his work had been conceived, accomplished, and confirmed in communion with God.

Like Jesus, therefore, they turned to prayer not as stern duty, but as high privilege; not as supplication for benefits so much as communion with their Father. Such communion, like the best intercourse between friends, they sought for the sake of the friendship itself. Yet, as a result of their friendship with God, they enjoyed more brotherly relations with men. They learned more of the bearing of prayer upon human fellowship and upon all the friendly interactions of community.

Thanksgiving Helps Increase Joy in Fellowship

Such experience led naturally to thanksgiving. The friendship of the disciples with Jesus, their new enjoyment of God and of universal brotherhood, the exhilarating news of the Kingdom of God, and their own calling to be its pioneers— all this, in addition to the common gifts of every day, gave occasion for such thanksgiving as the disciples had never known before. Thanksgiving on the scale of their enlarging discovery of God kept him vividly before them as the Author of all good. It went beyond gratitude for benefits received, and rose to adoration and praise of God, himself.

Thus Paul, beset by "conflicts without and fears within," discovered that thanksgiving is a way to hopeful initiative in prayer; and shared this discovery with his friends: "Maintain your zest for prayer by thanksgiving."[d] Paul himself is a striking illustration of the effects of thanksgiving. Out of his own experience of singing psalms of praise while fast in the stocks of the Philippian jail after his scourging, Paul could write later to his friends at Philippi: "Rejoice in the Lord always: again I will say rejoice. In nothing be anxious; but in everything by prayer and supplication *with thanksgiving* let your requests be made known to God; so shall God's peace, that surpasses all our dreams, keep guard over your hearts and minds in Christ Jesus."[e]

Conversely, by the neglect of thanksgiving, needless anxiety may increase; a positive and joyous confidence may be lost. Prayer may fall to the low level of uncertain pleading. Then it becomes an enervating habit of beseeching God for what he is waiting to bestow. Against this habit Jesus warned his disciples: "In praying do not heap up empty phrases as the Gentiles do; for they think that they will be heard for their many words. Do not be like them, for your Father knows what you need before you ask him."[f] Thanksgiving helps us to rise above this deadening routine. It changes pleading to praise, and envelops life in an atmosphere of confidence and courage. It does not evade hard facts; it faces facts in true perspective. A man whose contagious influence had much to do with a great spiritual awakening in India was noticed seldom to ask God for anything, but often to be thanking him for what others had not yet perceived to be within their reach.

Confession Helps Remove Barriers to Fellowship

While the new experiences of the early Christians led to thanksgiving, they led no less surely to confession. Facing difficulties and failures in the work committed to them, they found release in acknowledging their own shortcomings before God. To the Father, made known by Jesus, they could come confidently to discover whatever hindered communion with him and community among men. They found deeper meaning in the familiar prayer: "Search me, O God, and know my heart; try me, and know my thoughts; and see if there be any wicked way in me, and lead me in the way everlasting."[g] Confession for these disciples was not a discipline from which they shrank, but a liberation for fruitful service. It set them free from the trammels of the past and opened their lives more fully to the creative energy of love.

The value of such experience is now confirmed by applied psychology, even though psychology alone falls short of what is possible through religious confession. Dr. A. J. Hadfield shows how confession helps "by discovering and bringing into consciousness the latent cause of worry or failure, which normally tends to elude consciousness. Modern practice in psychotherapy confirms the old belief that confession, more especially confession of fears and anxieties, is good for the soul."[4] If fears or worries, antipathies, or other causes of maladjustment are to be cured, they must be brought up from the depths in which they work insidiously. They must be faced in the open for what they really are, and dismissed, to give no further trouble, rather than repressed and allowed to work unsuspected disaster. And they can be faced most effectively, as other studies in the psychology of religion show, when we come to a God "who sees us as we really are, and with whom alone we may be utterly frank."[5]

If confession is to go further than merely letting out the repressed cause of the trouble, if it is to open the way for the penetration of the entire personality by the spirit of love that can renew all life from within, then it must deal with sins of omission as well as of commission, and with corporate as well as personal wrongs. Nothing perhaps needs to come home more searchingly to the Christian conscience in our day than "the fact of personal complicity in collective sin." We are ready enough to confess the sins of others in business and politics. We need to recognize our own share in corporate wrongs. Confession, carried to this larger dimension, should move us to corresponding repentance—to a change of mind and will that enables us not only to perceive but also to overcome collective evil, and to take our full share in the business of righting public and social wrong.

The personal confession of early Christians was voluntary and spontaneous. It came through fellowship with a Master who knew them thoroughly, yet trusted them as they had never been trusted before. This surprising confidence in their better selves by a Friend, so discerning yet so devoted, seems to have brought to them at once a deeper consciousness of their own perversities, and a stronger desire to be rid of everything that would disturb their comradeship with him and with his other friends in their difficult adventure.[h]

Prayer for Others Helps to Bring the World Together

The more the disciples were set free from self through confession and thanksgiving, the less their prayer was confined to merely personal concerns. Rather, it became a way to apply the resources of God to the particular tasks of his Kingdom. Through Jesus the disciples discovered God to be the Author of true community. When, for instance, Jesus was moved with compassion for the helpless multitude whom he was teaching and healing, he saw with deeper insight than did his disciples that the real difficulty was not with the multitude: "The harvest is plentiful," he said, "but the laborers are few; pray therefore the Lord of the harvest to send out laborers into his harvest."[i] By such prayer, as his own life showed, Jesus meant to encourage the development of workers whose minds would be so quickened by the Spirit of God that they would work in harmony, aware of one another's needs, and aware of the needs of the multitude. The prayer that seeks increase of this awareness, Jesus evidently believed, would help to create a responsive community of love among men. For such a friendly community is developed through closer relations with a God who is love, and who communicates his own yearnings to his children. This is a process which true prayer makes possible by training men to think, to feel, and to exercise their powers in fellowship with One who so loves his children as to draw them into understanding sympathy with one another. Because true prayer works in this spontaneous, disinterested manner, it is beyond doubt an indispensable factor in developing the community of friendly workers typified by Jesus.

In the very nature, therefore, of this provision for developing a race of Christlike men there may be a reason for different levels of possible response between God and men. "Perhaps we should say," with A. G. Hogg, "that the difference between the so-called 'system of nature' and the so-called 'supernatural' is just the difference between the discovered and the undiscovered in God. The 'system of nature' means just the unity or plan which scientific thought believes itself to have discovered as prevailing in average human experience. And average human experience is determined by the character of average human activity; it is the response which God provides out of the infinitude of his resources to the demand which the average will and the average faith of man makes upon him. But what if there were a faith which, faced by a difficult situation, was inspired to a demand upon God grander than the ordinary man ever dreams of? Must not God, by virtue of the very uniformity of his nature, respond in a correspondingly exceptional manner? Only it would be a hitherto undiscovered manner of response, evoked by a previously unattempted act of will and faith. As Prof. A. E. Taylor has said, 'there is no philosophical justification for refusing to admit the possibility of incessant new departures.' There is always room for new creative thoughts. The establishment of the Kingdom of God was the creative new departure in the relations between God and man which our Lord made possible to the Father by his human life of faith."[6]

The more we take part in this new departure, the less we fear that prayer, which furthers it, will be misunderstood as an attempt of one person to influence another unduly. Rather it will be understood as an endeavor to come by way

of God into such personal relations as will help all concerned to work together in that Kingdom which enlists a
far-flung community of friendly workers. It is the experience
of many that the more faithful they are in the practice of
such prayer for persons and great causes, the more they become the confidants of people in perplexity or other need.
Aspirations and misgivings long hidden are confided to them,
and obscure good qualities are unconsciously revealed. They
come thus to a better understanding of widely differing needs
and of how to meet them in the enjoyment of common resources. They are brought more deeply into those "intimate
relationships that make the world of persons an organic
whole."[7]

Growth in Prayer Is Like the History of Religion

Even without specific theory, many a man has been led
by insistent need into illuminating experience of prayer. As
Abraham Lincoln said while dealing with a national crisis,
"I have been driven many times to my knees by the overwhelming conviction that I had nowhere else to go. My own
wisdom and that of all about me was insufficient for the day."

Prayer, then, may begin with need; but it should not end
there. Every man prays in a limited way by the demand he
makes habitually upon life, even though he thinks little, if
at all, about God.[8] But, in so far as he goes forward to know
and to serve a God of love, he brings all his concerns into
the light of God's love. Such growth in prayer corresponds
in general with the long history of religion. "At the beginning the attitude is more that of using the gods for men's
ends; at the culmination prayer puts men at the service of
God for the correction of human ends, and for the attainment of these corrected ends rather than the initial ones."[9]
So men have been led from prayers for meager personal
needs, befitting a limited, tribal God, to the universal prayer
which Jesus taught: "Our Father, Thy Kingdom come . . .
on earth."

As the early Christians saw the effects of these larger expectations, they were led to greater achievements in prayer for others. Both the effects that Paul perceived in others when he prayed for them and the effects in himself when his friends prayed for him impelled him to call for the same support from comrades whom he had never seen, but hoped to join later in Rome: "Brothers, I beg of you, by our Lord Jesus Christ and by the love that the Spirit inspires, rally round me by praying to God for me."[j] Such ventures in fellowship were encouraged also by the way Jesus had quickened love and courage in his disciples through his prayers for them. They remembered what he had told Simon Peter in a desperate crisis of his life, and how therefore he could strengthen Peter with convincing assurance of the final outcome: "I prayed for you, Simon, that your faith should not fail. And you, when you have returned to me, are to strengthen your brothers."[k] So these early followers of Jesus learned not to limit the range of prayer to their own inner life, but turned to it confidently in order to share a richer life, not only with their friends, but with others also for whom at first they seemed unable to do anything except to pray. For they had learned, however partially, what we can now discern on a larger scale—that the whole world is bound together in more intimate interdependence than has yet been realized; that there are subtle yet profound possibilities of interaction; and that the attitudes and conditions for realizing them can be learned more fully by those who venture to explore the ways of prayer.

Those who have thus ventured ever since that early day, including many of the most discerning men and women of their time, have become convinced in a school of well-tested experience that "there is nothing more powerful than prayer and there is nothing to be compared with it";[10] that "private prayer, when it is real action, is the greatest forge of personality; and that prayer on the scale of the whole gospel is for the religious life what original research is for science— by it we get direct contact with reality."[11] Therefore George Meredith could say: "Cast forth the soul in prayer, you meet

the effluence of the outer truth, you join with the creative
elements giving breath to you; and that crust of habit which
is the soul's tomb; and custom, the soul's tyrant; and pride,
our volcano peak that sinks us in a crater; and fear, which
plucks the feathers from the wings of the soul—you are free
of them, you live in the day and for the future, by this exercise and discipline of the soul's faith."

Questions for Further Thought and Discussion

In what sort of situation might prayer break fellowship rather than create it?
What has prayer done—or what should it have done—in such situations as:
   the church quarrel, the family estrangement, the nervous breakdown,
   alcoholism, mission work, the daily job?
Can such prayer as establishes communion in a Friends meeting have that
   effect in a wider circle of Christians? How can it affect non-Christians?
Granting that prayer is an essentially individual matter, what does the fact
   of community do for it and with it?

24

CONDITIONS AND TESTS FOR EFFECTUAL PRAYER

Harmonious Exercise of the Higher Faculties

FAITH IN PRAYER is not a first condition for Christian prayer. This might make prayer a fetish. A first condition is an adventurous faith, even though small as a mustard seed, that there is, or may be, a father-like Spirit in the universe seeking to co-operate with men. Prayer is a way of responding to this Spirit. By its very nature, therefore, prayer requires, not credulous wishing, but the harmonious exercise of our higher faculties. It calls the mind and the spirit into partnership; Paul said, "I will pray with the spirit, and I will pray with the mind also."[a] Prayer calls the will to high resolves. Willingness to act is a condition for clearer guidance through communion with God: "If any one is willing to do his will, he shall know about the teaching, whether it is from God."[b] Such prayer calls also for the best exercise of the emotions: "Above all you must be loving, for love is the link of the perfect life."[c] And love so exercised and disciplined becomes in turn the great wellspring of prayer: "We pray as much as we desire, and we desire as much as we love."

Love, therefore, is another essential for communion with a Christlike God. "Here we face the real trouble with our prayers. Not for the lack of a satisfying philosophy do our

313

prayers run dry, but for lack of love." Before a man blames
his lack of prayer for others and for great causes on intellectual perplexities, "he well may ask whether, if all his questions were fully answered, he has the spirit that would pour
itself out in vicarious praying." Such praying, Harry Emerson Fosdick suggests, "is the result of generous devotion, not
of logical analysis. We put our *lives* into other people and
into great causes; and our prayers follow after, voicing our
love, with theory or without it. We lay hold on God's alliance for the sake of the folk we care for and the aims we
serve. We do it because love *makes* us, and we continue it
because the validity of our praying is proved in our experience."[1]

Though for convenience we speak of emotion, mind, and
will, we would not suggest that they are divisible, or that
they are exercised separately in either faith or love. True
faith, as we have seen, "is an act of the whole nature, giving
the Eternal World the opportunity to verify itself in our
experience." And such verification needs the whole man,
thinking, feeling, working at his best. So also love is not a
separable part of us. As Walter Rauschenbusch remarked of
Jesus, "love with him was not a fluctuating and wayward
emotion but the highest and most steadfast energy of a will
bent on creating fellowship." Love is an equally important
factor in the proper functioning of the intellect. For intellect, as we can see in our day, when it tries to function without the sympathetic insights born of love, becomes a disintegrating factor in the man himself and in society. Whereas,
intellect, feeling, and will bent on creating fellowship grow
into a unified and co-operating person as one offers his entire
self to the Spirit of love in Christlike prayer. Thus also such
a person is brought into more creative fellowship with others
in a divine-human community.

A Two-fold Condition of Spiritual Health

The growth of such fellowship requires a two-fold condition of spiritual health, which is also a condition and test of

prayer. As Henry Drummond put it: "To get to man by way of God, and to God by way of man, is the only way to keep the entire health of the soul."[2] We need to come to men by way of fellowship with God in order to correct the distorting pressure of persons and things in the turmoil of the world. Withdrawal from time to time for communion with a God eager to fill the willing heart with his love does not isolate that heart from others. Rather it opens hearts and minds to the integrating Spirit of truth and love that is always seeking to develop harmonious interaction between all men and the rest of the universe.[3]

Yet our interactions with persons and with the rest of the universe will be distorted by our own immediate interests unless, also, we come to God by way of men—their true needs and aspirations. Early disciples saw such an approach to God, as important in the experience of Jesus: "He took upon him the form of a servant, and was made like other men." "He had to be made like his brothers in every respect, in order to prove a merciful and faithful high priest," representing the people.[d] It takes time and pains to become human in this deep and broad sense in which Jesus became human. Yet this also must be our aim, if we would pray and work with kindred sympathies and insight. Each of us, according to his ability and opportunity, needs to find a moral equivalent for the experience Jesus gained from sharing the common lot and dealing faithfully with all sorts of people. This means that we should enter with a spirit like his into states of mind and feeling foreign to our own, and into the purposes, the sufferings, and the needs of our fellows.

Thus prayer helps one to think and act as Jesus did, not merely in an individual but also in a representative capacity. This, in part, is what the early Christians meant by praying in the name or spirit of Christ. Because of his boundless love, and because he "learned obedience through what he suffered,"[e] being "made like his brothers," he not only was fitted to be, but *felt* himself to be the Representative of mankind. Similarly, every human being is intended to be a rep-

resentative of mankind, though we seldom get far beyond
the point of knowing it theoretically. "To make it real, and
to feel it, requires a lifelong progress in love. And love grows
by prayer, which brings us gradually to the realization of
the oneness of the life of men."[4]

A good test for our habits of prayer is whether our prayers do foster such lifelong progress in love and unity as
representatives of mankind. The need for some such test is
intensified by the ease with which we slip into deadening
routine. "Prayer too long continued," Canon Streeter observes, "especially if mechanical repetitions and the drill of
a devotional system be invoked to sustain it, may easily and
insensibly slip down to the level of mere autosuggestion. It
may even become a 'pious habit' of mental vacuity which
may blunt the edge of understanding, quench initiative, dull
the moral sense." This tendency explains "why it has so
often happened that those who have been the first to stone
the prophets have been among the most devout. It would
explain, too, the intellectual and moral sterility of so many
of the best-intentioned supporters of organized religion. True
prayer must be that which *succeeds* in being (what all prayer
aspires to be) a realized contact with Creative Spirit—the
Spirit that makes all things new. If so, the test in one's own
life whether prayer is really prayer, or merely pious autosuggestion, will be the extent to which it inspires to bold
and constructive action and to moral and intellectual initiative."[5]

Prayer, Memory, and the Subconscious

When real prayer opens the door for such inspiration and
initiative, as countless thousands know, the question arises
how far prayer can help us through better control of memory and of the subconscious working of the mind. "Christian
prayer," as George A. Buttrick shows, "sets Christ in the
center of the field of attention: we fix our thought on him,
and his light judges and transfigures the whole land of recollection. . . . He becomes the center of reference in our

'memory system': we recall naturally those facts that belong to him. We forget what we ought to forget, and remember what we ought to remember, yet without 'repressions' or surrender of honesty. We are saved from the snares by which memory goes wrong. His image [and influence] have expulsive power, until memory becomes his world"[6] (the world of the Realm of God, whose citizens he desires us to be even now).

Although this condition is not wholly attained in our present life, the more the Spirit manifest in Jesus is given control in our memory, the more we find similar help through the subconscious working of the mind. *"Prayer focuses the conscious mind on God made known in Jesus, and the conscious mind,* however much influenced by the secret city [of the subconscious], *still has wide dominance.* . . . For the subliminal is not separate, and to regard it with alarm would be surrender and finally chaos. Prayer can govern the conscious life, and the conscious life can direct the subconscious. If a man be faithful in prayer, not only morning and night, but 'in between times' in ejaculatory prayer, the impression on the conscious mind is always recent. Thus our awareness is shaped, and our awareness has priority and rule. The subconscious may even then rebel, but mainly with such weapons as the conscious self chooses to give, and often it will be a splendid ally."[7]

How prayer helps to release festering repressions that are related to fears, anxieties, antipathies, or other causes of maladjustment, and clears the way for more creative living, was considered in our preceding chapter. Now we may take heart also from the way "prayer gives the subconscious the relaxation necessary for its own best endeavors. . . . James Watt discovered the secret of the steam condenser while watching his mother's teakettle. In all such 'flashes' two elements are constant. There is, first, a long prior study and labor. Second, there is a period of relaxation, a time of incubation, during which the subconscious mind is secretly busy with the problem in its own laboratories; a quiet time, when there is no

conflict between the clamant will and the subliminal forces.
. . . Always there is need of rigorous thought and action. But
these do not suffice: the clever, too-busy conscious mind must
be stilled. When the mind is freed from the clamorous world,
when it is at home in God, answers flash—more important
answers than the steam engine. The world cannot solve its
problems of daily life or warring nations without this re-
source of prayer."[6]

Prayer Far More Than Autosuggestion

Whether prayer can be more than autosuggestion, whether
it can make possible creative relations with the deepest
Reality in the universe, helping us to control the depths of
our subconscious selves and producing evident changes in
the outer world, depends, after all, upon the nature of the
God with whom we have to do. Here is a basic and determining condition of prayer. "Plato and Aristotle represented
God as that absolute good which, unmoving and changeless
in itself, the soul pursues and longs for. To Christianity, it
is the soul that is pursued. The God of the Christian is one
who invades the earth in order to bring men to themselves;
to every soul of man he 'stands at the door and knocks.' "[7]
This must be so if God's love is like the highest kind of
fatherly love. "Men are called into the family of God, yet
only as men fulfill fraternal relations with one another can
God have the satisfactions that belong to a father. Thus it
is that Christian prayer has to be reciprocal as between God
and the worshiper. There is an ancient doctrine that our
prayers are inspired in us by God himself, so that he also
prays in our prayers. . . . Because the Father values so highly
every child of his, in prayer to him I must adopt his point
of view with respect to my fellows, desiring for each of them
full and joyous self-realization. This sort of submission—to
a God who values each individual—tends therefore toward
the deference for each individual which is the foundation
of democracy."[8] It produces observable and constructive
changes in society.

Further examination confirms this view of the difference between real prayer and mere autosuggestion. So careful a psychological observer as William Brown of Oxford concludes: "Autosuggestion where it succeeds is more nearly akin to prayer than is generally recognized by those interested only in the treatment of functional nervous diseases by autosuggestion. I mean that it is rarely successful unless the patient has at least a subconscious belief that the universe is friendly."[9] Another careful psychologist, James B. Pratt, says: "Psychology may and should point out that the subjective effects of prayer are almost invariably due, directly or indirectly, to some real faith in the objective relation. That meditation may have excellent subjective effects is not to be denied, but no one with any knowledge of the psychology of religion will claim for meditation an influence equal to that which results from the earnest prayer of the man of faith."[10] Still another penetrating student concludes from wide experience: "Nothing but a spiritual vision born of prayer will enable us to approximate Jesus' estimate of every man, woman, and child as precious in God's sight. And until we have this vision, nothing we do will be more than patchwork."[11] Such prayer at its best, as we have seen, is a mode of radical reorientation of the man who prays in his search for higher levels of co-operating life.

Therefore the prayer which helps to orient us with creative Reality, as any determined seeker may learn for himself, has far greater social effects than has the popular kind of autosuggestion. Much autosuggestion is too circumscribed by one's own physical and mental states to influence profoundly social reconstruction, or even one's own objective outlook. Because certain kinds of autosuggestion deny or avoid the existence of evil and the real plight of humanity, they can be used more or less complacently without facing the demands of a transforming love for one's fellow men. Temporarily, such treatment may ease tensions by ignoring some of life's obligations. But any method of dealing with physical or emotional ills, however soothing in itself, which ignores the deeper needs of men and the purpose of God for a community of brothers, tends to distort our relations with both God and men. This antisocial effect of self-centering auto-suggestion may not be detected in the first generation; for social habits often survive the convictions in which they originate. But time shows, perhaps in the second or third generation, which has never experienced the same character-shaping faith, that all the while the hidden streams which feed the larger social purposes had been cut off at their source. The way to recover the source is not to call God in as an afterthought to some formula of autosuggestion. The well-tried way to the most fruitful relations with God and men is through such range and depth of communion with him as the first Christians learned from Jesus. The more we seek God as they did, for his own sake and for the sake of his world-wide community, the more complete are the resultant benefits to all our faculties and to a world of brothers.

A Balance between Society and Solitude

To grow in such range and depth of communion as the disciples saw in Jesus we need to practice his balance between society and solitude. Phillips Brooks contrasts the lack of this balance in modern life with its unerring play in the life of Jesus, beginning with the solitude of his temptation in the wilderness. "That which would have remained only a talent in him, if he had stayed in the desert, becomes a life when he goes forth into the world. What Goethe wisely says of all men does not lose its truth when we are thinking of the Son of Man: 'A talent shapes itself in stillness, but a character in the tumult of the world.' This is Christ's balance between solitude and society. Each makes the other necessary. With us they often lose this value, because they are not set in any relation to each other. Solitude is barren, and so society is frivolous. Solitude creates no consciousness for society to ripen. Each craves the other, not because it wants its complement, but because it is tired of itself and longs to change."[12]

In the life of Jesus, however, we see the perfect play of this balance when his solitude fulfills itself with company. Once and again he goes apart into a mountain for a night of communion with his Father. Such communion, however, as his life and teaching show, brought him more closely in touch with the needs and aspirations of his brother men. And so the early morning finds him among them, choosing his first apostles, or joining his toiling disciples in their boat. "Everybody must have felt how the two needs tremble in response to one another in the intense atmosphere of that vivid night before his crucifixion. First there is the long conversation of the Supper. Then comes the terrible solitude of the Garden of Gethsemane. Again and again the Sufferer comes wandering back to where the tired and unconscious men are lying. . . . Even later, as the Lord's career sweeps into that channel where it must run alone, still the craving for society seems to beat responsive to every new throb of suffering. He turns and looks at Peter; he would almost open his heart to Pilate; he tells the women who follow him to Calvary about the future of the beloved land that murdered him; and at last, even upon the cross, he has mercy to give to the robber at his side, and care still for his mother and the disciple whom he loved. Every moment of deepening communion with his Father has its corresponding moment of sympathy with his brother men. . . . And this same poise and mutual supply which was between society and solitude in the life of Jesus himself he was always trying to establish in the lives of those whom he taught."[12]

Times and Places for Prayer

This same poise and mutual supply between society and solitude, which each of us should find according to his need, give special significance to the times and places devoted to prayer. With none of us, it seems, can spontaneous prayer and our various relations with both men and God be kept at their best in the whirl of modern life without certain times, faithfully set apart and guarded, for being alone with him.

The early morning has great advantage for such unhurried meditation and prayer as will most profoundly influence the entire day. This has been proved under different conditions of life by many of the world's most useful men and women. Some mothers of young children and wives of commuting husbands have found a time after breakfast more favorable. But even in such cases, an interval on first waking for recollection and thanksgiving is invaluable.

The deep influence of the evening upon our unconscious states of mind has led many of wide experience to emphasize also the importance of closing the day in communion with God. F. H. Barry shows "why the best protection against temptation is to give great prominence to praise and thanksgiving in our evening prayers. It is possible to overemphasize the practice of nightly self-examination with highly deleterious effect. Within limits, it is probably indispensable. We cannot afford to resign our consciousness with any memory upon it which will close the door to the divine influence in the mysterious world we enter in sleep. But it must be very strongly balanced by the prayer of contemplating God's perfection. For if we start the day, or go to bed, with our minds chiefly occupied with the suggestion of our sin and weakness we are simply, in the slang phrase, 'asking for trouble.' We are inviting the assaults of evil. But if our minds were stored with the suggestion of the glory and the power of God from the moment we wake to the moment we fall asleep, we should be to a very large extent immunized against wrong suggestions, and evil desires would have no dominion over us."[13]

For similar reasons the distorting pressure of things at midday points to the need of at least a brief time then to bring oneself in humility and quietness before God. That these different times bring unique and decisive influence into the day's work is demonstrated by many who have carried the heaviest responsibilities. Persevering experiment will discover what time is suited for each need, and how best to employ it.

Especially is alert experiment needed to discover the times, whether long continued or brief and frequent, in which to pray for people and causes. Here especially we need a flexible and faithful discipline for the whole day, so that its various events, the reading of the newspaper or of the day's mail, the unexpected encounters or the appointed duties, may be made occasions to further community by the outgoing of the soul with God.

The places for prayer are as various as the occasions for it. Jesus often resorted to a garden during his crowded days in Jerusalem. Peter chose a housetop where the solitude, and perhaps the outlook, helped to break the bondage of racial taboos. Philip found a place of vision on a desert highway and was prepared for fellowship with an Ethiopian official driving by. James discerned beside a bed of suffering a place for the healing influence that modern psychotherapy also attributes to prayer. Stephen, under the stones of his persecutors, prayed for them and helped Paul of Tarsus to come to his better self. In a shipwreck, Paul found prayer a decisive factor in bringing discipline and deliverance out of perilous confusion. At the first Church Council in Jerusalem the members turned to prayer in order to reconcile the differences which threatened to disrupt the church. Thus they found a way for unity of aim in diversity of opinion.

In the duties and distractions of the kitchen, Brother Lawrence learned "that we should establish ourselves in a sense of God's presence by continually conversing with him."[14] In a Chinese dispensary, under surveillance for months by bandits who expected to kidnap him and the women helpers in his mission, Dr. Walter Judd showed the value of a place for prayer in the thick of work. When the day came that the bandits must flee, they amazed even themselves by their inability to return cruelty for love, and they offered instead to pay for what had been done for them.

Walking behind the balustrade of a roof at Cambridge

University, Charles Simeon illustrated the importance of a convenient and secluded place that invites to prayer. He had chosen rooms under the roof because they opened out on a hidden gutter where he could walk unobserved. Many men of his day were more gifted than Charles Simeon, but when he had given prayer the primary place in his life, the students of Cambridge University, dimly discerning something unusual, came to his rooms week after week to learn the secret of a richer life. He had won his battle with sloth by forfeiting a sovereign every time he allowed oversleeping to interfere with his time for prayer. He literally prayed his way through opposition and ill treatment at Cambridge, and for fifty years profoundly influenced students who spent their lives in service throughout the Empire. Well might Lord Macaulay, looking back on his own student days, say of Simeon: "His influence extended from Cambridge to the most remote corner of England. His real sway over the Church was far greater than that of any Primate."

Charles Simeon illustrates also the varying effects of place and posture in prayer. The importance he attached to a convenient place where he could walk in the open air may have been accentuated by his extreme difficulty in rousing himself from sleep, perhaps also by the common tendency of kneeling, especially at night, to induce drowsiness. Like others with similar difficulties, he found release by walking or standing in the quiet of the early morning or under the stars at night.

A housewife in an east side tenement, whose crowded life denied such solitude, improvised seclusion by throwing her apron over her head, and then unconsciously through the day showed the radiance born of communion with God. Some find that turning the pages of a stimulating book, or working in a garden, a carpenter shop, or a kitchen enlivens meditation and the sense of human solidarity that makes prayer more vital. And some find that the mere presence of books, distilling rich experience, makes a library or quiet alcove a favorable place to realize the social implications of prayer.

How to keep these details of time, place, and posture in vital relation to life can be learned only by the actual experiment and steadfast practice of each person for himself. The experience of others may give invaluable hints, but rigid imitation is disastrous. Rules that help one may bind another to a deadening routine and close his eyes to passing opportunities.

The Need for More and Better Training in Prayer

If these attitudes and conditions for prayer are decisive for our lifelong progress in love, and for the very existence of a co-operating world, what about the question of adequate training for prayer? May it not be that the greatest *undeveloped* possibilities in the whole range of Christian service center in the problem of how best to encourage and direct prayer? For here we should be dealing with the diagnosis and cure of the social blindness and the other evils that are making chaos of the modern world. Why then has this whole subject of education in prayer "never yet received the careful thought and serious investigation that its importance deserves?"

This question was raised by a representative commission composed of educators and leaders of the Church throughout the world. In reporting their survey of the resources of the Church, they summarized an "overwhelming volume of testimony" showing the necessity and possibilities of prayer. Therefore, they stressed a need that is now even more urgent: "As in this Conference the Christian Church looks with a greater seriousness than ever before at the problem of the non-Christian world, the call that is most insistent is that Christian men and women should deeply resolve to venture out and make trial of the unexplored depths of the character and the resources of God. The missionary enterprise has led many adventurous spirits to explore unknown territories and tread unbeaten paths. The same spirit of adventure is needed to discover the wealth and resources of life in God. . . . The primary need is not the multiplication of prayer meetings, but that individual Christians should learn to pray. . . . We would, moreover, emphasize the fact that the encouragement and direction of the prayers of Christian people is one of the highest and most difficult forms of Christian service, and constitutes a special vocation. It is important that those to whom this work is entrusted should be chosen on account of their special gifts and aptitudes. . . . It needs to be born in mind that, after all, the issue of aids to prayer, however numerous, and of incentives, however excellent, does not thereby create a body of praying men and women, just as the free distribution of musical instruments does not create a body of musicians. . . . The question then which calls for the serious attention of the Church seems to be how best to develop and train in the Christian soul the desire and the capacity for prayer. The real problem is the securing of a body of Christian people who by earnest and sustained effort have become proficient in the practice of prayer."[15]

Questions for Further Thought and Discussion

How much of "a theology" does the practice of prayer demand?

In what ways does prayer change us as we pray? our picture of things for which we pray? persons and causes prayed for?

What examples can we list of the alternation between solitude and society, worship and work?

What are the dangers of setting a certain time for prayer daily—and of not doing so?

What aspects of psychiatric therapy have long been found in Christian prayer?

Of the people with whom you work every day, probably what percentage pray regularly? Does the answer have anything to do with the sense of community found there?

What are some ways of leading people to pray?

25

CONSUMMATION OF FELLOWSHIP

Redemptive Love Must Be a Suffering Love

WHY DOES MUCH of the Christianity and Judaism of our
time suggest a formal or complacent rather than a prophetic
and creative religion? Why does many a church or synagogue
seem to be an acquiescent congregation rather than a transforming fellowship? Is it because, like the rulers in the time
of Jesus, we prefer to play safe with existing institutions
rather than to take the risks of "projecting a new society
over against the existing world-order"?[1] It is because, ever
since the first great compromise with that existing order, the
majority of Christians have been thinking more in terms of
personal, national, or class interests than in terms of that
world-uniting community which Jesus called men everywhere to seek above all else?

However we may account for past failures, this much is
confirmed by both personal and corporate experience since
Calvary: Only as we are seeking and willing to suffer for
such a society as Jesus envisioned, can we understand his
suffering and the sacrificial life on which true community
depends. For nothing is more deeply imbedded in the experience we find in the New Testament, and in life itself,
than this: love, if it is to be a redemptive influence in the
individual and a transforming power in society, "must be a
suffering love—a love that involves pain and renunciation

and sacrifice and very death itself. The principle of this vicarious suffering may be seen in all family life and even in the lesser kinships of the animal creation, as when a mother gladly suffers pain for the sake of her child's welfare, or a mother-hen braves many a danger for the protection of her brood."[2] But what is distinctive about a truly Christian fellowship is that it realizes this self-giving of natural instinct as containing the main secret of the further spiritual development of the race, and that consequently it seeks to extend such giving to all those who in any way need help. To bear one another's burdens, as Paul said, is to fulfill the underlying principle of the Christian fellowship. It was the exercise of this noblest sort of love in the disciples that led many in the early third century to recognize the Christians of that period as a distinctly different kind of men. "See," it was said, "how these men love one another, and how ready they are even to die for one another." "This is the great spiritual discovery for which Christianity stands, and it is certain that it was in the nature of a discovery even to men who had been reared in the faith of Israel."[2]

Dr. Claude Montefiore explains this discovery in comparing Jewish benevolent righteousness (chesed) with Christian love (agapé). He says that agapé stands for "something more venturous, more self-sacrificing, more eager, more giving, than can honestly be said to be connoted by righteousness or goodness. It . . . does in its height 'cause a man to lay down his life for his friend.' It . . . drives a man forth to save, to redeem, and to forgive."[3] Or, as a great Catholic, Baron Von Hügel says, [it is] "a love which loves, not in acknowledgement of an already present lovableness, but in order to render lovable in the future what at present repels love."[4] Such love looks beyond suffering or death to more abundant life, beyond loveless and unsocial individuals to a community of loving and lovable persons.

So the Cross, in the experiences that accompanied and followed Calvary, convinced proud Jews and Romans, as well as hopeless slaves, that here was a way by which they could "get the better of evil"[a] and foster a new fellowship cemented by suffering. Thus the Cross became a symbol of the power of suffering in group action as well as in personal attitudes. It opened a way by which the early Christians could be articulate when all other ways were closed. In this way, even when they had to face lions in the arena, they became a transforming influence out of all proportion to their numbers. In this way they prevailed, even when the Jewish Church and the Roman Empire tried to silence them, and they won leaders like Paul of Tarsus from the very forefront of the opposition.

The winning of such men, who were at first exasperated at the unpatriotic ideas of Stephen, for instance, illustrates how this new insight and love, even to the point of death, induced opponents to embrace a new philosophy of life. The more these men and women, like Paul, whose habits of thought and life had been hostile to the "way of the Cross," saw its influence exerted through suffering for a universal brotherhood, the more it set them thinking that this influence might correspond with the deepest Reality that men can know. So they came to believe that "God was in Christ reconciling the world to himself," and that he had committed to them the same ministry of reconciliation.[b] In the light of the crucifixion of Jesus, and of the experience of those who followed the same road, these early converts learned the meaning of a ministry like his. They perceived that though they were not to seek physical death or suffering for its own sake, they were to die to all self-seeking, to "set no value on their own life as compared with the joy of fulfilling the commission received from him."[c] Coming thus to know Jesus, as Paul said, through "the fellowship of his suffering," they came to know him also in "the power of his resurrection."[d] They found that "he has taken away the power of death and brought life and immortality to light through the good news."[e] In proportion as they also lived "by virtue of a life beyond the reach of death,"[f] their fellowship, which could not be broken, was multiplied.

"A Spiritual Contact along the Path of Death to Self"

The power of this deathless fellowship is explained in Professor Berguer's psychological study of the early Christians' experience: "They had tasted the life and the triumphant power of him who had died. They saw that death did not destroy life; they had shared this unique experience, which had transformed the world, that to die was to live, since he whom they had seen die thenceforward lived in them. . . . That is the experience of the disciples. . . . The life of the Christian community, the change in the attitude of the disciples, the rapid development of the Church, its extension, and its missionary work would remain inexplicable save for some spiritual event of the first importance that had revolutionized the whole psychology of the first believers and transformed them completely. This event, according to their testimony, was *the Resurrection of Jesus Christ,* the certitude of his life, to which death has not put an end, the contact that has been effected between himself and them in such a way as to leave no room for doubt on their part." They discovered that "he reveals himself as living only to those who have, in some way . . . at least vibrated to the emotions and the experiences through which he passed. . . . It is the irrevocable testimony of a spiritual contact which takes place only along the path of death to self."[5]

So these earliest Christians, pondering the effects of the death and resurrection of Jesus in the light of their own experience, found the old problem of suffering illuminated by what the crucifixion and its sequel disclosed to them of the nature and work of God. For, as Canon Streeter says, "the spectacle of the ideally good man brought to an ideally bad end, as a consequence of his self-devotion to moral and religious reform, raises the problem of evil in its acutest form. The career of Jesus is a test case. Indeed, for all who ask the meaning of the Universe, it is *the* test case. The Cross of Christ must be, either the darkest spot of all in the mystery of existence, or a searchlight by the aid of which we may penetrate the surrounding gloom. And from reflection on that Cross there has dawned upon the mind of man a new vision of God—a vision of a God who himself enters into the world's pain, and thereby breaks the power of the world's sin. And with this has come a new perception of the possibilities of pain—an apprehension that there is a kind and quality of pain that is creative, curative, redemptive, and that this is a kind of pain which man is privileged to share with God. Evil is neither explained nor denied; it is defeated."[6]

This defeat of evil, and the new sense of victorious fellowship in suffering and resurrection, was no mere anticipation of something to come. Paul voiced a present experience: "Just as Christ was raised from the dead by a manifestation of the Father's power, so we may live and move in a new sphere of life. For if we have become united with him by the act symbolic of his death, surely we shall also become united with him by the act symbolic of his Resurrection, knowing as we do that our old self has been crucified with him in order to . . . free us from any further slavery to sin. . . . So you also must think of yourselves as dead to sin but alive to God, through union with Christ Jesus."[g] Or, as another early Christian put the immediately practical aspects of such fellowship in suffering and victory with Christ, "we know what love is by this, that he laid down his life for us; so we ought to lay down our lives for the brotherhood. But whoever possesses this world's goods, and notices his brother in need, and shuts his heart against him, how can love to God remain in him? . . . Let us put our love not into words or into talk, but into deeds, and make it real."[h]

This discovery of the power of suffering love to influence men began soon after the tragedy on Calvary, and has never since been wholly lost. "You have crucified the pioneer of life," was the charge that came home to the scoffing crowd on the day of Pentecost and moved many to repentance and sacrificial living. It is through perceiving the consequences of evil fall upon others, especially when they fall upon one

who endures them to set others free, that men often do discover their better selves and their godlike destiny. The great
literature of the world illustrates this fact,[7] as do the life and
testimony of many men and women who have most deeply
influenced their fellow men. Gandhi, voicing his conviction
that the sufferings of uncompromising Christians in Germany have not been in vain, added this personal testimony:
"Though I cannot claim to be a Christian in the sectarian
sense, the example of Jesus' suffering is a factor in the com-
position of my undying faith in nonviolence, which rules all
my actions, worldly and temporal. And I know that there
are hundreds of Christians who believe likewise. Jesus lived
and died all in vain if he did not teach us to regulate the
whole of life by the eternal law of love."[8]

The Love Symbolized by the Cross and Resurrection

What then does this eternal law of love, symbolized by
the Cross and the Resurrection, require of us, of churches,
and of kindred groups? We need not consider all its aspects
to find guidance for our time. It would show "ignorance of
the nature of the reaction of the Cross upon individuals and
upon the world," says Richard Roberts, "to suppose that any
single theory of the Cross would be an adequate interpretation of it. The Cross is as many sided as life itself; but at the
heart of it is the fundamental law that sacrifice is the supreme
condition of peace and increase of life, and that self-surrender
is the secret of self-realization." It follows from what we have
seen of the essential continuity of human life with the divine
life, and of the death and resurrection of Jesus as expressing
that continuity, that the Cross reveals not only a human
ideal, but the very life of God. "The Cross was the affirmation of the principle that the very deepest truth of the life of
God, translated into terms of history in the Crucifixion, was
to become the very deepest truth of the life of man."[9]

Because the Cross expressed this deepest truth of the life
of God and of man, it was to be translated into men's lives
continuously, not only singly but in a community. "The

Church was the community founded by Christ for the perpetuation of the achievement of the Cross into future ages. It is impossible to resist the feeling in reading the gospels, that after Jesus had recognized the futility of attempting to bring in the Kingdom of God through the channels of current Judaism, and had in consequence broken definitely with the synagogue, his chief aim was to build up a community of disciples by whom his work could be carried on. The special emphasis which he lays upon his death from the time of Peter's confession shows that he was preparing the disciples for some direct redemptive activity. That constituted them straightway into a body of an entirely different character from any voluntary association of men joined together by a common interest and committed to some common purpose. The Church was all this; but it was a good deal besides. It is significant that when the Church began to emerge from the confusion of its early years it learned to conceive of itself as 'the body of Christ,' . . . as that of which Jesus was the perfect embodiment and manifestation in history."[9] So the Church came to believe that it was to continue the Incarnation. Its members were "being built up together to be a dwelling place for God through the Spirit" so that God might be in them as he "was in Christ, reconciling the world unto himself."[i] And because the deepest influence in this work of reconciliation is found in the Cross, the Cross must be reproduced in the life of the Church and its members. The blood of the martyrs is the seed of the Church, is a true principle; "but it needs raising to larger dimensions—the blood of the Church is the seed of the Kingdom."[9]

The Church will raise this principle of self-giving to ever larger dimensions in our day if it will give itself in the spirit of the martyrs, rather than compromise with the forces that resist a world-uniting fellowship. We know that this principle can be raised to larger dimensions when we look at the early experience of the Church. It originally partook of the spirit of the martyrs, and in turn nourished and supported those who were willing to pass through death, if need

be, rather than surrender the principle and spirit of brotherhood on earth. At the beginning it attained an unusual
independence of all imperialisms, whether political, economic, or religious, because its members believed that at
any cost they "must obey God rather than men," and that
they were his ambassadors to serve the interests of a very
different kind of government from that prevailing at Jerusalem or Rome. Consequently, they held themselves free
from all alliances at variance with their commission, for they
had been called to seek first the Kingdom of God and to
pray for its coming on earth, even to the point of giving
their lives for it. In intention, therefore, "Christianity is
nothing less than a civilization, and in order to realize itself
as such it sets up in the world a community after its own
genius, a community which is not of the world but which
undertakes to fashion the world increasingly after the ideals
prevailing in its own fellowship."[10]

But later, as we have seen, the Church became entangled
with the Empire, and has never since recovered fully its
original independence or singleness of aim. After the second
century it set out upon "the unvarying path along which
original Christianity and practically all of its sects have
passed from revolutionary challenge to the principalities and
powers of this world to acceptance of its ways and works.
Just as ecclesiastical Rome took on the pattern of conquering, ruling Rome, so has modern Protestantism taken over
the ways and works of the trading, investing West. Its ethics
have confusedly mixed the concepts of profit and service. It
has come under increasing institutional dependence upon
successful money making for maintenance of activities."[11]

But along with this self-preserving tendency in the churches,
there has come another trend, more consistent with the
principle of the Cross in social development. "Today as never
before the leaders of organized Christianity are aware that
the West has never really accepted Jesus, that the religion
of the churches is not his religion. In other days rebel sects
like the Lollards, the Anabaptists, the Levellers, have had

this awareness. But it was induced largely by their own economic need and therefore somewhat limited to that interest. It should be our gain that the present widespread consciousness of the ethical nature of the gospel is more objective and general. Carried through, it requires a thoroughgoing and continuous transformation of society. It is an ethic of service and sacrifice, and it takes life in a different direction from the ethic of conquest and enjoyment. It offers renunciation by the privileged as the substitute for the class war."[11]

If this meaning of the Cross is to be taught effectively by the churches, it must be practiced by them institutionally. They must develop the capacity to perceive and eliminate institutional decay. Such decay begins when an institution becomes more concerned for itself than for the ends it should serve. If the churches are to diagnose and to cure this atrophy of self-centeredness, they must practice constantly a revaluation of themselves and their works with corresponding repentance and change of ways. Thus the churches may show how other institutions, as well as individuals, can be led to repent so that social change may come by constant renewal rather than by decay or revolution.

Science can aid in this work, but it cannot motivate it. So we are brought again to the necessity that religion join with science for the progressive revaluing and redirecting of life. "Under the impulse of the scientific method, organized religion has highly developed its critical faculty in recent years. Within the churches there is more revaluation going on than in any other social institution. The spirit of Protestantism is congenial to this effort. Its genius is more than protest, it is freedom to search for truth."[11] If the churches will pursue this search for truth in all that vitally concerns society, they may enlarge the motives of science and enlist many more who are scientifically minded in discovering and fulfilling the conditions for a better world.

Moreover, the churches and their members, in order to continue the Incarnation in our day, must show to the world

much more than a mere ethic; they must show in their own
life and work the power of the self-sacrificing love of God
that was shown by Jesus in his earthly life. For nothing less
has been found able to transform men "by the renewing of
their minds, so that they may learn by experience what the
will of God is, namely, what is good and acceptable to him."j

Therefore Protestantism must face a responsibility for its
members who are leaders in business and the professions.
Many of these leaders have been educated under its influence. Among Protestants are found in large part, especially
in English speaking lands, the technically trained people who
provide the community with its engineering, medical service,
law, finance, business management, and teaching. The attitude of these leading members of society may largely determine the manner of its transformation. "Unless there are
sufficient of them who see the need of change, and are willing
to embrace its discomforts, we shall get the next stage in
social development by the driving force of the needs of the
masses, without intelligent planning; and it will come with
the maximum of friction and waste."[11]

If citizens in general lack wise leaders, and fail to rise
above racial, class, and party prejudice in business and civic
relations at home, they cannot support effectively the larger
co-operation between nations on which the peace and prosperity of the world depend. And without adequate support
for such co-operation, the possibilities of general well-being
that are now within reach will be blasted, and modern civilization also will suffer the doom of persistent self-seeking.
"The crisis, then," says Lewis Mumford, "presses toward a
conversion, deep-seated, organic, religious in essence, so that
no part of political or personal existence will be untouched
by it. . . . And a Church that taught one part of mankind to
walk upright and unafraid through one Dark Age may yet
summon up the power that will enable us to avert another
Dark Age, or to face it, if it begins to descend upon us, with
unyielding courage."[12]

The Whole Life of Jesus Still Points the Way

Toward the needed courage and co-operation of individuals or of nations the whole life of Jesus still points the way. He began to draw the issues more clearly, as we have seen, after vested interests, following a practice still prevalent, "sent emissaries from Jerusalem, to catch him in his words." He saw that some of the people, at least, must be awakened to what was at stake before the forces of reaction could put him out of the way by stealth. So he "steadfastly set his face to go to Jerusalem," where the real issue could be clarified at a time of national assembly, instead of being stifled in some obscure corner of the provinces. He took the risks of facing entrenched interests where they were most powerful, yet also most vulnerable, at the very center of their machinations. By his raid on the hucksters and money changers in the temple, he exposed the connivance of rulers in the exploitation of the poor; and in still other ways he dramatized the issue so that it could be understood for all time.[13]

Yet, side by side with this more public work of education, Jesus devoted himself with characteristic concern to the disciples who soon would have to bear the heaviest responsibility. Thus the Fourth Gospel portrays him approaching the Cross: "When Jesus knew that his hour had come to depart out of this world to the Father, having loved his own who were in the world, he loved them to the end." And before the last supper with his apostles, he girded himself with a towel, that he might minister to them as a servant. When he had washed their feet, he said to them, "I have given you an example, that you also should do as I have done to you."[k] Going soon after to the lonely vigil in Gethsemane, he bore with patience the drowsiness of friends who failed to watch with him even for an hour.[l] Foreseeing Peter's denial, Jesus had prayed for him, then admonished him: "When you have turned again, strengthen your brothers." And after Peter's third denial, Jesus looked at him with such love that Peter went out and wept bitterly.[m] Throughout the abusive mockery of justice, Jesus spoke the truth in love, or kept the silence of a forgiving heart. When he found a penitent thief sharing the agony of crucifixion, Jesus welcomed him into everlasting fellowship. Thus identified to the last with the lot of "the unprivileged," he prayed for "the privileged" who had despitefully used him.[n] And then, "by the power of an indestructible life," he convinced the disciples that such love never ends.[o]

His whole life seems to be saying to us: "God so loved the world that he gave his only son." "Greater love has no man than this, that a man lay down his life for his friends. You are my friends, if you do what I command you. This is my commandment, that you love one another as I have loved you."[p]

The most concise form of his commission to his disciples is also the most comprehensive. A long life will not exhaust its meaning; yet to all who respond to him it gives assurance of light and strength for every step: "As the Father has sent me, even so I send you."[q]

Questions for Further Thought and Discussion

In what ways does the quality of fellowship among human beings depend on their idea of God and the universe?

How, in turn, do our experiences of human love provide a framework for Christian beliefs about ultimate reality?

On what do campaigners today base "brotherhood" when they declare it apart from "Fatherhood"?

If Christian love is indeed a revolutionary power, is it ever completely at home in the institutionalized Church?

Is suffering always redemptive among people, as was that on the Cross?

What happens to any person's sense of community when he realizes himself to be a part of the Incarnation?

Is there really hope that Christians in this age can achieve what Von Hügel calls "a love which loves, not in acknowledgment of an already present loveableness, but in order to render lovable in the future what at present repels love"?

In what ways does this book advance that possibility?

NOTES

THE NOTES, numbered consecutively in each chapter, refer not only to the titles, authors, and publishers of books and articles quoted in the text, or valuable for further reading, but also to other pertinent material for use in discussion or experiment, such as suggestive instances and projects that deserve attention, organizations which can give additional information, etc.

In order that the experience and teaching of Jesus, his predecessors, and early co-workers, may flow most naturally into our discussions, we have often used a translation of Old or New Testament into modern speech. References to the particular passage and translation used are marked by small letters, arranged alphabetically for each chapter.

When quotations, standing near each other in our text, are taken from the same author and book, this fact is shown by using the same numeral after each of the quotations, thus reducing the complexity of the notes, and showing in the text that these quotations are from the same source. The numerals given in the notes to show the pages of the book quoted are placed in the same order as the quotations to which they refer.

Some important general subjects of our inquiry extend over two or more chapters. We consider specific aspects of these general subjects in separate chapters in order to keep each chapter short enough to be read at one sitting. The title of a chapter and the section heads will suggest the part of the subject to be considered.

CHAPTER 1

LEARNING HARMONY THROUGH FELLOWSHIP

1 Arthur S. Morgan, *The Small Community, Foundation of Democratic Life, What It Is and How to Achieve It* (New York: Harper & Brothers), pp. xix, xx.

2 In other instances Alcoholics Anonymous, which holds group meetings in a near-by city, has been very helpful.

3 Richard Roberts, *For God and Freedom* (Sackville, New Brunswick, Can-

ada: Mt. Allison University Press), p. 45, and *The Red Cap on the Cross* (London: Headley Brothers), pp. 68–9.

⁴ Lecomte du Noüy, *Human Destiny* (New York: Longmans, Green and Co.), pp. 104 ff., 163–4, 177–180, 242–3, 273. See du Noüy in our index; Gerald Heard, *The Source of Civilization* (New York: Harper & Brothers), Conclusion, p. 293 ff., and sources cited later.

⁵ Eugene W. Lyman, *The Meaning and Truth of Religion* (New York: Charles Scribner's Sons), pp. 32–34, 439 ff.

BIBLICAL SOURCES

a "Helper," thus Moffatt, Goodspeed, and others, John 14:15–16 and 25–26; 15:26; 16:7 f.; Cf. Luke 11:13; b Phil. 2:1 and 1:5, R.S.V. use "participation" and "partnership" for the Greek *koinonia;* c Rom. 8:2, 11, 14, 23, R.S.V.

CHAPTER 2

THE RELEVANCE OF JESUS FOR ENDURING COMMUNITIES

¹ William Lecky, *History of European Morals* (New York: D. Appleton & Co.), Vol. II, pp. 1, 2, 12.

² Henry C. Link, *The Return to Religion* (New York: The Macmillan Co.), pp. 6, 7, 33, 34.

³ J. Arthur Hadfield, *The Psychology of Power,* chap. III in *The Spirit,* edited by B. H. Streeter (New York: The Macmillan Co.), pp. 108–112.

⁴ Edward I. Bosworth, *The Life and Teaching of Jesus* (New York: The Macmillan Co.), pp. 70 and 49, quoting Heb. 4:15 from A.V. with Heb. 5:8 and 2:18 from R.S.V.

⁵ Oscar Wilde, *De Profundis.*

⁶ James Hastings Nichols, *Primer for Protestants* (New York: Association Press), p. 101.

⁷ John Baillie, *The Roots of Religion in the Human Soul* (New York: Charles Scribner's Sons), p. 181.

⁸ George Bernard Shaw, Preface to *Androcles and the Lion* (New York: Brentano's), p. xiv.

⁹ Vladimir G. Simkhovitch, *Towards the Understanding of Jesus* (New York: The Macmillan Co.). John Kelman says of this little book, "I have never seen the immense intellectual grasp of Jesus put so strongly or convincingly before."

¹⁰ Ernest D. Burton, *Christianity in the Modern World* (Chicago: University of Chicago Press), chapter II, "Jesus as a Thinker."

¹¹ John Dewey, *Reconstruction in Philosophy* (Boston: Beacon Press), chapter VII quoted by Eugene W. Lyman in context of next reference.

¹² Eugene W. Lyman, *The Meaning and Truth of Religion* (New York: Charles Scribner's Sons), p. 186.

¹³ Robert Andrew Millikan, *Science and the New Civilization* (New York: Charles Scribner's Sons), p. 190.

¹⁴ Quoted by Henry Sloane Coffin in an article, "Can Jesus Maintain His Authority" in *The Christian Century,* Jan. 14, 1931, p. 53.

15 William Lecky, *The History of European Morals* (New York: D. Appleton and Co.), Vol. II, p. 9.

16 See Benjamin Kidd, *The Science of Power* (New York: G. P. Putnam's Sons), esp. chapter VIII, "Woman Is the Psychic Center of Power in the Social Integration," and chapter IX, "The Mind of Women."

BIBLICAL SOURCES

a Luke 6:7–11, R.S.V.;   b Matt. 18:21, 22, 20th Century N.T.;   c John 10:10, Moffatt's Translation;   d Matt. 11:29, Moffatt, condensed;   e Matt. 15:14, R.S.V.;   f Matt. 15:1–20 and Mark 7:3–4, 20th Century and Moffatt;   g Matt. 7:16 and 6:30 A.V.;   h Luke 8:1–3, 23–49; 24:19;   i Mark 9:38–39, Moffatt; j John 6:37, 20th Century, John 8:32, Charles B. Williams Translation, Bruce Humphries, Boston;   k Acts 3:15, Moffatt.

CHAPTER 3

THE SCOPE OF COMMUNITY INSPIRED BY JESUS

1 Eugene William Lyman, *The Meaning and Truth of Religion* (New York: Charles Scribner's Sons), pp. 85–86.

2 Henry Nelson Wieman, *Methods of Private Religious Living* (New York: The Macmillan Co.), p. 25.

3 Arthur H. Compton in *Herald-Tribune Magazine Section*, New York, Sunday.

4 Statement of 1920 on "The Moral Witness of the Church on Economic Subjects." Quoted in *Christianity and the Social Revolution* (New York: Charles Scribner's Sons), pp. 57–58.

5 David S. Cairns, *Christianity in the Modern World* (New York: George H. Doran), pp. 29–31.

6 H. N. Wieman, *The Wrestle of Religion with Truth* (New York: The Macmillan Co.), pp. 66–67.

7 William Temple, *The Hope of a New World* (New York: The Macmillan Co.), p. 67.

8 Harry F. Ward, *Which Way Religion?* (New York: The Macmillan Co.), pp. 141, 159–161, condensed.

9 Ralph W. Sockman, *Morals of Tomorrow* (New York: Harper and Brothers), p. 309.

10 John Oliver Nelson, *Young Laymen—Young Church* (New York: Association Press), chap. VI, p. 85, "We Traced Current Theologies." A book with many examples of young laymen co-operating effectively.

· 11 John Knox, "The Sustaining Community," closing *The Christian Answer* (New York: Charles Scribner's Sons), pp. 188–190. A symposium edited by Henry P. Van Dusen.

BIBLICAL SOURCES

a Matt. 6:31–33, Moffatt and R.S.V.;   b Isa. 3:14–15;   c Matt. 23:23, Weymouth;   d Matt. 6:28–33, and 7:7–8, 12, Moffatt;   e Matt. 5:44, 45, 48, compare Plato: Timaeus, 29s;   f Matt. 10:20, Goodspeed, and John 17:17–21; g Heb. 1:3, Moffatt; Col. 2:9–10;   h II Cor. 5:17–20.

CHAPTER 4

VERIFICATION BY PAUL OF TARSUS

[1] John Dow, "The Historical Element in Christianity," *The Canadian Student* for March, 1929.

[2] Dean William R. Inge's essay on Paul in *Outspoken Essays* (New York: Longmans, Green and Co.), p. 205.

[3] Frank Chamberlain Porter, *The Mind of Christ in Paul* (New York: Charles Scribner's Sons), pp. 17, 13–41.

[4] For an engaging view of the later Paul, whose influence was felt in Caesar's household and the Praetorian Guard even while he was chained to a Roman soldier, read continuously his letter of gratitude and encouragement to his devoted friends at Philippi. (Acts 28:16, 20, 30; Phil. 1:12–13; 4:18).

[5] C. H. Dodd, *The Meaning of Paul for Today* (New York: George H. Doran), pp. 82–83.

[6] Sholem Asch, *One Destiny, An Epistle to the Christians* (New York: G. P Putnam's Sons), pp. 5, 6, 83, 86, 87 condensed.

[7] John Cournos, *An Open Letter to Jews and Christians* (New York: Oxford University Press), pp. 167, 151, 166. Cournos seems not to appreciate all that was at stake for spiritual and political freedom when Paul opposed those who insisted that Gentile Christians must submit to the demands of Pharasaic legalism.

[8] Elton Trueblood, *Foundations for Reconstruction* (New York: Harper & Brothers), pp. 9–11.

[9] Elton Trueblood, *The Common Ventures of Life* (New York: Harper & Brothers), pp. 24–26 from chap. I, "The Recovery of Wholeness."

BIBLICAL SOURCES

[a] Gal. 5:22–23, Moffatt; [b] See II Cor. 11:24–30; 12:8–10; [c] I Cor., 13th chapter; [d] Acts 10:14 ff., Gal. 2:11 ff.; [e] Acts 15:10; [f] Acts 26:5; [g] Gal. 3:24, A.V.; [h] Rom. 7:14—8:2, Phil. 3:3–14; [i] Acts 7:58–60, 8:1, 9:4–6, 22:7 ff., 26:14 ff.; [j] Gal. 1:11 ff., II Cor. 4:5 ff.; [k] Rom. 8:28–29, Weymouth, compare Moffatt; Rom. 15:5–6, II Cor. 1:3 ff.; [l] Rom. 8:28–29, R.S.V.; [m] Rom. 12:21; [n] Rom. 8:19, 21, Moffatt and Goodspeed.

CHAPTER 5

CONTINUING VERIFICATION IN LIFE

[1] Harold Anson, *A Practical Faith* (London: George Allen and Unwin, Ltd.), chap. III.

[2] Gerald Heard, *The Source of Civilization* (New York: Harper & Brothers).

[3] See Lecomte du Noüy's conclusion quoted in last paragraph of this chapter. Also Ashley Montagu, *Being Human* (New York: Henry Schuman).

[4] Charles E. Raven, *The Creator Spirit* (Cambridge: Harvard University Press), pp. 117–127.

[5] Origen, speaking as a scientist in *Contra Celsum*, IV, p. 76, quoted by Raven as in Note 4.

6 W. R. Sorley, The Gifford Lectures, *Moral Values and the Idea of God* (3rd ed., New York: The Macmillan Co.), pp. 503–504, and 342–346, condensed.

7 Henry P. Van Dusen, *The Plain Man Seeks for God* (New York: Charles Scribner's Sons), pp. 196–7 and 186 condensed.

8 R. L. Stevenson, *Letters* (English ed.), Vol 1, p. 370.

9 *Journal of Katharine Mansfield*, edited by Middleton Murray, pp. 166, 167, 201, quoted by Lyman.

10 Jennie M. Bigham, *Life of the Seventh Earl of Shaftesbury, K.C.*, pp. 43–44, quoted by Lyman.

11 Eugene W. Lyman, *The Meaning and Truth of Religion* (New York: Charles Scribner's Sons), pp. 410–414.

12 George Tyrrell in letter to Baron Von Hugel, quoted by Richard Roberts on the flyleaf of *That Strange Man Upon His Cross* (Nashville: Abingdon-Cokesbury).

13 Paul Tillich, *The Shaking of the Foundations* (New York: Charles Scribner's Sons), pp. 106, 107, quoting Rom. 8:34–37.

14 Harold Dodd, *The Meaning of Paul for Today* (New York: George H. Doran), pp. 32, 33, condensed.

15 Edwin Grant Conklin, *The Direction of Human Evolution* (New York: Charles Scribner's Sons), pp. 240–241, 245, 246, condensed.

16 Lecomte du Noüy, *Human Destiny* (New York: Longmans, Green and Co.), pp. 104 ff. and 273, condensed. See our index under du Noüy.

BIBLICAL SOURCES

a John 12:32–33; Luke 23:42, 43; II Tim. 1:10; b Matt. 6:10, 33; II Cor. 5:18–20, 6:1; Phil. 3:20–21, Moffatt and R.S.V.; c Rom. 12:21, Moffatt; d I John 3:2–3, R.S.V.

CHAPTER 6

RELIGION AND SCIENCE IN PARTNERSHIP

1 Alfred North Whitehead, *Science and the Modern World* (New York: The Macmillan Co.), p. 253.

2 Charles E. Raven, *Science, Religion, and the Future* (New York: The Macmillan Co.), pp. ix, x, 11, 12, condensed.

3 Lecomte du Noüy, *The Road to Reason* (New York: Longmans, Green and Co.), pp. 239–240.

4 Vannevar Bush, *Modern Arms and Free Men* (New York: Simon & Schuster), pp. 78, 100, in large paper edition.

5 J. Arthur Thomson, *The Outline of Science* (New York: G. P. Putnam's Sons), Vol. IV, p. 1180.

6 William Adams Brown, *Beliefs that Matter* (New York: Charles Scribner's Sons), pp. 72, 73.

7 William Adams Brown, *Beliefs that Matter* (New York: Charles Scribner's Sons), p. 73, citing James Harvey Robinson's *The Mind in the Making* (New York: Harper and Brothers), and Justice Cardozo's chapter on "The Judge as Legislator" in *The Nature of the Judicial Process* (New Haven: Yale University Press), e.g., p. 135 ff.

[8] Adolf Harnack, *What Is Christianity?* (New York: G. P. Putnam's Sons), p. 73.

[9] Halford E. Luccock, *Jesus and the American Mind* (Nashville: Abingdon-Cokesbury).

[10] Van Wyck Brooks, Editor, *Journal of Gamaliel Bradford* (New York: Houghton Mifflin Co.).

[11] John Dow in "The Historical Element in Christianity" in *The Canadian Student* of March, 1929.

[12] L. H. Bailey, *Cyclopedia of American Agriculture,* Vol. I (New York: The Macmillan Co.), p. 395 ff. and pp. 594–5.

[13] Frank Fritts and Ralph W. Gwinn, *Fifth Avenue to Farm, A Biological Approach to the Problem of the Survival of Our Civilization* (New York: Harper and Brothers), pp. 242, 244 ff. and 11 ff. For "A Practical Guide to the Selection and Management of the Small Farm" see M. G. Kains, *Five Acres and Independence* (with bibliography) revised and enlarged (New York: Greensburgh). For our agriculture, its problems and possibilities in relation to society as a whole, see Arthur Moore *The Farmer and the Rest of Us* (Boston: Little, Brown and Co.).

[14] Hugh A. Moran, "Co-operation Where It Counts," from *American Agriculturist,* Oct. 22, 1938, p. 1f.

[15] Gove Hambidge, *Your Meals and Your Money* (New York: Whittlesey House, McGraw-Hill Book Company).

[16] Rackham Holt, *George Washington Carver,* (an authorized biography) (New York: Doubleday, Doran Co.), pp. 242, 311, 312. James G. Wilson was Carver's teacher at Iowa State College of Agriculture and was later the Secretary of Agriculture in the cabinets of three Presidents. See also an inspiring sketch of Carver's life and work in Edwin R. Embree, *13 Against the Odds* (New York: Viking Press), pp. 97 to 116. (A book of short, lucid, and colorful biographies on the greatest of living Negroes.)

[17] Arthur P. Chew, *Plowshares Into Swords, Agriculture in the World War Age* (New York: Harper and Brothers), pp. ix, xi, 219, 220.

[18] Mr. Taylor is Agricultural Economist, The Farm Foundation; formerly Chief of the Bureau of Agricultural Economics, U.S. Department of Agriculture.

[19] Fairfield Osborne, *Our Plundered Planet* (Boston: Little, Brown and Co.), and William Vogt, *Road to Survival* (New York: Sloan Associates), though unduly pessimistic about some matters, show the urgency for international team-work to feed the world. A more hopeful view, with many interesting examples, is given in *New Worlds Emerging* by Earl Parker Hanson, who during twenty-five years worked intermittently in the tropics and the sub-arctic as an engineer, geographer, economist and government planner. He shows how distorted much writing about these regions has been, and why white men and others should experiment further with better ways of living there in productive communities. (New York: Duell, Sloan, & Pearce.) We quote pp. 151, 170.

[20] "Is Peace Still Possible?", *The Nation,* April 8, 1950, pp. 319–20.

[21] "A Way to Lessen World Hunger," *Reader's Digest,* March, 1950, p. 131 ff., (from the *Minneapolis Tribune,* Jan. 22, 1950).

[22] Robert A. Millikan, in a statement to James M. Spears as Chairman of the Sponsoring Committee of a National Preaching Mission, July 28, 1936.

The organization, Koinonia, hopes to train men, especially those going abroad, to implement this union of religion and science. Address care of Mount Vernon Place Methodist Church, Baltimore, Md.

BIBLICAL SOURCES

a Matt. 7:16–20.

CHAPTER 7

APPRAISALS BY SCIENTISTS AND PHILOSOPHERS

1 Albert Einstein, *The World as I See It* (New York: Covici-Friede), pp. 19–24. See pages 25, 26, 29, 32 ff., 45, 46, 101 ff., for further illustration of scientific procedure; see also p. 170 for Einstein's high evaluation of the Jewish Prophets and "Christianity as Jesus Christ Taught It," and the corresponding duty of men.

2 Albert Einstein in *The New York Times Magazine,* November 9, 1930, quoted by Allyn K. Foster in *The New Dimensions of Religion* (New York: The Macmillan Co.), p. viii.

3 Max Planck, *Where Is Science Going?* (London: George Allen and Unwin, Ltd.) quoted by N. Bishop Harman in *Science and Religion* (New York: The Macmillan Co.), pp. 35, 36.

4 Quoted by Ernst Mach in his *Popular Science Lectures* (LaSalle, Ill.: Open Court), p. 184, Third American edition.

5 D. S. Cairns, *The Reasonableness of the Christian Faith* (London: Hodder & Stoughton), pp. 75–86; 178–182. For an answer to the question, "How is it that the impact of science has tended to weaken men's hold on God?", see Henry P. Van Dusen, *God in These Times* (New York: Charles Scribner's Sons), pp. 40–45.

6 Georgia Harkness, *The Resources of Religion* (New York: Henry Holt and Co.), p. 155.

7 Alfred North Whitehead, *Science and the Modern World* (New York: The Macmillan Co.), pp. 267, 268, and *Religion in the Making* (New York: The Macmillan Co.), pp. 143, 144.

8 Walter Marshall Horton, *A Psychological Approach to Theology* (New York: Harper and Brothers), pp. 14–22.

9 J. S. Haldane, *The Sciences and Philosophy* (London: Hodder and Stoughton, Ltd.), pp. 260 and 302. J. S. Haldane should not be mistaken for his son, J. B. S. Haldane.

10 Eugene William Lyman, *The Meaning and Truth of Religion* (New York: Charles Scribner's Sons), pp. 164–165. See also p. 20. John Bennett considers this probably the best all-round book on the philosophy of religion.

11 Albert Einstein, *On the Method of Theoretical Physics* (New York: Oxford University Press).

12 Lecomte du Noüy, *Human Destiny* (New York: Longmans, Green and Co.), pp. 163–164.

13 W. R. Matthews, *God in Christian Experience* (New York: Harper and Brothers), pp. 114, 116 ff.

14 Bertrand Russell, quoted by H. B. Streeter in *Reality* (New York: The Macmillan Co.), pp. 22, 29, from Introduction to new edition of Lange's

History of Materialism (Kegan Paul), p. xii, and from *The A.B.C. of Relativity* (Kegan Paul), p. 226 ff.

[15] A. S. Eddington, *The Nature of the Physical World* (New York: Cambridge University Press), p. x of Introduction and pp. 323-324.

[16] *The New Republic*, Editorial, August 27, 1945, p. 241, "Atomic and Human Energy."

[17] Kirtley F. Mather, *Science in Search of God* (New York: Henry Holt and Co.), pp. 44-47, 54, 156.

[18] Albert Einstein in his Foreword to *The Universe and Dr. Einstein* by Lincoln Barnett (New York: William Sloane Associates). This book, written for laymen with delightful clarity, has been subjected throughout to the scrutiny of experts.

[19] Robert A. Millikan. On this whole subject Charles E. Raven also speaks from first-hand experience in *Science, Religion and the Future* (New York: The Macmillan Co.), quoted on p. 1 of our Chap. VI.

BIBLICAL SOURCES

[a] Luke 15:11-32.

CHAPTER 8

RELEASE OF ENERGY THROUGH THE INFLUENCE OF JESUS

[1] Alexis Carrel, *Man the Unknown* (New York: Harper and Brothers), pp. 145-6.

[2] F. R. Barry, *Christianity and Psychology* (New York: George H. Doran Co.), p. 149.

[3] Harold Anson, an essay, "Prayer and Bodily Health," in *Concerning Prayer* by Canon Streeter and others (New York: The Macmillan Co.), p. 335. See also D. S. Cairns, *The Faith That Rebels* (New York: Richard R. Smith).

[4] George W. Gray, *The Advancing Front of Medicine* (New York: Whittlesay House), pp. 228, 229, condensed. Entire Chapter X, "Anxiety," is illuminating.

[5] See "Does Our School System Make for Health?", Chap. XIII and the rest of *Health for the Having*, a handbook for physical fitness by William R. P. Emerson, M.D., Professor Emeritus of Pediatrics, Tufts College Medical School; Medical Consultant in Physical Fitness for the Aetna Life Insurance Co., formerly for Dartmouth College (New York: The Macmillan Co.), pp. 102, 123.

[6] Irving Fisher and Eugene Lyman Fisk, *How to Live, Rules for Healthful Living Based on Modern Science*, prepared in collaboration with the Hygiene Reference Board of the Life Extension Institute, Inc. (New York: Funk & Wagnalls), third edition, pp. 105-107.

[7] David Harold Fink, *Release from Nervous Tension* (New York: Simon & Schuster), p. 105 ff. Gives good suggestions about relaxing, good posture, etc., in Chapters VI to VIII. Taken by themselves, however, good physical habits are inadequate.

[8] Robert S. Woodworth, *Psychology* (New York: Henry Holt & Co.), third edition revised, pp. 318, 319, 330.

[9] Robert Lowry Calhoun, *God and the Day's Work* (New York: Association Press), p. 72. How we made vocations out of jobs is summarized in *Young Laymen—Young Church* by John Oliver Nelson (New York: Association Press). *So You Want to Help People* by Rudolph M. Wittenberg is valuable to parents and teachers as well as professional and amateur leaders in dealing with individuals and groups (New York: Association Press).

[10] Ministers and teachers need to be well acquainted with the various social agencies of the neighborhood, county, and state, and with the particular services which they are able to provide.

[11] See Daniel J. Fleming, *Bringing Our World Together, A Study in World Community* (New York: Charles Scribner's Sons).

BIBLICAL SOURCES

[a] Matt. 17:17–20; [b] John 10:10, Moffatt; [c] Matt. 13:58, Weymouth; [d] Acts 2:4; 9:17; I Cor. 2:4, 5, adapted; [e] Acts 3:1–16, Moffatt; [f] I Cor. 6:13, 19, 20, Goodspeed and Moffatt; [g] II Cor. 5:18–20; Rom. 8:19–24, Moffatt or R.S.V.; [h] Ps. 90:17; Ps. 127:1; Ne. 2:20; [i] Heb. 11:8–10 and 24 ff.; [j] Luke 10:1 ff.; [k] I Cor. 12:4–7 ff., Moffatt, also Rom. 12:4 ff.; [l] Luke 19:1–10.

CHAPTER 9

THE AVAILABILITY OF ENERGY

[1] J. A. Hadfield, *The Psychology of Power*. Chapter III of *The Spirit* edited by B. H. Streeter (New York: The Macmillan Co.), pp. 78, 100–111.

[2] William James, "The Energies of Men," an essay published originally as a magazine article and reprinted since in many forms.

[3] William James, chapter, "The Gospel of Relaxation," in *Talks to Teachers on Psychology and to Students on Some of Life's Ideals* (New York: Henry Holt and Co.), pp. 219, 224 f.

[4] Henry Nelson Wieman, *Methods of Private Religious Living* (New York: The Macmillan Co.), p. 83.

[5] Henry Nelson Wieman, *The Wrestle of Religion with Truth* (New York: The Macmillan Co.), pp. 75–6. *The Issues of Life* (Nashville: Abingdon-Cokesbury), pp. 232, 237.

[6] Report of Commission IV, World Missionary Conference, Edinburgh, 1910. David S. Cairns, Chairman; Chapter VII, General Conclusions, pp. 215–216, 228–229, 235, 255, (New York: Fleming H. Revell).

[7] John Dewey, *Human Nature and Conduct* (New York: Henry Holt and Co.), pp. 123–4, condensed from chapter on "Changing Human Nature."

[8] L. P. Jacks, *A Living Universe* (New York: George H. Doran Co.), p. 77.

BIBLICAL SOURCES

[a] Matt. 10:8 R.V. and Acts 20:35; [b] Rom. 7:18 and Mark 9:23; [c] Phil. 4:13; Acts 1:8, Moffatt.

CHAPTER 10

HOW JESUS EXPANDS FELLOWSHIP

1 John Oman, *The Church and the Divine Order*, p. 44 (English edition).

2 John Oman, *Grace and Personality* (New York: The Macmillan Co.), p. 85.

3 Ernest F. Scott in *An Outline of Christianity* (New York: Dodd, Mead and Co.), Vol. I, p. 58.

4 William Newton Clarke, *The Ideal of Jesus* (New York: Charles Scribner's Sons), p. 73 f.

5 W. Douglas Mackenzie, *The Christ of the Christian Faith* (New York: The Macmillan Co.), pp. 162, 163, 166.

6 A. C. Hogg, *Christ's Message of the Kingdom* (New York: Association Press), p. xiii.

7 Sholem Asch, *One Destiny: An Epistle to the Christians* (New York: G. P. Putnam's Sons), p. 5.

8 Luther A. Weigle, in *Contemporary American Theology Autobiographies, Second Series* edited by Virgilius Ferm (New York: Round Table Press), p. 338.

9 Friedrich Rittelmeyer, *Behold the Man* (New York: The Macmillan Co.), p. 159. Also George A. Buttrick, *Jesus Came Preaching* (New York: Charles Scribner's Sons), p. 205.

BIBLICAL SOURCES

a Mark 1:15, Weymouth;   b Mark 8:35, Weymouth;   c Matt. 18:3, Moffatt;   d Luke 17:20–21, Goodspeed. The Greek may mean "in the midst of you," as rendered by some modern translators. In either case it is an emphatic assertion that the Kingdom is present, though Jesus also taught it is to be more fully realized in the future;   e John 1:35–48, Moffatt; cf. Acts 1:21–22 to show that Peter had known Jesus from the baptism of John;   f Luke 4:31–44; Mark 1:16–39, R.S.V.;   g Mark 12:37, A.V.;   h Luke 19:1–9, Moffatt;   i Mark 3:13;   j Mark 6:30–31, R.S.V.; Luke 11:1 ff.;   k Luke 17:5–6; Matt. 17:19–20;   l Hebrews 2:9;   m Mark 8:34–35, Moffatt.

CHAPTER 11

HIS WAY TO RECONCILE LOYALTIES

1 James Stalker, *The Life of Christ* (New York: Fleming H. Revell), pp. 95–96.

2 Frederick C. Grant, *The Economic Background of the Gospels* (New York: Oxford Univ. Press), pp. 11, 105.

3 J. H. Leckie, *Jesus' Claim to be the Messiah* in *Outline of Christianity* (New York: Dodd, Mead and Co.), Vol. 1, p. 159.

BIBLICAL SOURCES

a Matt. 12:46–50, 20th Century N.T.;   b Acts 1:6, R.S.V.;   c Luke 19:11, R.S.V.;   d John 6:12–15;   e Luke 10:25–37, Moffatt;   f Luke 20:19–26, Weymouth, condensed.

Chapter 12

THE LOYALTY THAT CREATES COMMUNITY

[1] See *The Outline of Christianity* (New York: Dodd, Mead and Co.), Vol. I, Chapter VIII "The Entry into Jerusalem" and p. 103 of Chapter X "The Trial and the Crucifixion." Also Anthony C. Deane, *Jesus Christ* (New York: Doran), Chapter VII, Sec. II.

[2] Encyclical letter from the Bishops of the Anglican Communion, meeting at Lambeth, 1920. W. R. Inge, (*Outspoken Essays*, 2nd series) p. 115 shows that "the duty of unconditional obedience was not taught in the Middle Ages" and that a Christian "must follow his conscience even against the command of the authorities of the church."

[3] John Middleton Murry, *Europe in Travail* (New York: The Macmillan Co.), pp. 58–60.

BIBLICAL SOURCES

[a] Luke 9:51; Mark 10:32; [b] Luke 13:31–33, R.V. margin; [c] Luke 19:41–42, A.V. and Weymouth; [d] Mark 11:11, 15–18, Ballantine, referring to Isa. 56:7 and Jer. 7:11; [e] Matt. 26:45; Luke 23:34; [f] Acts 5:41–42, Goodspeed and 20th Century; [g] Acts 4:18–20, R.S.V. and Acts 5:29; [h] e.g. Stephen's speech, Acts 7:1 ff.; [i] Mark 2:27; [j] Acts 1:14, Riverside.

Chapter 13

AWAKENING TO SOLIDARITY

[1] C. Harold Dodd, *The Meaning of Paul for Today* (New York: George H. Doran Co.), pp. 144–5.

[2] C. Harold Dodd, *The Meaning of Paul for Today*, giving his own translation on pp. 144–5 of Phil. 2:5; compare Moffatt.

[3] Charles E. Raven, *The Creator Spirit* (Cambridge: Harvard Univ. Press), p. 267.

[4] Basil Matthews and Harry Bisseker, *Fellowship in Thought and Prayer* (New York: Edwin S. Gorham), pp. 22, 23.

[5] Condensed from Rufus Jones, *Social Law in the Spiritual World* (Philadelphia: John C. Winston Co.). Chapters on "The Meaning of Personality" and "The Realization of Persons."

[6] Bishop Francis J. McConnell, *An Outline of Christianity* (New York: Dodd, Mead & Co. distributors), Vol. IV, pp. 189 and 201.

[7] John Bennett, "Christianity and Class Consciousness" in *The World Tomorrow*, Feb., 1932.

[8] "The Church and the Disorder of Society," pp. 193–4 from official report of Section III, of The First Assembly of the World Council of Churches, also in one-volume editions including papers and reports of Sections I, II, III, and IV, and in *The Official Report* of the actual proceedings at Amsterdam, Edited by W. A. Visser 't Hooft, all published by Harper & Brothers, New York.

[9] Elton Trueblood, *Alternative to Futility* (New York: Harper and Brothers), pp. 31, 34, 123, 112 and 49 ff.

[10] David S. Cairns, *Christianity in the Modern World* (New York: George H. Doran Co.), pp. 30, 31.

BIBLICAL SOURCES

[a] Acts 2:22–24, and 36 ff. See also 3:12–16; 4:10–13, and 7:50–52. Moffatt's translation makes especially vivid the repeated charges of corporate responsibility; [b] Acts 3:13–14, Moffatt; [c] Acts 4:1–4, Weymouth; [d] Acts 7:35 ff.; [e] I Tim. 5:22, R.S.V.; [f] Acts 10th Chap. and 15:5–12; [g] Acts 8:5–14; 26–40. Compare also Peter's later yielding for a time to the pressure of social and religious exclusiveness. Gal. 2:11–14; [h] Acts 11:19–26; 12:25 and 13:1 ff.; [i] I Cor. 12:26–28, R.V. margin and Moffatt. See also Col. 1:18 and 24; [j] Eph. 4:25–29, Weymouth; [k] Eph. 4:3–16, Moffatt and Goodspeed, condensed; [l] I Cor. 12:26 and 24–25, Moffatt; [m] Rev. 21:2, 25–26, R.S.V.; [n] Rev. 21:22–24, R.S.V.; [o] John 1:35 ff.; [p] Luke 15:3–7, 11–22.

CHAPTER 14

FELLOWSHIP IN SOCIAL DISCOVERY

[1] Acts 2:42, translation by C. Anderson Scott in "What Happened at Pentecost," Chapter IV of *The Spirit* by B. H. Streeter and others (New York: The Macmillan Co.), pp. 133, 137, 138, also the section on "The Fellowship the Organ of Insight," p. 141 ff.

[2] C. Harold Dodd, *The Meaning of Paul for Today* (New York: George H. Doran Co.), p. 139 ff.

[3] William Temple, *Essays in Christian Politics and Kindred Subjects* (New York: Longmans, Green and Co.), Chapter I on "Fellowship," p. 3 f.

[4] *By an Unknown Disciple,* Chap. VI, p. 56 ff., in illustrated edition printed from new plates by Harper and Brothers.

[5] Charles Fiske and Burton S. Easton, *The Real Jesus* (New York: Harper and Brothers).

[6] Friedrich Rittelmeyer, *Behold the Man* (New York: The Macmillan Co.), p. 138.

[7] M. P. Follett, *The New State, Group Organization the Solution of Popular Government* (New York: Longmans, Green and Co.), pp. 24–27, 31, 39–42.

[8] Walter Donham, *Education for Responsible Living* (Cambridge: Harvard University Press), p. 139 ff., from Chap. X, "The Humanities, Religion and Purpose."

BIBLICAL SOURCES

[a] Acts 15:1–33; [b] Acts 13:1–4; [c] Phil. 1:5, Weymouth; 4:14–15, Weymouth and R.V.; [d] Phil. 1:9, Moffatt, and 2:1–4, Weymouth and C. A. Scott; [e] Phil. 2:5, Moffatt, compare R.S.V.; [f] I John 1:1–7 and 2:10–11, Goodspeed; [g] Mark 6:31; [h] Matt. 16:23, Weymouth, also Mark 8:33, "Your outlook is not God's, but man's," Moffatt; [i] John 13:4–5, 12–17, 34–35, and 16:12–13, Goodspeed. Compare Luke 22:24–27. Chapters 13–17 of John should be read in their entirety to get the full effect.

CHAPTER 15

BETTER PROCEDURES FOR DEMOCRATIC FELLOWSHIP

[1] Eduard C. Lindeman, *Social Discovery* (New York: The New Republic Publishing Co.), p. 195.

[2] George A. Coe, *Motives of Men* (New York: Charles Scribner's Sons), Chapter on "Cooperative Thinking."

[3] Prepared by the Inquiry, *Creative Discussion* (New York: distributed by Association Press), pp. 3–8.

[4] Harrison Elliott, *The Process of Group Thinking* (New York: Association Press), p. 8.

[5] For Quaker procedure in business meetings see William Comfort, *Just Among Friends* (New York: The Macmillan Co.), p. 41 ff.

[6] George B. Huszar, *Practical Applications of Democracy* (New York: Harper and Brothers), pp. 28, 32, 33, 104, 105, 122, 127, condensed, with Selected Bibliography.

[7] Charles W. Ferguson, *A Little Democracy Is a Dangerous Thing* (New York: Association Press), condensed, pp. 90, 102–107, 120–122.

[8] D. Elton Trueblood, *The Predicament of Modern Man* (New York: Harper and Brothers).

[9] In introduction to the *Official Report*, The Oxford Conference (New York: Harper and Brothers).

[10] J. W. Studebaker, *The American Way, Democracy at Work in the Des Moines Forum* (New York: McGraw-Hill), pp. ix, x.

[11] M. P. Follett, *Creative Experience* (New York: Longmans, Green and Co.), Chapter XII "A Participant Electorate."

[12] M. P. Follett, *The New State* (New York: Longmans, Green and Co.), Condensed from Chapter I.

[13] A pamphlet to help participants as well as leaders in *How to Lead Discussion: A Guide for the Use of Group Leaders* by LeRoy E. Bowman (New York: Woman's Press). See series of Public Affairs Pamphlets and Foreign Policy Association Pamphlets for information and suggestion on particular problems.

[14] Arthur E. Morgan, *The Small Community, Foundation of Democratic Life, What It Is and How to Achieve It* (New York: Harper and Brothers), Chap. XII, "The Community Council." Community Service, Inc., Yellow Springs, Ohio, and in some states strong state councils are prepared to help local communities. See thirty-four good illustrations of *Small Communities in Action* by Jean and Jess Ogden (New York: Harper and Brothers).

[15] Robert D. Leigh, *Group Leadership with Modern Rules of Procedure* (New York: W. W. Norton Co.), pp. 65, 66, 56, 57.

[16] Biographical note by B. F. Streeter to Lily Dougall's *God's Way with Man* (New York: The Macmillan Co.), p. 10 ff.

[17] B. F. Streeter, *Immortality* (New York: The Macmillan Co.), Introduction, p. x, xi.

[18] A. Clutton Brock, *What Is the Kingdom of Heaven* (London: Methuen and Co. Ltd.), pp. 80–86. Chapter on "The Kingdom of Heaven and Politics."

CHAPTER 16

FELLOWSHIP IN EDUCATION

[1] C. Delisle Burns, *Challenge to Democracy* (New York: W. W. Norton and Co.), p. 170 ff.

[2] William Ernest Hocking, *Human Nature and its Remaking* (New Haven: Yale University Press), revised edition, p. 253.

[3] Richard C. Cabot, M.D., *What Men Live By* (Boston: Houghton Mifflin Co.), Chapter XI, p. 101.

[4] George A. Coe, *What Ails Our Youth* (New York: Charles Scribner's Sons), pp. 16–17, 11–13, 31, condensed.

[5] Condensed from *Colliers*, March 1, 1947 and in *Reader's Digest*, May, 1947, p. 21 ff.

[6] John Dewey, "How Much Freedom in New Schools," *The New Republic*, July 9, 1930, p. 206; Richard C. Cabot, M.D., *Adventures on the Borderlands of Ethics* (New York: Harper and Brothers), Chap. I.

[7] William Temple, *Christianity and Social Order* (New York: Penguin Books), p. 67.

[8] Theodore Gerald Soares, *Religious Education* (Chicago: University of Chicago Press), p. xvi.

[9] J. W. Studebaker, *The American Way, Democracy at Work in the Des Moines Forums* (New York: McGraw-Hill), pp. 29–32.

[10] Dorothy Canfield Fisher, *Why Stop Learning* (New York: Harcourt, Brace and Co.), p. 262 ff.

[11] Sir Richard Livingstone, *The Future in Education* (New York: Cambridge University Press), pp. 44 to 60 and 75 ff., published with another small book by the same author, *Education for a World Adrift*, in one volume called *On Education*.

[12] Edward P. Westphal, *The Church's Opportunity in Adult Education* (Philadelphia: The Westminster Press), p. 15.

[13] Frank C. Laubach, *The Silent Billion Speak* (New York: Friendship Press), pp. 181–190 ff. and 3 ff. condensed. Inquire of Conference on World Literacy and Christian Literature, 156 Fifth Avenue, N.Y.C.

[14] *Christian Century*, editorial notes on pp. 1203–4, Oct. 9, 1946.

[15] See books on *The Springfield Plan*.

[16] H. Crichton Miller, M.D., *The New Psychology and the Parent* (New York: Albert & Charles Boni), pp. 2–8 condensed.

[17] Benjamin Kidd, *Social Evolution* (New York: G. P. Putnam's Sons).

[18] The National Recreation Association, 315 Fourth Avenue, New York City 10, gives bibliographies and other suggestions on various phases of recreation.

[19] *Reader's Digest*, June, 1947, "The Teacher Goes a Visiting," pp. 41–44.

[20] Paul H. Vieth, Editor, *The Church and Christian Education* (St. Louis: Bethany Press); reports an important study by a special committee of the International Council of Religious Education, pp. 168 ff. and 191 ff.

[21] Very helpful in their special fields are: *Children and Religion* by Dora P. Chaplin (New York: Charles Scribner's Sons); *The Modern Parent and the Teaching Church* by Wesner Fallaw (New York: The Macmillan Co.);

The *Church-School Teacher's Job* by Mildred Moody Eakin and Frank Eakin (New York: The Macmillan Co.) and *The Community and Christian Education* by Tilford Swearinger (St. Louis: Bethany Press).

BIBLICAL SOURCES

a Mark 9:33–36; Matt. 18:3–6, and Luke 9:48, Moffatt.

CHAPTER 17

EDUCATING THE WHOLE MAN

1 Alfred Edersheim, *The Life and Times of Jesus* (New York: A. D. F. Randolph & Co.), pp. 146–148, 252–253, Vol. I, 5th Edition.

2 S. J. Case, "Jesus in Sepphoris" in *Journal of Biblical Literature*, Vol. XLV (1926) Parts I and II.

3 John and Evelyn Dewey, *Schools of Tomorrow* (New York: E. P. Dutton and Co.).

4 George A. Coe, *What Ails Our Youth* (New York: Charles Scribner's Sons), pp. 7–9.

5 Matthew Arnold, *Civilization in the United States* (Boston: De Wolfe Fiske & Co.), pp. 8–10, quoting from Grant's *Personal Memoirs*, Chapter I, (Chas. Webster & Co.).

6 W. F. Luder, "Science—Idol or Method," *Christian Century*, Sept. 18, 1946, pp. 1118, 1119.

7 Lecomte du Noüy, *Human Destiny* (New York: Longmans, Green and Co.), condensed from pp. 182–185, 228–230, 205, 250–253.

8 Phillips Brooks, *The Influence of Jesus* (New York: E. P. Dutton and Co.), condensed from pp. 219–222, 192, 142.

9 Benjamin Kidd, *Social Evolution* (New York: G. P. Putnam's Sons), pp. 307–8.

10 William E. Hocking, *Human Nature and Its Remaking* (New Haven: Yale University Press, revised edition), pp. 259–261.

11 George A. Coe, *Educating for Citizenship* (New York: Charles Scribner's Sons), p. 88 ff., also Paul Hutchinson, *The New Leviathan* (Chicago: Willett, Clark and Co.).

12 Paul H. Veith, *Objectives in Religious Education* (New York: Harper and Brothers), pp. 73–74.

13 Alfred North Whitehead, *The Aims of Education*, p. 106, quoted and amplified by Sir Richard Livingston, "Education for a World Adrift," p. 49 ff., in *On Education* (New York: The Macmillan Co.).

14 William Temple, *The Hope of a New World* (New York: The Macmillan Co.), p. 12.

15 H. Richard Neibuhr, Wilhelm Pauck, and Francis Miller, *The Church Against the World* (New York: Harper and Brothers), pp. 106–112.

16 "One World for Religion Too," from an address by Harry Emerson Fosdick before the Protestant Council of the City of New York. *Reader's Digest*, May, 1946, p. 73.

[17] Paul Vieth, Editor, *The Church and Christian Education* (St. Louis: Bethany Press), pp. 301, 302.

[18] *The Relation of Religion to Public Education—The Basic Principles,* by a Special Committee of the American Council on Education, Washington 6, D. C., 1947. Salient features reported in *Information Service,* April 12, 1947.

BIBLICAL SOURCES

a Luke 2:43 ff.;   b Luke 10:1 ff., 9:1 ff., Mark 6:7, Matt. 10:1 ff.

CHAPTER 18

RECURRING HINDRANCES TO FELLOWSHIP
AND COMMUNITY

[1] T. R. Glover, *The Influence of Christ in the Ancient World* (New Haven: Yale University Press), p. 35.

[2] John Macmurray, *Freedom in the Modern World, Broadcast Talks on Modern Problems* (London: Faber and Faber), pp. 70–77.

[3] Henry P. Van Dusen, *God in These Times* (New York: Charles Scribner's Sons), pp. 17–18, 34–36, condensed.

[4] A. N. Whitehead, *Nature and Life* (Chicago: Univ. of Chicago Press) quoted by Van Dusen as above pp. 32 and 16.

[5] *The Return of Christendom* by a group of Churchmen, with an Introduction by Bishop Gore, and Epilogue by G. K. Chesterton (New York: The Macmillan Co.), p. 104 ff.

[6] James Denney, quoted in *The Return of Christendom,* as above.

[7] Robert Lowry Calhoun, *God and the Common Life* (New York: Charles Scribner's Sons), p. 14.

[8] Julian W. Mack, in Introduction to *Law and the Modern Mind,* by Jerome Frank (New York: Coward-McCann), pp. x-xi.

[9] H. A. Overstreet, *A Declaration of Interdependence* (New York: W. W. Norton and Co.), pp. 51–53. Pages 46–51 deal with hindrances to the physician, the lawyer, and the minister; pages 53–59 with abuses in politics and finance.

[10] Louis D. Brandeis, *Other People's Money,* Chapter I, (New York: Frederick A. Stokes Co.), or inexpensive reprint by Nat. Home Library Foundation, Washington, D. C., with biographical introduction by Norman Hapgood.

[11] Francis J. McConnell, *Christianity and Coercion* (Nashville: Abingdon-Cokesbury), p. 43.

[12] *Towards the Christian Revolution,* A Symposium by Canadian scholars, with foreword by Richard Roberts, edited by R. B. Y. Scott and Gregory Vlastos (New York: Harper and Brothers), pp. 155 and 160–161.

[13] Harry F. Ward, *Which Way Religion* (New York: The Macmillan Co.), p. 146.

BIBLICAL SOURCES

a Matt. 23:23 ff., Moffatt. Cf. Luke 11:42.

CHAPTER 19

HALF RELIGION VERSUS COMPLETE COMMUNITY

[1] David S. Cairns, "The Need for a Common Christian Mind," in the *Intercollegian*, New York 1921, p. 2.

[2] Winfred Ernest Garrison, *The March of Faith* (New York: Harper and Brothers), pp. 146–7.

[3] John C. Bennett, *Social Salvation, A Religious Approach to the Problems of Social Change* (New York: Charles Scribner's Sons), Chap. II "The Interdependence of Individual and Social Salvation."

[4] R. Coupland, *The Life of William Wilberforce*, p. 265. Quoted by John Bennett.

[5] G. M. Trevelyan, *British History in the Nineteenth Century*, p. 54. Quoted in footnote by Bennett.

[6] B. C. Plowright, *Rebel Religion—Christ, Community and Church* (New York: Round Table Press), pp. 179, 180, 87–89, 180–185.

[7] C. Harold Dodd, amplified in our Chapter XIII, Section II.

[8] John Macmurray, *Creative Society* (New York: Association Press), Chapter II.

[9] John Bennett in concluding paragraph of *Christianity and Communism* (New York: Association Press), p. 127.

[10] A. J. Muste, in *Federal Council Bulletin*, Jan., 1938, p. 5. Summarized here with permission.

[11] As summarized in *Radical Religion*, Autumn number 1937, p. 1. See the *Report on the Church and the Social Order* of the Oxford Conference of 1937, published by Willet, Clark & Co.

[12] A. Herbert Gray, *The Christian Adventure* (New York: Association Press), pp. 20, 21, condensed.

[13] Kenneth Scott Latourette, *The Christian Outlook* (New York: Harper and Brothers), p. 221–23.

[14] "Christians in the Secular World," by the Archbishop of Canterbury, William Temple, as reprinted in *The Christian Century*, March 1, 1944, pp. 269–271. (Also in *The Christian Newsletter*, London). The few sentences in parenthesis are from his last book, *The Church Looks Forward* (New York: The Macmillan Co.), p. 3.

BIBLICAL SOURCES

[a] Matt. 21:33–46, Weymouth. Cf. Goodspeed, and Torrey, who translates "given to a people yielding its fruit"; [b] Luke 12:32.

CHAPTER 20

THE USE OF POSSESSIONS TO FOSTER FELLOWSHIP

[1] Adolph Harnack, *The Mission and Expansion of Christianity*, Vol. 1, p. 176.

[2] From conclusion (p. 193) of the C.O.P.E.C. Commission on Industry

and Property. This conclusion is in striking agreement with the results of a similar investigation in the U.S.A. See Notes 5, 6, 13 and 14 below.

[3] Samuel Dickey, *The Constructive Revolution of Jesus* (New York: George H. Doran Co.), p. 134.

[4] Harry F. Ward, *Our Economic Morality and the Ethic of Jesus* (New York: The Macmillan Co.), p. 5.

[5] *The Church and Industrial Reconstruction* by the Committee on the War and the Religious Outlook, assisted by a special subcommittee. (New York: Association Press), pp. 182–187.

[6] From Conclusion of the report of the Commission on Industry and Property of the Conference on Christian Politics, Economics and Citizenship. We quote from these American and British findings not only because they are so pertinent *now*, and so clearly and concisely stated, but also because the representative character and the procedure of the group authorship illustrate the conditions for attaining a common Christian mind on these complex issues.

[7] R. H. Tawney, *The Sickness of an Acquisitive Society*, published in the United States as *The Acquisitive Society* (New York: Harcourt, Brace & Co.).

[8] H. L. Gantt, *Organizing for Work* (New York: Harcourt, Brace & Co.), p. 14.

[9] Walter Lippmann, *A Preface to Morals* (New York: The Macmillan Co.), pp. 238–240, referring to Graham Wallas, *Our Social Heritage*, Chap. I.

[10] C. Delisle Burns, *Industry and Civilization* (New York: The Macmillan Co.), Conclusions, pp. 247–251.

[11] Julian Huxley, *Science and Social Needs* (New York: Harper and Brothers), p. ix.

[12] Julian Huxley, cited by Halford E. Luccock, *Christian Faith and Economic Change* (Nashville: Abingdon-Cokesbury), p. 100.

[13] *The Proceedings of C.O.P.E.C. Being a Report of the Meetings of the Conference on Christian Politics, Economics, and Citizenship, held in Birmingham, England, April 5-12, 1924.* (New York: Longmans, Green and Co.), p. 182 ff.

[14] *Industry and Property*, Vol. IX, of C.O.P.E.C. Commissions' Reports, (New York: Longmans, Green and Co.), pp. 195–7.

[15] Copies with list of signers obtainable from Federal Council of Churches, 297 Fourth Avenue, New York City, Social Action Department, National Catholic Welfare Conference, 1312 Massachusetts Avenue, N.W., Washington, D. C., Synagogue Council of America, 110 W. 42nd Street, N.Y.C.

[16] See *Amsterdam* (Chicago: Christian Century Press), 25c. A booklet with the story of, and statements by, the 1st Session of the World Council of Churches, Sec. III of The Church and the Disorder of Society, pp. 19–22, or the official report.

[17] Arnold J. Toynbee, *Civilization on Trial* (New York: Oxford University Press), pp. 147 ff., 31.

BIBLICAL SOURCES

[a] Acts 4:32, R.S.V.; [b] Acts 5:4; [c] I Cor. 16:1–4; II Thess. 3:10; [d] Luke 12:13–21, R.S.V. and Weymouth; [e] Luke 12:22–32, Moffatt and Weymouth, adapted; [f] Luke 18:18–30; Mark 10:17–31, Moffatt; [g] Matt. 6:21, 24, Good-

speed; h Mark 8:36, 37, Weymouth; i Mark 10:23–27, Moffatt; j James
4:2–3, Weymouth & R.V. condensed; k I Tim. 6:9–10, Weymouth.

CHAPTER 21

INTERRACIAL AND WORLD-UNITING FELLOWSHIP

1 E. Stanley Jones, *The Christ of the Indian Road* (Nashville: Abingdon-
Cokesbury), pp. 125–128, 216–217.

2 Daniel J. Fleming, *Whither Bound in Missions* (New York: Association
Press), pp. 63–66.

3 C. C. Montefiore, *The Synoptic Gospels* (New York: Macmillan), Vol. II,
p. 520.

4 Edmund D. Soper's *Racism: A World Issue* (Nashville: Abingdon-
Cokesbury), pp. 32–40 and 31, from which the preceding quotations are
taken. Similar conclusions published by a UNESCO commission in 1950.

5 Arnold J. Toynbee, *A Study of History* (New York: Oxford Press),
pp. 51–59, 249–251.

6 Wilfred Wellock, "To Hold or to Share?" in *Fellowship*, February, 1939,
p. 4.

7 *The Scientific Monthly*, April, 1948, pp. 322–26, "A Great African Project"
by Mrs. Edith Tilton Penrose, who worked with the Economic and Social
Council of the U.N.

8 David C. Williams, "The Last of Britain's Empire" in *The Nation*,
August 20, 1949, p. 179 f.

9 Liston Pope, Report of his investigations in Africa, quoted in *Time*,
Aug. 29, 1949, and closing sentences from his leading article, "About Face
for Foreign Missions" in *Christianity and Crisis*, Nov. 28, 1949.

10 Gerald Heard, "Colonies and Civilization," in *Fellowship*, Feb., 1939,
p. 3 f.

11 Foreign Policy Association pamphlet No. 73, Feb., 1949, 22 E. 38th St.,
N.Y.C., includes *Man and Food: The Lost Equation?* by C. Lester Walker,
and *Food and Diplomacy*, by Blair Bolles, giving examples of international
cooperation for food as evidence of greater possibilities.

12 Statement signed by Henry Sloan Coffin, John Dewey, Charles K. Gilbert,
Alice Hamilton, Millicent C. McIntosh, Ernest O. Melby, Ralph W. Sockman, Gerard Swope, and others, *The Christian Century*, Nov. 30, 1949,
p. 1428. The speech they commend and fourteen others are published under
the title, *Visit to America* by Jawaharlal Nehru (New York: John Day Co.).

13 "The North Atlantic Road to Prosperity," William Hard and Andre
Visson, *Reader's Digest*, July, 1949.

14 Gunnar Myrdal, *An American Dilemma: The Negro Problem and
Modern Democracy* (New York: Harper and Brothers), condensed from Section 9 and 10 of Chap. 45.

15 Condensed from a vivid story of Hill City, "The Gang Goes Up-hill" in
The Survey Graphic, March, 1940, pp. 182–185.

16 Carey McWilliams, "Equality—A Political Problem" in *Survey Graphic*
for Dec., 1947, p. 690 ff.

17 *To Secure These Rights*, Chap. IV, "A Program of Action," pp. 139–175.
The fifteen full-page charts are in themselves an impressive summary of

need and opportunity. U.S. Government Printing Office, Washington, D. C., 1947, also in cheap reprints.

CHAPTER 22

THE CHURCH AS A WORLD-UNITING FELLOWSHIP

[1] Lecomte du Noüy, *Human Destiny* (New York: Longmans, Green and Co.), p. 264.

[2] Arnold Toynbee, *A Study of History* (New York: Oxford University Press), pp. 13 ff., 24, 358, 558, 386 ff., and 244 ff., in Abridgement of volumes I-VI by D. C. Somerwell.

[3] Arnold Toynbee, *Civilization on Trial* (New York: Oxford Press), pp. 265, 214–216, 39–40; also, as background for this summary, pp. 14–15, 70–71, 93–94, 127–8, 133 ff., 141–148, 159 and Chap. 12, "Christianity and Civilization" from p. 230 to 252.

[4] International and related issues that need an informed public opinion are treated in the *News Letter* of The World Alliance for International Friendship through Religion—offices with The Church Peace Union, 170 East 64th St., N.Y.C.

[5] Henry P. Van Dusen, *World Christianity, Yesterday, Today, Tomorrow* (Nashville: Abingdon-Cokesbury), pp. 115–122, 136 ff., 158 ff., 95 ff., also final Ch. 9.

[6] See Henry P. Van Dusen, *They Found the Church There: The Armed Forces Discover Christian Missions* (New York: Charles Scribner's Sons).

[7] James Hastings Nichols, *Primer for Protestants* (New York: Association Press), pp. 83–84.

[8] Walter H. Horton, *Toward a Reborn Church, A Review and Forecast of the Ecumenical Movement* (New York: Harper and Brothers), from concluding pages 108–120.

[9] See pamphlet by Walter H. Horton: *Centers of New Life in European Christendom* issued by the American Committee, World Council of Churches, 297 Fourth Avenue, New York.

[10] Elmore M. McKee, "Implementing the Ecumenical Ideal at the Parish Level," in Vol. IV, *Toward World-Wide Christianity* of the Interseminary Series (New York: Harper and Brothers).

[11] John Oliver Nelson, *Young Laymen—Young Church* (New York: Association Press).

[12] Headquarters of the Laymen's Movement, 347 Madison Ave., New York.

[13] *Information Service* is published weekly from 297 Fourth Avenue, N.Y.C., to give currency to such matters.

[14] For suggestions on how to help in this field ask The Committee on Friendly Relations among Foreign Students, 291 Broadway, N.Y.C.

CHAPTER 23

PRAYER, A WAY TO BETTER FELLOWSHIP

[1] Quoted by Leon H. Barnett, *Cosmic Christianity* (New York: Fleming H. Revell Co.).

2 W. R. Matthews, *Following Christ* (New York: Longmans, Green and Co.), pp. 60–61.

3 Henry T. Hodgkin, *Lay Religion* (London: Headly Bros.), p. 202.

4 Dr. A. J. Hadfield, "The Psychology of Power" in *The Spirit* (New York: The Macmillan Co.), p. 103.

5 James B. Pratt, *The Religious Consciousness* (New York: The Macmillan Co.), p. 327.

6 A. C. Hogg, *Christ's Message of the Kingdom* (New York: Association Press), p. 69.

7 Harry Emerson Fosdick, *The Meaning of Prayer* (New York: Association Press), p. 188, from a chapter called "Unselfishness in Prayer," which has helped many to appreciate and practice prayer for others.

8 See Harry Emerson Fosdick, chapter on "Prayer as Dominant Desire" in *The Meaning of Prayer* (New York: Association Press), p. 142 ff.

9 George A. Coe, *The Psychology of Religion* (Chicago: University of Chicago Press), pp. 318–319.

10 Chrysostom, quoted in concluding the great study of *Prayer* by Friedrich Heiler (New York: Oxford Univ. Press), p. 363.

11 P. T. Forsythe and Dora Greenwell, *Prayer* (London: Hodder and Stoughton), pp. 111–112.

BIBLICAL SOURCES

a Ps. 46:1; b Luke 6:12–13; c Mark 1:33–38; d Col. 4:2, Moffatt; e Acts 16:23–25 and Phil. 4:4, 6–7, R.V. and Moffatt condensed; f Matt. 6:7–8, R.S.V.; g Psalm 139:23, 24; h e.g. Luke 5:3–11; i Matt. 9:35–38, R.S.V.; j Rom. 15:30–33, Moffatt; k Luke 22–32, 20th Century.

CHAPTER 24

CONDITIONS AND TESTS FOR EFFECTUAL PRAYER

1 Harry Emerson Fosdick, *The Meaning of Prayer* (New York: Association Press), pp. 184–193.

2 Henry Drummond.

3 See Henry Nelson Wieman, *Methods of Private Religious Living* (New York: The Macmillan Co.), pp. 22 and 148.

4 A. H. McNeile, *Self-Training in Prayer* (New York: Longmans, Green and Co.), third edition, p. 34.

5 B. H. Streeter, *Reality* (New York: The Macmillan Co.), p. 292 ff.

6 George A. Buttrick, *Prayer* (Nashville: Abingdon-Cokesbury), pp. 175, 179, 182, from two priceless chapters, "Prayer, Memory, and the Subconscious" and "Prayer, Imagination, and Thought."

7 William Ernest Hocking, *Human Nature and Its Remaking* (New Haven: Yale University Press), revised edition, p. 398.

8 George A. Coe, *The Psychology of Religion* (Chicago: University of Chicago Press), pp. 319–320.

9 Quoted by William Adams Brown in *The Life of Prayer in a World of Science* (New York: Charles Scribner's Sons), p. 45.

10 James B. Pratt, *The Religious Consciousness* (New York: The Macmillan Co.), p. 335.

11 Georgia Harkness, *Prayer and the Common Life* (Nashville: Abingdon-Cokesbury), p. 214.

12 Phillips Brooks, *The Influence of Jesus* (New York: E. P. Dutton and Co.), pp. 103–108 condensed.

13 F. R. Barry, *Christianity and Psychology* (New York: George H. Doran Co.), p. 114.

14 *The Practice of the Presence of God, Being Conversations and Letters of Brother Lawrence.* Various editions.

15 From Chapter I, Report of Commission VI on *The Home Base of Missions* at the World Missionary Conference at Edinburgh (New York: Fleming H. Revell).

BIBLICAL SOURCES

a I Cor. 14:15, R.S.V.;   b John 7:17, Weymouth;   c Col. 3:14, Moffatt; d Phil. 2:7, A.V.; Heb. 2:17, Goodspeed and Moffatt;   e Heb. 5:8–9, R.S.V.

CHAPTER 25

CONSUMMATION OF FELLOWSHIP

1 Charles Clayton Morrison, *The Social Gospel and the Christian Cultus* (New York: Harper and Brothers), p. 198.

2 John Baillie, *The Place of Jesus Christ in Modern Christianity* (New York: Charles Scribner's Sons), pp. 45–47, quoting Tertullian.

3 Claude Montefiore, *The Old Testament and After*, p. 209 f. Quoted by John Baillie as in Note 2.

4 Baron Von Hügel, *Essays and Addresses on the Philosophy of Religion*, Second Series, p. 160. Quoted by John Baillie as in Note 2.

5 George Berguer, *Some Aspects of the Life of Jesus from the Psychological Point of View* (New York: Harcourt, Brace & Co.), pp. 266, 281, 292–3.

6 B. H. Streeter, *Reality* (New York: The Macmillan Co.), pp. 63–4.

7 Charles Allen Dinsmore, *Atonement in Literature and Life* (New York: Houghton Mifflin Co.).

8 P. O. Philip in correspondence from India, *The Christian Century*, Feb. 22, 1939, p. 254.

9 Richard Roberts, *The Renascence of Faith* (New York: Fleming H. Revell), pp. 213–220.

10 *The Christian Century*, an editorial, "The Christian Church," April 18, 1934, p. 519.

11 Harry F. Ward, *Which Way Religion* (New York: The Macmillan Co.), pp. 185, 183, 184, 180, 186, 187.

12 Lewis Mumford, *Faith for Living* (New York: Harcourt, Brace and Co.), pp. 4, 6, 173, 193 with similar testimony from Albert Einstein, Walter Lippmann, and Lord Tweedmuir (John Buchan) quoted by Elton Trueblood, *The Predicament of Modern Man*, Chapters IV and V, "The Insufficiency of Individual Religion" and "The Necessity of a Redemptive Society" (New York: Harper and Brothers).

BIBLICAL SOURCES

a Rom. 12:21, Moffatt; b II Cor. 5:18–20; c Acts 20:24, Moffatt, adapted;
d Phil. 3:10, Moffatt; e II Tim. 1:10, Goodspeed; f Heb. 7:16, Twentieth
Century; g Rom. 6:4, 5, 6, 11, 20th Century, Moffatt, Goodspeed; h I John
3:16–18, Moffatt; i Ephesians 2:22, 20th Century, and II Cor. 5:18–20;
j Romans, 12:1–2, Weymouth and Moffatt; k John 13:1, 2, 4–15, R.S.V.;
l Mark 14:32–42; m Luke 22:32, 61, 62, R.S.V.; n Luke 23:34, (cf. Luke 6:28)
and Luke 23:39–43; o Heb. 7:16, 24, 25 and I Cor. 13:8, R.S.V.; p John 3:16,
15:12–14, R.S.V.; q John 20:21 with 17:18, R.S.V.

ACKNOWLEDGMENTS

GRATEFUL acknowledgment is made to the following who kindly granted permission to reprint material from their publications. Where any selections appear without proper acknowledgment, it is to be understood that diligent search has been made, and is still being made, and that upon further information due credit will be given in future editions.

Abingdon-Cokesbury Press for quotations from *The Christ of the Indian Road*, by E. Stanley Jones; *Christianity and Coercion*, by Francis J. McConnell; *Racism—A World Issue*, by Edmund Davison Soper; *Prayer*, by George Arthur Buttrick; *World Christianity—Yesterday, Today, Tomorrow*, by Henry P. Van Dusen.

George Allen and Unwin, Ltd. for quotations from *A Practical Faith*, by Harold Anson.

American Agriculturist for quotations from the article in the issue of October 22, 1938, by Hugh A. Moran, entitled "Co-operation Where It Counts."

Bethany Press for quotations from *The Church and Christian Education*, by Paul H. Vieth, editor.

Cambridge University Press for quotations from *The Future in Education*, by Sir Richard Livingstone; *The Nature of the Physical World*, by A. S. Eddington.

The Canadian Student for quotations from the article in the issue of March, 1929, entitled "The Historical Element in Christianity."

Christian Century Foundation for quotations from correspondence signed by P. O. Philips in the February 22, 1939 issue of *The Christian Century;* "Science—Idol or Method," by W. F. Luder in the September 18, 1946 issue of *The Christian Century;* Editorial Notes in the October 9, 1946 issue of *The Christian Century*.

Coward-McCann for quotations from *Law and the Modern Mind*, by Jerome Frank.

Crown Publishers for quotations from *The World As I See It,* by Albert Einstein (Covici Friede).

Doubleday and Company for quotations from *George Washington Carver,* by Rackham Holt.

Duell, Sloan and Pearce for quotations from *New Worlds Emerging,* by Earl Parker Hanson. (Copyright by Earl Parker Hanson.)

Friendship Press for quotations from *The Silent Billion Speak,* by Frank Laubach.

Funk and Wagnalls Company for quotations from *How to Live,* by Irving Fisher and Eugene Lyman Fisk.

George W. Gray for quotations from his book, *The Advancing Front of Medicine,* published by Whittlesey House. (Copyright by George W. Gray.)

Harcourt, Brace and Company for quotations from *Faith for Living,* by Lewis Mumford; *Some Aspects of the Life of Jesus,* by Georges Berguer; *Why Stop Learning,* by Dorothy Canfield Fisher.

Harper and Brothers for quotations from *Toward A Reborn Church* and *A Psychological Approach to Theology,* by Walter Marshall Horton; *Plowshares Into Swords,* by Arthur P. Chew; *Morals of Tomorrow,* by Ralph W. Sockman; *Alternative to Futility, The Common Ventures of Life,* and *Foundations for Reconstruction,* by Elton Trueblood; *God in Christian Experience,* by W. R. Matthews; *The Small Community,* by Arthur E. Morgan; *Toward the Christian Revolution,* by R. B. Y. Scott and Gregory Vlastos, editors (Willett, Clark); *The March of Faith,* by Winfred Ernest Garrison; *By An Unknown Disciple; Practical Applications of Democracy,* by George B. Huszar; *An American Dilemma: The Negro Problem and Modern Democracy,* by Gunnard Myrdal; *The Church Against the World,* by Francis P. Miller (Willett, Clark).

Harvard University Press for quotations from *The Creator Spirit,* by Charles E. Raven; *Education for Responsible Living,* by Wallace B. Donham.

Hodder and Stoughton, Ltd. and the Dr. J. S. Haldane Trust

for quotations from *The Sciences and Philosophy,* by J. S. Haldane.

Henry Holt and Company for quotations from *The Resources of Religion,* by Georgia Harkness; *Human Nature and Conduct,* by John Dewey; *Talks to Teachers on Psychology and to Students on Some of Life's Ideals,* by William James; *Psychology,* by Robert S. Woodworth; *Science in Search of God,* by Kirtley F. Mather.

Houghton Mifflin Company for quotation from *What Men Live By,* by Richard C. Cabot.

Longmans, Green and Company for quotations from *Human Destiny* and *The Road to Reason,* by Lecomte du Noüy; *The New State,* by M. P. Follett.

McGraw-Hill Book Company for quotation from *The American Way, Democracy at Work in the Des Moines Forum,* by J. W. Studebaker.

The Macmillan Company for quotations from *The Church Looks Forward* and *The Hope of a New World,* by William Temple; *Immortality, Reality,* and *The Spirit,* three books by B. H. Streeter; *The Christ of the Christian Faith,* by W. Douglas Mackenzie; *The Return of Christendom,* by a group of Churchmen; *Science and the Modern World,* by Alfred North Whitehead; *Science, Religion and the Future,* by Charles E. Raven; *The Synoptic Gospels,* by C. C. Montefiore; *Moral Values and the Idea of God,* by W. R. Sorley; *Industry and Civilization,* by C. Delisle Burns; *A Preface to Morals,* by Walter Lippmann; *The Religious Consciousness,* by James B. Pratt; *Which Way Religion?* by Harry F. Ward.

The Nation for quotations from the article in the issue of April 8, 1950, by John Boyd Orr, entitled "Is Peace Possible?"

W. W. Norton and Company for quotations from *A Declaration of Interdependence,* by H. A. Overstreet; *Challenge to Democracy,* by C. Delisle Burns; *Group Leadership with Modern Rules of Procedure,* by Robert D. Leigh.

Oxford University Press for quotations from *Civilization on Trial* and *A Study of History* (Abridgment by D. C. Somervell), by Arnold Toynbee; *The Economic Background of the Gospels,* by Frederick C. Grant; *An Open Letter to Jews and Christians,* by John Cournos.

Penguin Books, Ltd. for quotation from *Christianity and Social Order,* by William Temple.

G. P. Putnam's Sons for quotations from *One Destiny,* by Sholem Asch; *Social Evolution,* by Benjamin Kidd; *The Outline of Science,* edited by J. Arthur Thomson.

Reader's Digest for quotations from the article in the issue of July, 1949, by William Hard and Andre Visson, entitled "The North Atlantic Road to Prosperity"; and for quotations from "A Way to Lessen World Hunger" reporting Norris E. Dodd, condensed in *Reader's Digest,* March, 1950, from the *Minneapolis Tribune* (January 22, 1950), by Edwin Muller.

Fleming H. Revell Company for quotations from *The Renascence of Faith,* by Richard Roberts.

Richard Roberts for quotations from his book, *The New Man and the Divine Society,* published by The Macmillan Company.

Ernest F. Scott for quotations from his book, *An Outline of Christianity,* originally published by Bethlehem Publishers.

Charles Scribner's Sons for quotations from *Beliefs That Matter,* by William Adams Brown; *The Direction of Human Evolution,* by Edwin Grant Conklin; *The Christian Answer* and *God in These Times,* by Henry P. Van Dusen; *God and the Common Life,* by Robert Lowry Calhoun; *The Ideal of Jesus,* by William Newton Clark; *The Meaning and Truth of Religion,* by Eugene W. Lyman; *The Motives of Men* and *What Ails Our Youth,* by George A. Coe; *Science and the New Civilization,* by Robert A. Milliken; *The Place of Jesus Christ in Modern Christianity,* by John Baillie; *Social Salvation,* by John C. Bennett; *The Shaking of the Foundations,* by Paul Tillich.

Simon and Schuster for quotations from *Modern Arms and Free Men,* by Vannevar Bush (Copyright by Trustees of The Vannevar Bush Trust); *Release from Nervous Tension,* by David Harold Fink (Copyright by David Harold Fink).

Survey Associates for quotations from the article by Webb

Waldron in the March, 1940, issue of *Survey Graphic,* entitled "A Gang Goes Up Hill."

University of Chicago Press for quotations from *The Psychology of Religion,* by George A. Coe.

Henry Nelson Wieman for quotations from his books, *The Issues of Life,* published by Abingdon-Cokesbury Press; and *The Wrestle of Religion with Truth,* published by The Macmillan Company.

Yale University Press for quotations from *Human Nature and Its Remaking,* by William Ernest Hocking.

G.A.B.